COMPLETE
LOW-FAT
COOKBOOK

Sue Kreitzman, described by *The Times* as 'the queen of low-fat cookery writing', has been writing cookbooks since the mid 1970s. In the early 1980s she adapted standard cooking techniques to create Slim Cuisine, which uses no or only minute amounts of fat.

Sue lectures and demonstrates all around the country, and regularly appears on radio and television. She contributes to many national magazines and newspapers, including *BBC Good Food*, *Woman's Own*, *Woman's Realm*, *Chic* and *Living*.

Sue Kreitzman's Complete Low Fat Cookbook is her seventeenth cookbook. Her other books include *Sue Kreitzman's Low-Fat Vegetarian Cookbook, Slim Cuisine Italian Style, Slim Cuisine Quick and Easy* and *Slim Cuisine Indulgent Desserts*.

Sue wholeheartedly believes in good food with maximum flavour and minimum fat.

COMPLETE LOW-FAT COOKBOOK

Sue Kreitzman

PIATKUS

DEDICATION
For my friends (and relation)
on and around the Roman Road

ACKNOWLEDGEMENTS

Thanks so much to Julie Haylock for introducing me to Terence Fisher, and to Terry for providing a mail order source of excellent low-fat chocolate. As always, a million thank-yous to Mandy Morton for our monthly free-wheeling forum of food chat and gossip on BBC Radio Cambridgeshire. Warm gratitude to Heather Rocklin, my editor at Piatkus, for being such a delight to work with, and to my assistant Sandie Mitchel-King for her hard work, support, and good nature.

I am very grateful to the garden-team at The Prospect Trust for keeping my garden overflowing with fragrance and flavour (a herb garden is one of the great joys of life!), and to Brenda Huebler who ensures that life at Tiptoft runs smoothly. Much love and many thanks to my husband, Dr Stephen Kreitzman, for his help and support, as well as for his many cuddly qualities.

Finally hugs and kisses to my friends in Bow who have been so much fun to cook, eat and schmooze with – in particular Keith Brewster and Peter Novis, Googie Woodham and Jeanette Hoare, Peter and Katie King, Shawm Kreitzman, and all the smiling faces up and down the Roman Road.

Copyright © 1996 Sue Kreitzman

First published in 1996 by
Judy Piatkus (Publishers) Ltd
5 Windmill Street
London W1P 1HF

The moral right of the author has been asserted
A catalogue record for this book is available from the British Library

ISBN 0–7499–1545–5 (hbk)
ISBN 0–7499–1661–3 (pbk)

Designed by Sara Kidd
Photography, including cover, by Steve Baxter
Food preparation by Meg Jansz
Styling by Helen Payne
Artwork by Paul Saunders

Typeset by Selwood Systems, Midsomer Norton
Printed and bound in Great Britain by
Butler & Tanner Ltd, Frome and London

CONTENTS

INTRODUCTION

I love food. I love everything about it. I love to cook it, think about it, smell it, look at it, feed it to other people, learn new things about it, and savour its history. Most of all, I love to eat it – no wonder I eventually tipped the scales at 15½ stone. In 1982, when I lost a considerable amount of weight, I realized that if I wanted to continue my ongoing love affair with food, I would have to investigate seriously a low-fat lifestyle. But I soon discovered that the problem with most low-fat recipes is that one might as well cook the paper the recipe is printed on – it would surely taste better than the recipe itself. So I set out to reinvent all of the foods I love. I spent (and I continue to spend) my time lovingly developing new ways of putting foods together so that the result is low in fat, high in nutrients, yet comforting, delicious and joyously edible in large portions.

This volume comprises a complete guide to my low-fat cooking expertise. Everything has been updated to encompass the wealth of wonderful ingredients now available in supermarkets all around the country (how things have changed since 1982!), the harried, rushed lives everyone seems to lead these days, and all of the new techniques I have developed since my original low-fat cookbooks (the *Slim Cuisine* series) were printed.

This book overflows with recipes for the kind of food people really like to eat every day – spag. bol., sausages and mash, pizza, roasted chickens and joints, fish and chips, nursery puddings, chocolate cake – but even more important, it is full of techniques and ideas. Once you gain a feeling for and an understanding of the basics of low-fat cookery, you will be able to adapt almost anything you like to the low-fat method. It is an easy way to cook – there are no mysterious and intricate procedures that have to be mastered – and it is exciting as well. Food cooked without its usual blunting cloak of fat and oil is vibrant, fresh-tasting and bursting with clear flavours and textures. And once you get into a rhythm of low-fat cooking and eating, the constant guilt that accompanies so many of our eating experiences ('I shouldn't have eaten this. I'll be good tomorrow, I promise!') just disappears. How wonderful to be able to cook, eat, feed family and friends, and enjoy every moment of it, without a backlash of guilt, fat or ill health.

WHY LOW FAT?

There are three components of food that provide calories: proteins, carbohydrates and fats (including *oils* which are simply liquid fats). Proteins and carbohydrates provide 4 Calories per gram, while fats provide 9 Calories per gram. In practical terms, that works out to approximately 120 Calories per tablespoon. And not only is fat much higher in calories, it is also metabolized differently; dietary fat goes to body stores in an extremely quick and easy fashion. In other words, fats literally make one fatter faster than carbohydrates and proteins do.

It's important to remember that *all* fats provide 9 Calories per gram, and are quickly metabolized to fat stores. That includes animal fats (such as poultry fat, lard, dripping, suet and the butterfats in butter and other dairy products); polyunsaturated and monounsaturated oils; margarines of all sorts; vegetable shortenings and even low-fat spreads. (Low-fat spreads contain *less* fat than butter or margarine, because they have been diluted – with water, air or buttermilk, for instance – but they still contain substantial amounts of fats which provide 9 Calories for each gram of fat.)

A low-fat lifestyle is a painless way to *lose* weight while still enjoying oodles of delicious food, and it is the only sensible way to *maintain* a weight loss. It is a necessity for those with medical problems that are compromised by dietary fat – high cholesterol levels, arterial or cardiac problems, gall bladder problems, and so on – but I have learned over the years that a low-fat lifestyle is also for people who want to follow a healthier way of life, so that they do not develop dietary-fat-related diseases and obesity later in life; who want – through wise food choices – to maintain a high degree of 'wellness', and who want to avoid the eventual need for serious dieting by avoiding in the first place the insidious weight-gain that creeps up on those who eat thoughtlessly.

A LOW-FAT LIFESTYLE

A totally fat-free diet would be very difficult to achieve, and dangerous as well. A very small amount of essential fatty acids (3–4 grams a day) are needed to maintain health, and the 'fat-soluble' vitamins (A, D and E), found in fatty substances, are vital to our well-being too. A sensible low-fat diet derives 20–25 per cent of total calories from fat. That amounts to approximately 50 grams of fat. How does one achieve this ideal? Well, first of all, obsessively counting fat grams is *not* the way to go about it. Food is pleasurable above all, and grimly attempting to calculate the fat grams in everything you eat, and trying to keep a running daily sum, is a depressing, pleasure-killing and unnecessary activity. Cutting out added fats (butter, oils, margarine and so on), fatty meats and poultry, whole milk products and high-fat processed foods will automatically bring your daily fat intake into the recommended range, so there will be no need to juggle charts and figures, and turn each meal and snack into a grim accounting exercise.

There is another quite important reason for cutting out these fatty ingredients. The more fat you eat, the more you crave it. In a very real sense, fat is an addictive substance, although – once through the first low-fat week or so – it is surprisingly easy to do without. A good example is switching from full-fat milk to skimmed milk. At first, the skimmed variety seems strange – too thin and watery – but after a week or so, you will most likely find it quite acceptable, and if you then try to switch back to full-fat, your palate will probably recoil in disgust. How, you wonder, did you ever manage to ingest such an unpleasantly thick, fatty substance? Give yourself a chance. After a spell of low-fat eating, you'll be tasting pure and vivid tastes, uncloaked by grease, that you have never before imagined. Switching back again becomes unthinkable, because the tastes and textures of high-fat food become actively unpleasant. The less you eat fat, the less you want it, which is why an on-again, off-again, low-fat lifestyle really won't work. And replacing one kind of fat (saturated animal fats) with another (highly mono- or polyunsaturated oils or the artificially resaturated fats in margarines) does not make a low-fat lifestyle. It simply switches one high-fat régime for another, and will do nothing to cure fat-craving. It will certainly do nothing for weight loss or weight maintenance, and the health benefits of such a switch are not all that clear-cut; diets high in fats and oils – both highly saturated *and* highly unsaturated – have been implicated in a host of diseases. A total reduction, therefore, is the wisest move.

HOW TO DO IT

Here is a list of simple steps to take to achieve a low-fat cooking style. As you work your way through the book, you will find lots more detail about each of the following points, but this list will give you an overview.

1 Grill, poach or oven-'fry' instead of frying in fat or oil.

2 Sauté (pan-fry) or stir-fry in stock (or stock and wine) instead of fat and oil. (If you make your own chicken or meat stock, chill it overnight so that the fat rises to the top and solidifies. Discard the fat before using the stock. If you make your own vegetable stock, prepare it without added fat. Homemade stocks freeze well – freeze them in small containers.)

3 Substitute olives for olive oil. Instead of sautéing onions and garlic in oil (120 Calories and 14 grams of fat per tablespoon), make a **flavour infusion** using a few black olives (10 Calories and 1 gram of fat for 2 olives). To make the infusion, combine chopped onion (or thinly sliced spring onion) and crushed garlic with the flesh (slivered off the stone) of 2–3 black olives. Sauté in stock, or stock and wine, until the onions and garlic are tender, and the liquid just about gone. The flavour will be superb. Intensify the flavour even more by adding 2 chopped, dry-pack, sun-dried tomatoes (page x) and a pinch of crushed dried chillies, to the onions and garlic.

4 Buy an oil spray, or make your own (page ix). These sprays deliver a minuscule dose of oil for those times when you need to grease a pan or lightly lubricate something on the grill.

5 If you eat poultry and meat, eat the poultry without the skin, and always de-fat the pan juices. (Quick-chilling them in the freezer makes the fat rise quickly to the top, so that it can easily be skimmed off.) Buy *lean* meat only. Buy extra-lean mince, and buy joints and chops that have no visible fat marbling *within* the meat. Always trim away any visible fat surrounding the meat.

6 If you eat meat every day (or even twice a day), try decreasing the amount of meat you eat per meal, and the number of meat meals you have per week. Learn to 'stretch' meat with vegetables (see the Meat chapter) so that, although you are eating less of it, you are still getting plenty of meaty satisfaction.

7 Eat vegetarian meals several times a week – nice big pasta dishes, for instance, or vegetable curries, or paella-type rice dishes. Eat plenty of vegetables, potatoes, pulses, grains and fruit every day. Eat fish frequently; if you eat canned fish, buy the kind packed in brine.

8 Eat unbuttered, unmargarined toast, and don't use butter, margarine or low-fat spreads (or mayonnaise) in sandwiches either. For every *tablespoon* of fat that you leave off, you save about 120 Calories and 14 grams of fat. See the Spreads chapter (page 73) for plenty of delicious alternatives.

9 Dress your salads with non-fat dressings (conventional dressings pile on the fat grams like nobody's business). See pages 95–101 for plenty of no-fat dressing ideas, and check out the supermarket as well; many bottled non-fat dressings are available and you might find one you like.

10 Get into the habit of reading labels, even if it means taking a magnifying glass to the supermarket. Ingredients on the label are listed in descending order of amount – the first ingredient is the one there is the most of in the food. That's your first clue as to a product's suitability. The label will also tell you how much fat the food contains per 3½ oz (100 g), and how much fat each serving contains (but does their idea of a serving match yours?). This information is your second clue. The product may be labelled 'low-fat' or 'reduced fat' or 'healthy eating'. This is no clue at all. A reduced-fat crisp, for instance, although lower in fat than a standard crisp, still spells disaster for a low-fat régime. And a product labelled 'healthy eating' may be medium fat rather than low or no fat. So read the small print, and use some common sense.

11 Substitute skimmed-milk dairy products for full-fat or part-skimmed ones. Look for quark

(a non-fat, smooth curd cheese that is very useful in all sorts of recipes), very low-fat fromage frais (beautifully rich and creamy), non-fat yoghurt (it can be a bit thin, but it can be drained to make it more like Greek yoghurt – see page 100), buttermilk (cultured from skimmed milk and as thick as pouring cream), and, of course, skimmed milk itself. Add skimmed milk powder to skimmed milk to give it added richness, and added nutrition as well (the powder is fortified with vitamins A and D, two of the fat-soluble vitamins, and so provides a no-fat source of those valuable nutrients).

12 Use a few well chosen medium-fat dairy products to add taste and texture to your cooking. You won't need much – a little goes a long way. Look for Italian-style mozzarella cheese in liquid-filled pouches or larger blocks (20 per cent fat for the full-fat version, 10 per cent in the half-fat version), ricotta cheese (beautifully sweet and creamy and only 15 per cent fat), Parmesan cheese (use the real thing, in blocks, and grate it by whirling cubes of the cheese in a blender until powdered). Parmesan has a gorgeous, strong cheese flavour; a little goes a long way, and adds wonderful depth of flavour. Look, too, for Boursin Léger (a low-fat version of the well known French garlic and herb spread), and medium-fat creamy goat's cheese (it comes in little pots, usually with a picture of an adorable goat on the side).

SOME VALUABLE INGREDIENTS

OIL SPRAY

If you look in the section of the supermarket devoted to bottled oils, you will find a delightful surprise: Frylight oil spray. It is available with either olive oil or sunflower oil; both are extraordinarily useful. You can make your own spray with a small plastic perfume spray atomizer (available in some chemists and department store cosmetic departments). Needless to say, use clean, new bottles that have never been used for perfume. A new plastic plant mister works well, too. Fill the bottle with oil and water. You want the bottle to deliver a fine oily mist, rather than an oily stream. Experiment until you get the oil–water mix that delivers a mist, rather than a stream, when you *shake* and *spray*. (Since oil and water don't mix, you will always have to *shake* just before you spray.) Depending on the spray delivery on your particular bottle, the water–oil ratio may need to be half and half, three quarters to one quarter, or even seven eighths to one eighth. When spraying filo pastry, however, use the pure (Frylight) spray only as the oil and water mix may make the filo a bit soggy. If you love to make Chinese stir-fries, keep one bottle for a sesame oil and water spray to give your low-fat stir-fries the proper fragrance.

EGGS

Eggs are a highly nutritious food, but the yolk contains fat (6 grams) and cholesterol. Current medical thinking suggests that two or three whole eggs a week should do no harm, *unless* you have a medical problem that precludes added dietary cholesterol. When in doubt, check with your doctor. Egg whites are virtually fat and cholesterol free, and so can be used with abandon as a wonderful cookery ingredient, especially for baking (see the Dessert chapter, page 209).

Omelettes and scrambled eggs can be prepared with several of the yolks removed first. The colour will be paler than normal, but the taste will be good. Cook them in a non-stick pan with a spritz of oil spray.

STOCK

This is one of the most important and basic ingredients in the low-fat kitchen. If you make your own, it is essentially *free* because it can be made from vegetable scraps and carcasses that you have saved from roasted chickens. But wonderful store-bought stocks (vegetable, chicken, beef or fish) are now available in little pots in the chill cabinets of many supermarkets. The stock is concentrated, so the little pots yield 3–4 times their volume (dilute them with water) and the pots can be stored in the freezer until needed. They thaw in the microwave in a trice.

Stock cubes tend to be too salty (and they contain too much fat), but there are excellent vegetable bouillon powders available. Look for Marigold Vegan and Vegetable Bouillon powders – they are quite indispensable. You'll find them in good supermarkets, or in wholefood and health food shops. To use them as a sauté medium, simply put some water (and wine if you wish) into the pan with the garlic and onion, then sprinkle in some bouillon powder.

WINES AND SPIRITS

Wine adds richness and gorgeous deep flavour to low-fat cooking. When wine is boiled or simmered briskly, as it is in the recipes in this book that call for it, the alcohol (and the alcohol calories) are boiled away, so it will not compromise your weight loss or weight maintenance régime, and it will not send you reeling into the gutter in a drunken stupor! Dry white vermouth, Côtes de Rhône and dry sherry are the wines that you will find endlessly useful as you cook your way through this guide. Buy one of those little vacuum pumps to pump the air out of a partially used bottle

of wine. They are not expensive and will keep the unused portion of wine fresh. Liqueurs and brandies are valuable as well, as flavourings in low-fat puddings; a few well-placed splashes here and there work wonders.

BALSAMIC VINEGAR

I have absolutely no interest in what's 'in' and what's 'out' of fashion. What interests me is what is delicious. And balsamic vinegar is delicious. So what if it was once chic and is now passé? The stuff is sweet, treacly and gorgeous, and dresses up low-fat food like nothing else. A sprinkling of balsamic (I carry some with me always, in a little hip flask) adds instant pizzazz to a salad, a jacket potato, a fish fillet, even a dish of strawberries! Balsamic vinegar is made from the juice of Trebbiano grapes. The real stuff is aged in wood (for years) and is expensive. I mean *very* expensive. It is fabulous (you could drink it in a glass) but you may not feel willing – quite understandably – to mortgage your house or sell your first-born for a drizzle of vinegar, however orgasmic. The more down-to-earth supermarket bottles of balsamic are very good indeed, and will brighten your low-fat meals in many ways.

SUNDRIED TOMATOES

When I first started writing about low-fat cookery, sundried tomatoes were only available in posh food halls, and then only packed in olive oil. How times have changed! Cellophane packs of dry-pack (no oil) sundried tomatoes are almost universally available now in supermarkets the length and breadth of the country. How sweet life is! Some supermarkets may even have more than one brand to choose from. (Italian brands are saltier than American ones.) A few sundried tomatoes, snipped with scissors and added to a flavour infusion, bring a subtle, smoky, slightly caramelized flavour to your stews, soups and sauces. They are a seasoning rather than a main ingredient, and help to deepen the flavour of lower-fat dishes.

HERBS

Fresh herbs bring an exquisite dimension to low-fat cooking. Fresh, clear flavours are what low-fat cooking is all about, and the herbs help the food to shine with that freshness. All sorts are available in the supermarket, year round, and many people have discovered the joy of growing their own. To substitute dried for fresh, use a third of the amount and add it early in the cooking (usually in the flavour infusion). Never use dried herbs for garnish. Always sniff dried herbs before using; if they are musty, they will ruin the dish.

Where large quantities of fresh herbs are called for, I measure them in a measuring jug. It sounds odd to specify 3/4 pint (450 ml) fresh basil, or 1/2 pint (300 ml) fresh parsley, but it *is* the most efficient way of measuring out large amounts of the herbs.

BOTTLED CONDIMENTS

There are some incredible ethnic and ethnic-influenced bottled sauces out there, just waiting to be tried. Look for spicy ketchup, hoisin sauce, teriyaki marinade, Sambal Oelek (I'm sure the name translates to 'Eek – this is hot!') and interesting mustards.

OLIVES

A few black olives in a flavour infusion (page viii) as a replacement for olive oil saves a lot of fat calories over a week's cooking. Buy stone-in olives, packed in brine (no oil) or dry-packed, in jars or vacuum packs. Canned, stoned olives tend to be flabby and tasteless.

BEFORE YOU BEGIN

1 Read the recipe through so that you know what you need as far as equipment and ingredients are concerned, and what you are doing.

2 Gather all the ingredients and equipment together and put them on your work surface. If the recipe calls for a spice mix, measure out the spices into a small bowl. Prepare the vegetables, trim the meat, measure the liquids, preheat the oven, prepare everything so that they are ready to go. The more organized you are, the faster the actual cooking will be.

3 All quantities are given in Imperial measurements and in the approximate metric equivalents. Follow one or the other.

4 If your only oven is a fan oven, reduce the oven temperature given in the recipe by 20 degrees. If you have a cooker that has a main fan oven, but an upper grill compartment that doubles as a (non-fan) oven, then opt for the upper non-fan oven whenever possible.

CALORIE AND FAT NOTE

I don't include calorie and fat counts for the recipes in this book for several reasons:

1 It is almost impossible to provide an accurate nutritional analysis for a recipe – there are too many variables in the food itself, and in personal interpretations of the particular recipe.

2 Nothing encourages joyless food obsession the way trying to balance the calories and fat grams does.

3 If you take on board all the advice given about low-fat, high-nutrition cookery contained in this book, you will have no need for number balancing – things will fall very nicely into place.

A NOTE ON SERVING SIZES

The number of servings you get out of a particular recipe depends on the 'shape' of the meal (what else is being served with the recipe, and how you are using it – as a main dish, accompaniment or starter), your appetite and the appetites of those you are feeding, and the kind of day you have had. That's why, in many cases, I give the yield of a recipe in volume so that you can visualize the amount a recipe makes, and then use it as you wish. When a number of servings is given, it is an approximate suggestion – your idea of how much a 'serving' is might be much more, or much less, than mine.

EQUIPMENT

THE MICROWAVE OVEN AND THE FREEZER

If you have a busy lifestyle (who doesn't these days?), a microwave and a freezer will save you a significant amount of time. A microwave cooks things that the conventional oven may have problems with – very low-fat white sauces and milk puddings, for instance – but its quick thawing capability is very useful as well. With a freezer, you can cook large portions of various staple dishes (shepherd's pie, bolognese, sausages and burgers, soups, etc.), eat some on the night, and then freeze some for future quick meals. And with the microwave/freezer partnership you can cook and freeze staple low-fat ingredients: roasted aubergine pulp or pan-braised aubergine (pages 157–8), tomato sauces, stocks, sautéed onions, and so on, so that they are on hand at a moment's notice.

BLENDERS AND PROCESSORS

Both a blender and a processor are useful: a blender for puréeing soups and sauces to exactly the right consistency, and a food processor for pâtés, spreads and dips; for easy slicing and grating (although an old-fashioned four-sided grater does a wonderful job of grating and slicing as long you mind your knuckles); and for making instant no-fat ice creams and sorbets. It is worth investing in a processor for the ice cream alone, but the investment doesn't have to be a big one – the smaller, inexpensive processors work perfectly well.

COOKWARE

Heavy-bottomed, non-reactive pots and pans will give very good results. A non-reactive pan is one that will not react with acid ingredients (such as wine, citrus juice, spinach and tomatoes) to produce off colours and tastes in the finished dish. Non-reactive materials include stainless steel, enamelled cast-iron, non-stick coatings and flameproof glass and ceramic (Pyroflam, Pyrex, etc.). Reactive materials to avoid include tin, uncoated cast-iron and uncoated aluminium.

There is a wide choice of good cookware to choose from. Here are a few suggestions:

A wide flameproof casserole with a tight-fitting lid is one of the most useful of all pans. It can be used as a frying pan, a sauté pan, a gratin or baking dish, a roasting tin and a serving dish. Le Creuset makes an excellent heavy-bottomed enamelled cast-iron pan called a 'buffet casserole'; Lakeland Plastics (see mail order, page 242) offers another. These are pricey, but they *are* good investments and will last for ages.

There are lower-priced alternatives: a large non-stick wok with a lid, for instance. Such a wok is incredibly useful, and not just for stir-frying. Most cookware shops and departments stock large, flat-bottomed woks with good non-stick coatings and tight-fitting lids. Often they come with a steamer insert as well. This versatile pan can be used as a frying pan, a saucepan and a steamer. You can make almost anything in one, including sauces, stews and soups. Another possibility is a 3 inches

(7.5 cm) deep, 11 inches (28 cm) wide non-stick frying pan with a tight-fitting lid. Again, this can be used for all sorts of preparations, and is not very expensive.

Other invaluable cookware and utensils for a low-fat lifestyle include:

Non-stick baking sheets
3 ½ pint (2 litre) measuring jugs for microwave sauces and puddings
Rubber spatula
Slotted spatula (fish slice)
Flexible palette knife
Kitchen scissors
Citrus zester

Swivel-bladed vegetable peeler
Thin metal skewer for testing
Efficient can opener
Sharp knives (dull knives are dangerous, and will slow you down)
Measuring jugs and spoons
A reliable set of kitchen scales
Four-sided grater (for grating *and* paper-thin slicing)
Brush (for brushing on marinades, milk and egg washes, etc.)
Whisk
Colander
Non-reactive sieves and strainers

FOLLOWING RECIPES

There is no such thing as a recipe that is guaranteed to 'work'. There are too many variables. A gas oven works differently from a fan oven; a ceramic hob is not the same as an electric coil or a gas flame. Some people have a food processor but no blender (or vice versa); some have neither but prefer to depend on a whisk, a sieve and a sharp knife. Types of cookware vary wildly, and every brand, size and wattage of microwave oven seems to have a mind of its own. Ingredients vary as well – a tomato, carrot or potato that I buy in Cambridgeshire in June will not be the same as one bought in Devon in October or Newcastle in January. Add to this confusion variables of personal taste, and it becomes clear that a universal recipe that works everywhere and pleases everyone is an impossibility. Use your common sense, and adjust recipes to suit your taste and equipment. If you hate chillies, for instance, the spicier recipes will work beautifully without them. I have had two tasters complain simultaneously, as they sampled a bean chilli at a demonstration, that it was too spicy, and not spicy enough. You know your palate, and the palates of those you feed, so adjust recipes accordingly.

Adjust, too, to the vagaries of your equipment. Cooking times especially must be taken with a grain of salt. The size and shape of the oven, the thickness of the pots and pans, the number of things you are baking at one particular time, the state of the thermostat – all these variables and more will affect the total cooking time. And microwave ovens (although I think they are invaluable and important machines) are even worse as far as consistency is concerned. There can be no standard microwave recipe. The size of the oven cavity and the wattage obviously affect the timing, but often two identical ovens – same size, same wattage, same model, same brand – give different results. And, I have found to my chagrin, if you move your microwave for any reason, you may find that, when you next make a tried and true recipe, the timing has completely changed. So always treat cooking times as a very rough guide. If you are prepared to be flexible and observant, and to trust your own taste and judgement, you should be able to cook very successfully indeed, and to enjoy the process as well.

A GUIDE TO THE SYMBOLS USED IN THIS BOOK

V suitable for vegetarians

☉ quick and easy to prepare (less than 30 minutes)

❋ can be frozen

VEGETABLES

Of all the things I hope to communicate in this guide, the most important is the value of vegetables. That importance can hardly be overstated; to health, well-being and gastronomic enjoyment. This chapter includes low-fat vegetable cooking techniques, as well as recipes for vegetable main dishes and side dishes. Because vegetables are the foundation of a high-nutrition, low-fat way of life, you will use all of this veggie advice over and over again. The clever use of vegetables' natural goodness will increase the nutrition and decrease the fat in your daily diet, as well as increase the total amount of food that you will be able to eat without gaining weight. For convenience and ease of reference, the vegetables are presented in this chapter in alphabetical order.

VEGETABLES AND HEALTH

Before vegetables became part of gastronomy and everyday cooking, they were used medicinally to treat every known physical complaint and every part of the body: cabbage for pleurisy, garlic for leprosy, parsnip for toothache, celery for impotence ... it all makes rather quaint reading today. However, modern books and reports on health and nutrition are not all that different. Vegetables are hot stuff right now in the medical literature, and every

week sees new publications lauding their health benefits: beans for their cholesterol-lowering fibre; dark green, yellow and orange vegetables for their vitamins and minerals and anti-oxidant activities; brassicas (cabbage and all its relatives) for their cancer protection ... I could go on for pages. It *is* quite true that the health benefits of vegetables can hardly be exaggerated, but to start glumly munching carrots, cabbages and broccoli like vitamin pills in the dogged search for eternal health would be to miss the point. Vegetables are delicious above all. For the low-fat cook, it is vegetables that make it possible to keep low-fat dishes luscious, sumptuous, lavish and deeply satisfying. The current government recommendation is that we should consume 5–7 servings of vegetables every day. Those servings can be slipped in, to great advantage, everywhere – not just in neat little piles, next to the roast (although, for vegetable lovers, those neat little piles can bring much pleasure as well). Vegetables can also be puréed to make vividly coloured, richly textured sauces; added to extra-lean mince to give bulk and succulence; simmered in soups to deepen flavour and improve texture; blended with herbs and spices to be spread smoothly and seductively on to crusty bread. A wealth of vegetables makes a low-fat lifestyle no hardship whatsoever.

ASPARAGUS

Asparagus was once deemed a good treatment for male sexual disfunction, just as beetroot was once believed to be a blood tonic – logical conclusions, albeit totally erroneous. The seasonal appearance of asparagus was once a glorious harbinger of spring; now, the slender stalks seem to be available at any time of year. Still, despite the proliferation of foreign asparagus, the appearance of the locally grown stuff, during its brief springtime season, remains one of the most exciting culinary experiences of the year. And it is, I sheepishly admit, a great treat to be able to feast on asparagus (even though of far-flung origins and far less flavourful) at virtually any time of year.

Asparagus can be steamed, stir-fried or roasted. Unless the stalks are pencil thin, peel them first to get maximum taste and texture out of the vegetable. To my palate, the juicy meatiness of peeled thick stalks is far preferable to the delicate crispness of pencil-thin asparagus. Prepare them this way:

1 Cut off the tough woody bottom of each stalk. With a paring knife, or with a swivel-bladed peeler, peel each stalk from the bottom up to the buds. Rinse the stalks under cold running water.

2 If you are not going to cook them at once, stand them in a glass of water as if they were a bunch of flowers, cover with a plastic bag, and refrigerate until needed.

STEAMED ASPARAGUS

V ⊘

Simply steamed asparagus served with an interesting sauce is not an accompaniment to anything; it is a meal in itself. As a general rule of thumb, 8 oz (225 g) equals one serving, but most people could easily polish off 12 oz (350 g). Since 3½ oz (100 g) asparagus (about 7 stalks) weighs in at 35 Calories, the only limits are set by finances, availability, and your patience for peeling. For maximum pleasure, eat the stalks with your fingers, dipping them into the sauce between each bite. For just-picked, seasonal, locally grown asparagus, ignore all references to sauces and dips, and just serve lemon wedges with the succulent stalks.

1 Prepare fresh asparagus stalks as described above.

2 Place the stalks in the basket of a steamer, and steam over boiling water for 3–7 minutes (depending on size) or until just tender but retaining a hint of crispness. To test, hold up a stalk with tongs. It should bend just a *little*.

3 If you plan to serve asparagus cold, refresh under cold running water to stop the cooking and set the bright green colour, then drain and cool. Otherwise, drain on a clean tea-towel over a wire cooling rack. Either way, serve with an interesting sauce or dip (or two different dips to make it even more interesting). Possibilities include any of the pepper sauces (pages 87–89) or the red and yellow pepper relishes (page 82) or the 'mayonnaise'-type sauces (pages 97–99). If you are allowing yourself 2–3 eggs per week (see page ix), a soft poached egg is a lovely thing to serve with asparagus. Grind some pepper on to the egg, then dip the asparagus stalks into the yolk, as you eat them. Fabulous!

STIR-FRIED ASPARAGUS

V ⊙

For a stir-fry, use thick asparagus, prepared as on page 2, or pencil-thin asparagus which will need no peeling. Cut into 1 inch (2.5 cm) lengths. Many supermarkets sell packs of thin asparagus tips that are perfect for stir-frying.

2–3 fl oz (50–75 ml) stock
juice of 1 lime
fresh asparagus stalks, prepared (see above) and

cut into 1 inch (2.5 cm) lengths, or fresh
asparagus tips
salt and freshly ground pepper

1 Heat the stock and half the lime juice in a non-stick wok or frying pan. Throw in the asparagus, and stir and turn (use two wooden spoons) in the hot stock for about 2 minutes.

2 Add the remaining lime juice and season lightly with salt and pepper. Stir-fry for another 1–2 minutes or until the asparagus is cooked but retains its bright green colour and more than a hint of crispness. Scoop it out with a slotted spoon and put it in a serving bowl.

3 Briefly boil down the cooking juices until syrupy (unless they are already syrupy), pour and scrape over the asparagus, and serve.

ROASTED ASPARAGUS

V ⊙

Roasting is the favourite vegetable preparation of the nineties, and very good it is too. Usually it is done in an oil-swamped dish; here the dish is merely misted. As a result, you get a mouthful of asparagus flavour with only a hint of olive oil, not the other way round!

olive oil spray (page ix)
thick asparagus spears, prepared (page 2)

freshly ground pepper

1 Preheat the oven to 220°C, 425°F, Gas Mark 7.

2 Spray a baking dish with the oil spray. The dish should be of a size to hold the asparagus in one uncrowded layer. Spread the stalks in the dish, and grind over some pepper. Bake in the oven for 20 minutes, then turn the stalks and bake for 5–10 minutes more.

AUBERGINE

Very low in calories and fat, an aubergine is also low in vitamins, but it packs a nice dose of trace minerals. Once it was necessary to salt them before cooking to draw out any bitterness. Today's aubergines have no bitterness and salting is unnecessary.

I find aubergine one of the most useful of all vegetables – low-fat cooking just wouldn't be the same without it. Oven-roasted or pan-sautéed in a flavourful infusion, then puréed in a blender or processor, it makes an extraordinarily successful filler for lean mince, enabling you to eat juicy low-fat sausages, meatballs, etc., that contain maximum meaty flavour, yet minimum meat and fat (see pages 156–7). But aubergine is not just a filler; as a vegetable in its own right it is superb. It has a satisfying substantial meaty texture, and an ability to soak up flavours; as the centre of a meatless meal it will please vegetarians and meat eaters alike. Its beautiful shiny purple skin is edible, although it is tougher than the flesh; whether or not to peel depends on the recipe. Often the best thing to do is to peel it in 'stripes' by removing alternate strips, peeling from stem to stern, so that the aubergine has alternating purple stripes. This way, you keep some of that wonderful colour, but the texture is better when the aubergine is cooked. When peeling is specified, it is easily done with a swivel-bladed peeler.

GRILLED AUBERGINE

V ⊙ ❄

Aubergine grills very well, and grilled aubergine slices can be used to form satisfying main dishes. They can be refrigerated for several days. Grilled aubergine is wonderful as a sandwich filling in crusty bread. Try it with one of the salsas, pestos, or 'mayonnaise'-type dressings (pages 76, 79–82 and 97–9). What with the meaty aubergine, the dripping salsa, the creamy dressing, and the bread crust that shatters as you bite into it, this is a magnificently messy sandwich.

1 aubergine, weighing about 8 oz (225 g)   *olive oil spray (page ix)*

1 Peel the aubergine lengthways in alternate stripes, then cut it across into ¼ inch (0.5 cm) slices.

2 Preheat the grill to high. Lightly mist a non-stick baking sheet with oil spray.

3 Spread out the aubergine slices on the baking sheet in one layer (cook in two batches if necessary). *Lightly* spray the slices with oil spray, and grill, close to the heat, for 3–5 minutes or until tender and very lightly speckled with brown. Turn the slices, spray *very* lightly, and grill for a moment or two on the second side.

CRUMBED GRILLED AUBERGINE

V

I first learned to make this (although it was a high-fat version, battered and pan-fried in butter and oil) from chef Louis Szathmary in Chicago. He served aubergine and courgettes, sliced lengthways, crumbed and fried, as a vegetarian main course. Before dipping them into batter, he would trim the slices into fish shapes. On the menu, he called this offering 'Zucchini (courgette) Fish' or 'Eggplant (aubergine) Fish'. Everyone loved this culinary pun, and devoured great shoals of the piscine vegetables.

1 quantity Fromage Frais Mayo (page 97)
10–12 tablespoons plain breadcrumbs
4–5 tablespoons freshly grated Parmesan cheese
salt and freshly ground pepper

1 aubergine, weighing about 8 oz (225 g)
olive oil spray (page ix)
lemon wedges or balsamic vinegar, to serve

1 Preheat the grill to high.

2 Spread some 'Mayo' on a large plate. Combine the breadcrumbs with 1–2 tablespoons cheese. Season with salt and pepper, and spread on a second large plate. (You won't need much salt; both the cheese and the Mayo contain plenty.)

3 Trim the ends off the aubergine. Peel and cut the aubergine *lengthways* into slices about ¼ inch (0.5 cm) thick.

4 Lightly mist a non-stick baking sheet with olive oil spray.

5 Dredge each vegetable slice in the Mayo (using a rubber spatula to spread it evenly on each side), then dip in the crumb–cheese mixture. Make sure both sides are well coated. Add more Mayo, crumbs and cheese to the plates as needed. As the aubergine slices are ready, place them on the baking sheet. When they are all on the sheet, *lightly* mist the slices with olive oil spray. Position the baking sheet 5 inches (12.5 cm) from the heat and grill for 3–5 minutes until nicely speckled with brown. *Carefully* ease a palette knife or spatula under each slice and flip over. (If part of the coating on the underside is disturbed, sprinkle a little more crumb–cheese mixture on before sliding back under the grill.) Grill for a further 3–5 minutes or until speckled with brown on both sides.

6 Serve hot or cold, with lemon wedges or balsamic vinegar.

AUBERGINE GRATIN

SERVES 4

V ☙ ❋

In this gratin, because some of the aubergine skin is left intact, flashes of purple skin show through the creamy sauce, in an enchanting manner. The cheese sauce is made in minutes in the microwave (pages 93–94).

two 8 oz (225 g) aubergines
6 spring onions, trimmed and sliced
4–5 sun dried tomatoes, diced with scissors (optional)
1–2 garlic cloves, crushed
1–2 pinches crushed dried chillies

about ½ pint (300 ml) stock
2–3 teaspoons dry vermouth
about ¾ pint (450 ml) Cheese Sauce or Garlic Sauce (page 94)
2–3 tablespoons freshly grated Parmesan cheese

1 Preheat the grill. Peel the aubergines lengthways in alternate stripes, then cut across into ¼ inch (0.5 cm) slices.

2 Grill the aubergine slices according to the directions on page 4.

3 Spread the aubergine slices in a single layer in a 10 inch (25.5 cm) square, 2 inches (5 cm) deep baking or gratin dish. Set aside.

4 Put the spring onions, sun dried tomatoes, garlic, dried chillies, stock and vermouth in a heavy-bottomed, non-reactive frying pan. Cover, bring to the boil, and boil for 5 minutes. Uncover, reduce the heat and simmer until the garlic and onions are tender and the liquid almost gone (the mixture will be syrupy). Spread this mixture evenly over the aubergine slices, using a rubber spatula to scrape out every bit.

5 If the cheese sauce is not freshly made and hot, warm it according to the directions on page 94. Pour and spread the sauce evenly over the aubergine. Sprinkle evenly with grated Parmesan.

6 Grill, a few inches from the heat, for 3–5 minutes or until speckled with brown and beginning to bubble. Serve at once.

AUBERGINE PARMIGIANA

V ❄

Aubergine Parmigiana is flexible – make as little or as much as you like. One aubergine, 300 ml (½ pint) tomato sauce, a ball of Italian mozzarella and a few spoonfuls of grated Parmesan will feed two nicely. If you plan to freeze, freeze *before* baking.

grilled aubergine slices (page 4)
Basic Tomato Sauce (page 85)

Italian mozzarella cheese, drained and slivered
freshly grated Parmesan cheese

1 Preheat the oven to 180°C, 350°F, Gas Mark 4.

2 Place a layer of grilled aubergine in the bottom of a gratin dish. Spread with tomato sauce, then scatter on the mozzarella and a little Parmesan. Top with more aubergine, then more sauce, and a final scattering of Parmesan.

3 Cover and bake in the oven for 20 minutes, then uncover and bake for a further 20 minutes.

CAPONATA

MAKES 1 PINT (600 ML)
V ❄

Caponata is a Sicilian sweet and sour aubergine stew, originally prepared with aubergine cubes that have been either deep-fried or sautéed in *plenty* of olive oil. It takes astonishingly well to the low-fat olive infusion method, and would be splendid as a first course, snack or lunch, served with (or spread on to) crusty bread. Serve cool or at room temperature.

4–5 black olives in brine, drained and slivered
  off their stones
2 tablespoons drained capers
1–2 tablespoons raisins
3–4 garlic cloves, crushed
1–2 good pinches crushed dried chillies
½ pint (300 ml) stock

¼ pint (150 ml) dry red wine
1 aubergine, weighing about 9 oz (250 g),
  unpeeled and diced
two 14 oz (400 g) cans whole tomatoes, drained
  and cut into strips
2–3 tablespoons shredded fresh basil leaves
4–5 tablespoons chopped fresh parsley

1 Combine the olives, capers, raisins, garlic, chillies, stock and wine in a large non-reactive, flameproof casserole or saucepan. Cover, bring to the boil, and boil for 5–7 minutes.

2 Add the aubergine and tomato strips, and season with salt and pepper. Simmer, uncovered, for 20 minutes. Stir in the herbs, and simmer, stirring occasionally, for 10 minutes more.

BEANS AND PULSES

First come 'snap' beans – immature pods that break with a crisp, clean snap and can be eaten whole. Then, as they mature, they become shell beans – mature fresh seeds (beans) that must be removed from their pods. Finally, they are dried beans, and must be rehydrated in liquid. All beans are available in these three forms, but different beans are best at different stages.

Mature, dried beans brim over with nutritional goodness. Their protein levels are high, and although their complement of amino acids (the building blocks of protein) is not complete, a diet rich in vegetables and grains, and/or small amounts of animal protein (meat, fish, poultry, dairy products) rounds it out nicely. Bean fibre is reported to lower blood cholesterol, and the beans also provide B vitamins. Their fat levels are very low. Of course, good nutrition counts for nothing if the food providing it is boring, insipid and unsatisfying. How fortunate that beans provide such pleasure, and that they take so well to no-fat and low-fat cooking methods. It is no longer necessary to go through the time-consuming ritual of soaking and cooking dried beans – a trawl of the supermarket shelves nets a spectacular array of canned beans of all types from borlotti to lentil. A good cupboard supply of canned beans and pulses of all descriptions is a guarantee of nutritious and delicious meals at a moment's notice.

RED AND WHITE BEAN STEW

YIELDS 1 ½ PINTS (900 ML)

V ⊙ ❄

You could make this lively stew with any beans but the finished dish looks wonderful with red kidney and white cannellini beans peeking through the herb-speckled sauce.

12 spring onions, trimmed and sliced
3 celery stalks, de-strung and diced
1 carrot, peeled and diced
3–4 garlic cloves, cut into chunks
3–4 sundried tomatoes, chopped with scissors
*   (optional)*
½ pint (300 ml) stock
3–4 fl oz (75–100 ml) dry white vermouth
½ teaspoon each of ground cumin and ground
*   coriander*

1–2 pinches crushed dried chillies
15 oz (425 g) can cannellini beans, drained and
*   rinsed*
15 oz (425 g) can red kidney beans, drained and
*   rinsed*
1 pint (600 ml) passata
salt and freshly ground pepper
2 tablespoons chopped fresh parsley
1–2 tablespoons chopped fresh coriander
juice of ½ lime

I Combine the spring onions, celery, carrot, garlic, sundried tomatoes (if using), stock, vermouth, cumin, coriander and chillies in a heavy-bottomed saucepan. Cover, bring to the boil, and boil for 5–7 minutes. Uncover and simmer briskly, stirring occasionally, until the liquid is reduced and syrupy, and the vegetables are tender.

2 Add the beans and stir to coat them with the vegetable and spice mixture. Stir in the passata and season with salt and pepper. Simmer, uncovered, for 15 minutes.

3 Stir in the chopped herbs and the lime juice before serving.

MIXED BEAN SALAD

MAKES 2 PINTS (1.1 LITRES)

V ☺

Beautiful on a buffet, this bean salad is made with cans of mixed beans – cannellini, chick peas, flageolet, limas, haricot, and so forth, all in one can.

¾ pint (450 ml) stock
1 carrot, peeled and chopped
2 celery stalks, de-strung and thinly sliced
1 red or yellow pepper, deseeded, peeled (page
  48) and chopped
1 red onion, chopped
1–2 garlic cloves, crushed
1 teaspoon each of ground cumin and crumbled
  dried oregano
½ teaspoon each of ground coriander and mild
  chilli powder

pinch of crushed dried chillies
2 ripe tomatoes, peeled, deseeded and chopped
two 15 oz (425 g) cans mixed beans, drained
  and rinsed
salt and freshly ground pepper
DRESSING
juice of 1 orange
juice of 1 lime
1 tablespoon balsamic vinegar
1 tablespoon each of chopped fresh parsley,
  chives and mint

1 Combine ½ pint (300 ml) stock with the carrot, celery, pepper, onion, garlic, spices and chillies in a heavy-bottomed frying pan. Cover, bring to the boil, and boil for 5 minutes, then uncover and simmer briskly until the vegetables are tender and 'frying' in their own juices.

2 Stir in the tomatoes, beans and remaining stock, and season with salt and pepper. Simmer, uncovered, for 10–15 minutes. Leave to cool slightly while you make up the dressing.

3 Stir together the dressing ingredients and mix gently with the bean mixture. Serve at room temperature.

LENTIL–AUBERGINE BOLOGNESE SAUCE

MAKES 1½ PINTS (900 ML)

V ⊙ ❋

Good old spag. bol. is delicious made with lentils in place of meat – and you don't have to be a vegetarian to love it. It's quick, nourishing, not terribly expensive, and everyone seems to enjoy it. I first started experimenting with the idea when I was working on my low-fat vegetarian cookbook. It has become one of those recipes that people take to right away, and pass on to others. In this version of my (I now consider it a classic!) lentil bolognese, aubergine lends 'meatiness' and carries the flavour of the garlic, wine and chilli. Canned lentils are a great convenience and make it possible to prepare the sauce quickly.

2 aubergines, peeled and chopped
2 onions, chopped
2 garlic cloves, crushed
2 sundried tomatoes, chopped (use scissors)
pinch of crushed dried chilli

4 fl oz (100 ml) red wine
½ pint (300 ml) stock
two 15 oz (425 g) cans lentils, drained and rinsed
two 14 oz (400 g) cans chopped tomatoes
salt and freshly ground pepper

1 Combine all the ingredients, except the lentils, canned tomatoes and salt and pepper, in a heavy-bottomed frying pan. Cover and simmer for 5–7 minutes, then uncover and simmer until the vegetables are very tender and the liquid absorbed.

2 Stir in the lentils and tomatoes, and season with salt and pepper. Simmer, uncovered, for 15–20 minutes or until thick and savoury. Remove from the heat.

3 Ladle out a quarter to one third of the sauce and purée in a food processor or blender. Combine the puréed and unpuréed portions, reheat, and serve with pasta, rice or couscous.

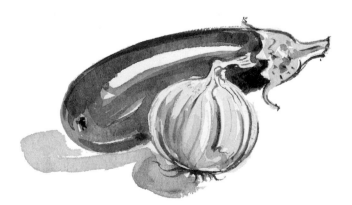

BEETROOT FLAGEOLET SALAD

MAKES 1 PINT (600 ML)

V ⊙

Beetroot and flageolet beans make a delicate and very pretty salad; the beetroot juices dye the flageolets a blushing pink. The earthiness of the beetroot and the delicacy of the beans are very effective together.

9 oz (250 g) vacuum-packed beetroot in natural juices (no vinegar)
15 oz (425 g) can flageolet beans, drained and rinsed
2 tablespoons chopped fresh parsley, to serve

DRESSING
1 garlic clove, crushed
1 tablespoon balsamic vinegar
juice of ½ lime, ½ orange and ½ lemon
2–3 drops teriyaki sauce
½ teaspoon Dijon mustard

1 Whisk together all the dressing ingredients and leave to marinate for about 15 minutes.

2 Open the beetroot package and drain off and reserve the juices. Stir 1 tablespoon of the juices into the dressing. Dice the beetroot and toss with the beans. Add the dressing and toss gently with two spoons to coat the beans and beetroot with the dressing.

3 Fold in the parsley just before serving.

Butter Bean Sausages

MAKES 10

V ⊙ ❊

These vegetarian sausages are crusty croquettes made from butter beans that have been enriched with an aubergine–garlic–olive infusion. The interior of the sausage is creamy-tender, a spectacular foil for the crisp exterior. Serve an interesting sauce such as the Orange Mango on page 92 alongside the sausages for dipping.

15 oz (425 g) can butter beans, drained and
* rinsed*
1 tablespoon fromage frais
4–5 tablespoons freshly grated Parmesan cheese
9 tablespoons dry wholemeal breadcrumbs
juice of ½ orange and ½ lemon
salt and freshly ground pepper
1 egg white, lightly beaten
oil spray (page ix)
Orange Mango Sauce (page 92) or lemon or
* lime wedges, to serve*

INFUSION
4 oz (125 g) aubergine, peeled and diced
1 small onion, chopped
3 black olives in brine, drained and slivered off
* their stones*
3–4 sundried tomatoes, chopped (use scissors)
1–2 pinches crushed dried chillies
2 garlic cloves, crushed
4 fl oz (100 ml) dry red wine
4 fl oz (100 ml) stock

1 Combine all the infusion ingredients in a frying pan. Cover and simmer briskly for 5–7 minutes, then uncover and simmer until the vegetables are very tender. Cool.

2 Put the aubergine mixture in the bowl of a food processor with the butter beans, fromage frais, 1 tablespoon Parmesan, 1 tablespoon breadcrumbs and the fruit juices. Season with salt and pepper, and process to a purée. Process in the egg white, then, if you have time, chill the mixture in the fridge for about 1 hour.

3 Preheat the grill. Mist a baking sheet with oil spray.

4 Mix the remaining crumbs and cheese and spread on a plate. Scoop up a spoonful of the bean mixture and drop on to the plate. Roll it into a sausage shape and coat with the crumb mixture. Toss it gently from one palm to the other to help shape the sausage. The mixture is rather soft (especially if it has not been chilled) so bits may fall off as you shape it. Just pick them up and mould them back on. Place on the misted tray, and repeat until the mixture is all used.

5 Grill the sausages, about 3 inches (7.5 cm) from the heat until golden brown and crusty, turning carefully with a fish slice every 3 minutes or so. Serve with lemon or lime wedges.

FRENCH BEANS (SNAP BEANS)

As with many of our treasured and familiar foodstuffs, beans originated in the New World, and probably came over to Europe with the Spanish Conquistadors. Immature snap beans, fresh in taste and snappy-crisp in texture, are effective raw, as part of an array of crudités. To cook, no more than a brief steaming is needed – the beans should conform to that holy grail of vegetable cookery, 'crisp-tender'. In other words, they should be cooked but should retain a hint of 'bite'. At one time (during the height of the rage for nouvelle cuisine), it was considered the thing to undercook vegetables so they were *much* more crisp than tender; in fact, a meal at a restaurant that specialized in such cuisine could resemble a rabbit convention: crunch, crunch, crunch, at every table! But these days, just a hint of crispness is what to aim for.

SAUTÉED FRENCH BEANS

MAKES 1½ PINTS (900 ML)

V ⊙

French beans can be steamed, or very simply stir-fried or pan-sautéed in a combination of stock and lime or lemon juice. And they are delectable briefly steamed first, then sautéed in an olive–garlic infusion, as here. Turn the beans into a main dish salad by serving at room temperature with 2–3 tablespoons crumbled half-fat feta cheese scattered on, and, if you like, some drained, flaked tuna in brine.

1 lb (450 g) French beans, topped and tailed,
  and de-strung if necessary
½ pint (300 ml) stock
1–2 garlic cloves, crushed
pinch of crushed dried chillies
3–4 sundried tomatoes, diced (use scissors)

3–4 black olives in brine, drained and slivered
  off their stones
1 tablespoon balsamic vinegar
salt and freshly ground pepper
6–7 fresh basil leaves, shredded

1 Steam the beans until half cooked. Refresh under cold running water, to stop the cooking, then drain well and set aside.

2 Pour the stock into a heavy-bottomed, non-reactive frying pan. Add the garlic, chillies, sun-dried tomatoes, olives and balsamic vinegar. Cover, bring to the boil, and boil for 4–5 minutes or until reduced by half. Add the beans.

3 Toss and cook for 2–3 minutes. Season with salt and pepper, and stir in the basil. Stir and cook for a further 4 minutes. Serve warm or at room temperature.

BEETROOT

So sweetly earthy, so crunchy when raw, yet so mouth-fillingly tender when cooked, and so magnificently *red*! What a vegetable – I love it. Although vacuum packs of ready-cooked beetroot are quite good, and very convenient (buy the kind packed *without* vinegar), it really is worth trying the fresh roots, when they are available – they have a much deeper, richer flavour. Boiling is the worst thing to do to these scarlet orbs as they lose colour and flavour. Baking brings out their best; steaming their second best. Raw, they are delicious (and stunning) peeled and grated into salads.

To prepare beetroots for cooking, trim off the greens and stems, leaving 1–2 inches (2.5–5 cm) of the stem. Scrub them, but take care not to pierce them or they will 'bleed' as they cook. Leave them unpeeled. The greens of young beetroots are good to eat (they look lovely, with red veins threading through the green). Wash them well, and steam them like spinach. The stems are good too; slice them and sprinkle raw over a sliced beetroot salad.

BAKED BEETROOTS

Choose beetroots of a similar size if possible. Wrap the prepared beetroot in heavy duty foil (shiny side in). With smaller beetroot, put 2–3 in a packet. Wrap them so that the beetroots are in roomy, well-sealed packets. Bake in the oven at 200°C, 400°F, Gas Mark 6 for 1–2 hours (the timing depends on the age and size of the roots). Use a skewer to test for doneness; the skewer should go in easily, but the roots should not be mushy. Also, the skins will give slightly when pressed. Cool slightly, then slip off the skins.

STEAMED BEETROOTS

Try to choose beetroots of a similar size (steaming works best with smaller beets), and prepare as described above. Put into the steamer basket, and steam over boiling water, replenishing the water as needed, for 40–60 minutes. Test, cool and peel as described above.

BEETROOT IN MUSTARD CREAM

MAKES 1¼ PINTS (750 ML)

V ☉

Band B (buttermilk and balsamic) make a marvellous dressing for beetroot. If your supermarket doesn't have buttermilk, use non-fat fromage frais. If you use ready-cooked beetroot, make sure they contain no vinegar.

4–6 small cooked beetroot, peeled
1 tablespoon Dijon mustard
6 fl oz (175 ml) buttermilk or non-fat fromage frais
1 tablespoon balsamic vinegar
1–2 tablespoons snipped fresh chives
freshly ground pepper

1 Cut each beetroot in half, and thickly slice each half. Put the pieces into a bowl, with their juices.

2 Put the mustard in a small bowl, and slowly whisk in the buttermilk or fromage frais, then the vinegar. Stir in the chives and season with pepper.

3 Pour the dressing over the beetroot and gently fold together. Don't mix too efficiently; the white of the dressing should be swirled with red. Refrigerate until needed.

RED AND RED SALAD

MAKES 1 PINT (600 ML)

V ⏲

If blood oranges are unavailable, or too expensive, juicy, seedless ordinary oranges will do nicely. This is a *brilliant* (in several senses of the word) combination! To add even more red, garnish the salad with rings of red onion.

2 large Baked Beetroots (page 14)
3 blood oranges
juice of 1 lemon
1 tablespoon balsamic vinegar
2 tablespoons shredded fresh basil
2 tablespoons chopped fresh parsley
½ tablespoon snipped fresh chives
freshly ground pepper

1 Peel and coarsely dice the beetroots, and place in a bowl.

2 Peel two oranges of all peel and pith, segment them, and dice each segment. Add to the beetroot. Squeeze the juice of the remaining orange over the contents of the bowl.

3 Mix in all the remaining ingredients and season with pepper.

CHINESE BEETROOT SALAD

MAKES 1 PINT (600 ML)
V ⊙

This is quick and easy pantry cooking at its best! Just grab a vacuum pack of beetroot, and add a splash of teriyaki, hoisin sauce and vinegar for a salad of ruby slices that sing with flavour.

*9 oz (250 g) vacuum-packed cooked beetroot
    (no vinegar)*
juice of ½ orange
dash of teriyaki sauce
1 tablespoon hoisin sauce

1 tablespoon cider or malt vinegar
½ tablespoon mild runny honey
*1 thin slice of fresh root ginger, peeled and
    crushed*
1 garlic clove, crushed

1 Drain the juices from the beetroot into a small saucepan. Stir in all the remaining ingredients, except the beetroot, and bring to the boil.

2 Slice the beetroot into a bowl and pour the sauce over the slices. Mix gently with two spoons to combine. Eat at room temperature, or chilled.

BROCCOLI

(Calabrese)

Mark Twain called cauliflower a cabbage with a college education; broccoli must be the cousin that went to finishing school. Like cauliflower, it is a member of the brassica family, and so includes cabbages and brussels sprouts among its relatives. Brassicas have an impressive nutritional profile – no fat to speak of, but plenty of vitamins and minerals, and, according to some nutritionists, an ability to help fight cancer and to lower blood cholesterol. Broccoli is a particularly good source of calcium.

When you buy broccoli, you essentially get two vegetables: the florets and the stalks. The florets are good briefly steamed, and then served with lemon wedges, or used in soups (page 104). The stalks, peeled and sliced (the slices have an endearing, lop-sided star shape), have that wonderful, crisp succulence that makes some vegetables so perfect for serving raw with a dip or in salads. The sliced stalks are also perfect for stir-frying with interesting herbs and spices.

STIR-FRIED ROMAN BROCCOLI

MAKES 1 PINT (600 ML)

V ☉

For a simple stir-fry treatment for peeled, sliced broccoli stems, toss them in stock and lemon or lime juice until they are tender with just a hint of crispness, and the pan juices are scant and syrupy. A clove or two of crushed garlic, stir-fried with the sliced stalks, wouldn't hurt. But the stalks can also be jazzed up a bit with Mediterranean seasonings, as in this recipe.

1 lb (450 g) broccoli stalks
3 black olives in brine, drained and slivered off
  their stones
½ teaspoon each of ground cumin and
  coriander
1–2 pinches crushed dried chillies
½ tablespoon drained capers
2 garlic cloves, crushed

2–3 sundried tomatoes, snipped with scissors
  (optional)
juice of about 1 ½ lemons
slivered rind of ½ lemon
about 1 pint (600 ml) stock
½ teaspoon each of caper brine and olive brine
salt and freshly ground pepper

1 Cut the tough, woody bottoms from the stalks, and peel the stalks, then slice them into thin rounds.

2 In a heavy-bottomed frying pan (or wok) combine the olives, spices, chillies, capers, garlic, sundried tomatoes, juice of ½ lemon, the lemon rind, half the stock, and the brines. Bring to the boil, then reduce the heat and simmer briskly until the garlic is tender and the liquid reduced and syrupy.

3 Stir in the broccoli stalks, remaining stock and juice of ½ lemon. Season with salt and pepper, and stir-fry until the broccoli is tender (with just the merest hint of a crunch) and the liquid greatly reduced. (If, during the simmering, the liquid cooks away too fast, add a bit more as needed.) Taste and add a bit more lemon juice if you think it is needed. Serve warm or at room temperature.

BRUSSELS SPROUTS

Adorable mini-cabbages, members of the health-giving brassica family, sprouts are dreadful when overcooked, but delicately delicious when cooked properly. Small, young sprouts are effective halved, so that their elegant tightly packed cross-sections are visible, and served as part of a crudité selection. To cook, leave whole, but trim the base, and strip away any loose outer leaves. Steam over boiling water for 6–10 minutes (depending on size) until tender with a bit of crispness remaining at the base of each sprout. As with most vegetables, you can gorge on these should you have a mind to: a good dozen sprouts contains only 50 fat-free Calories, and overflows with vitamins and minerals.

CREAMED SPROUTS

MAKES ¾ PINT (450 ML)

V

This is a medium-fat (as opposed to non-fat) treatment for sprouts, for those who can afford a bit of medium-fat cheese now and then. This gloriously creamy, garlic- and herb-flavoured dish tastes richer and more indulgent than it actually is.

1 lb (450 g) brussels sprouts, trimmed and
* halved*
5 oz (125 g) tub Boursin Léger

½ pint (300 ml) stock
2–3 tablespoons freshly grated Parmesan cheese

1 Preheat the oven to 220°C, 425°F, Gas Mark 7.

2 Spread the sprouts in a gratin dish. Put the Boursin and stock in a blender, and blend until very smooth. Pour over the sprouts.

3 Bake, uncovered, in the oven for 25 minutes, stirring occasionally.

4 Sprinkle on the grated Parmesan and bake for another 10 minutes or so, stirring once halfway through, until the sprouts are tender, and the sauce thick and creamy.

Opposite, clockwise from top: Cucumber and Fennel Salsa (page 80), Aubergine Gratin (page 6), Rice Pilau (page 115)

SWEET AND SOUR SPROUTS

MAKES 1 PINT (600 ML)

V ⊙

Frozen sprouts are great with a Chinese sweet and sour sauce. Serve them as they are, or make tiny meatballs (the same size as the sprouts) according to the Paprika recipe (page 171) and fold them into the sauce with the sprouts. If you choose to serve meatballs with the sprouts, make twice the amount of sauce: double up on all the sauce ingredients except the cornflour and water. The sweet and sour sauce can be served with almost any steamed vegetable you like.

1 lb (450 g) frozen baby sprouts
about ¼ pint (150 ml) stock
1 tablespoon soft brown sugar
2 fl oz (50 ml) cider or malt vinegar
1 tablespoon teriyaki sauce

1½ tablespoons tomato ketchup
1½ tablespoons hoisin sauce
1 tablespoon cornflour, whisked into 3
*   tablespoons cold water*

1 Put the frozen sprouts in a non-stick wok or frying pan with 2 fl oz (50 ml) stock. Simmer, stirring occasionally, until the sprouts are cooked the way you like them (I like them with a bit of a crunch, but you may like them softer). Drain in a sieve set over a bowl. (Reserve the liquid.)

2 Put the stock that has drained from the sprouts into a measuring jug. Add more stock to make ¼ pint (150 ml). Pour the stock into the wok.

3 Stir in all the ingredients, except the cornflour and water mixture, and bring to the boil. When boiling, stir in the cornflour and water paste, and boil for a moment or so until thickened. Turn the heat to low, stir in the sprouts and warm through. Serve at once.

Opposite, clockwise from top: Red and White Bean Stew (page 8), Pepper Salsa (page 80), Tzatziki (page 101), Corn Bread (page 202)

CABBAGE

In varied shades of green and red-purple, the tightly packed heads nestled into wild profusions of petal-like leaves, cabbages look like enormous edible roses. When cut in half, the convoluted cross-sections show their fascinating, complex designs. Like fingerprints, no two are the same. Why is such an amazing vegetable considered so plebeian? Eaten raw (crisp, juicy and satisfying to snack on), steamed, stir-fried in stock, braised or stuffed, cabbage has to be one of the best foods in the world. But not only is cabbage versatile and delicious, it also – as with all the other brassicas – bursts with health benefits. Overboil it, though, and it turns nasty: smelly, mushy and totally horrid.

BRAISED CABBAGE AND BEANS

MAKES ABOUT 2½ PINTS (1.4 LITRES)

☉ ❇

Gentle braising in a flavourful infusion, so that the cabbage soaks up flavour as it softens, is a very good way to treat the vegetable. Borlotti beans and a bit of smoky bacon set it off nicely. Serve with mashed potatoes for a stick-to-the-ribs meal.

2 black olives in brine, drained and slivered off
   their stones
1 onion, halved and sliced into thin half moons
3 garlic cloves, crushed
1–2 pinches crushed dried chillies
2 rashers lean smoked back bacon, trimmed of
   all fat and diced
1 pint (600 ml) stock

1 lb (450 g) savoy cabbage, trimmed of tough
   outer leaves, cored and sliced into thin shreds
1 tablespoon tomato purée
15 oz (425 g) can borlotti beans, drained and
   rinsed
freshly ground pepper
2–3 tablespoons chopped fresh parsley

1 Combine the olives, onion, garlic, dried chilli, bacon and 4 fl oz (100 ml) stock in a deep heavy-bottomed frying pan. Cover and bring to the boil. Reduce the heat a little, and simmer briskly for 5 minutes. Uncover and cook until the onions are browning and the liquid almost gone.

2 Add the shredded cabbage and stir to coat with the onion mixture. Stir together the remaining stock and the tomato purée and add to the cabbage. Cover and cook for 20 minutes, stirring occasionally.

3 Stir in the beans, season with pepper and cook for 3–4 minutes. Stir in the parsley.

STIR-FRIED CABBAGE

MAKES 1 PINT (600 ML)

V ☉ ❄

Thisextremely quick and easy, gently spicy cabbage stir-fry can be served as a vegetable side dish, or as a garnish for the Indian Sausage Patties on page 101. Serve the patties in a pita pocket with the cabbage, and a drizzle of yoghurt with tandoori spices stirred in.

1 small savoy cabbage
6 fl oz (175 ml) stock

juice of ½ orange and ½ lemon
½ tablespoon mild Korma curry powder

1 Discard the tough outer leaves of the cabbage, cut the cabbage in quarters, remove the core, and shred the leaves.

2 Put the remaining ingredients into a wok or frying pan and bring to the boil. Stir in the cabbage. Stir and cook for 3–5 minutes or until tender and the liquid almost gone.

BRAISED RED CABBAGE AND APPLES

MAKES 3 PINTS (1.7 LITRES)

V ☉ ❄

Whaen Bramleys are in season I use these. The dish tastes wonderful but the apples break down into a purée. Use tart eating apples and you will end up with bits of apple in the cabbage. It's good both ways.

2 lb (900 g) red cabbage
1 lb (450 g) tart apples (see above)
4 fl oz (110 ml) orange juice
1 large red onion, halved and sliced into thin
* half moons*

4 fl oz (110 ml) red wine
2 tablespoons balsamic vinegar
2 tablespoons soft brown sugar
salt and freshly ground pepper
juice of 1 lemon

1 Remove the tough outer leaves from the cabbage. Cut the cabbage into quarters and remove the core. Shred the leaves. Peel, core and dice the apples, and stir them into the orange juice.

2 Combine all the ingredients, except the lemon, in a large, heavy-bottomed saucepan, and season with salt and pepper. Bring to the boil, then reduce the heat, cover and simmer gently for 20–30 minutes or until tender, stirring occasionally. Add half the lemon juice. Taste and add more lemon juice and salt and pepper if necessary. Leave to cool and then chill.

MUSHROOM-FILLED CABBAGE PARCELS

MAKES 8 PARCELS
V ❄

Stuffed cabbage – magic words. In this recipe a mushroom mixture is folded inside crinkly savoy cabbage leaves.

2 lb (900 g) brown-cap mushrooms, roughly diced
½ teaspoon dried tarragon
2 fl oz (50 ml) dry sherry
several dashes teriyaki sauce
14 fl oz (400 ml) stock

2 tablespoons Dijon mustard
1 savoy cabbage
18 fl oz (500 ml) passata
juice and grated zest of ½ small lemon
salt and freshly ground pepper
chopped fresh parsley, to serve

1 Combine the mushrooms, tarragon, sherry, teriyaki and 4 fl oz (100 ml) stock in a heavy-bottomed frying pan. Simmer until the mushrooms have exuded a great deal of liquid. Let the liquid reduce a little, then stir in 1 heaped tablespoon Dijon mustard. Simmer until the mushrooms are tender and the liquid greatly reduced.

2 Meanwhile, remove and discard the tough outer leaves from the cabbage. Peel off eight leaves and, using a vegetable peeler, pare down the tough central vein of each one. Steam the leaves for 5 minutes, then refresh under cold running water to stop the cooking. Drain well, and dry by rolling in a clean tea-towel. Quarter, core and shred the remaining cabbage.

3 Lay a leaf flat on the work surface. Place a spoonful of the mushroom mixture on the centre of the leaf, fold the end and the sides over the filling and roll to form a neat parcel. Place, seam-side down, on a platter or large plate. Repeat with the remaining leaves. Set aside the leftover mushrooms.

4 Put the shredded cabbage in a large heavy-bottomed frying pan with the remaining stock. Bring to a simmer, cover and cook for 2 minutes. Uncover, and stir-fry until the cabbage is almost tender. Stir in the passata, the remaining mustard, the lemon zest and juice and the reserved mushrooms. Season with salt and pepper. Set the cabbage parcels, seam-side down, on the tomato mixture, cover and simmer for 30 minutes. To serve, sprinkle with parsley.

CARROTS

Nibbling on raw carrot sticks is a dieting cliché, but there is nothing punishing about such munching – quite the contrary. As far as I'm concerned, raw carrots are as compelling as sweets – they are loaded with natural sugar (although, of course, they are very low in calories), which makes them burst with sweetness, and they have that heavenly crunch when you bite down on them.

Carrots are much improved by peeling lightly with a swivel-bladed peeler; the best way to handle them is to peel and cut them when you want them, so that their nutrients stay intact.

To cook carrots, try braising them, or roasting them, wrapped in foil, in a hot oven (see below).

BRAISED CARROTS

Peel and slice as many carrots as you like (the more, the merrier), and put them in a frying pan with a little stock and a squeeze of lemon juice (and orange juice, too, if you like) or a splash of sherry, and ½ teaspoon sugar. Cumin is wonderful with carrots – add a big pinch if you like it, but not with sherry. With sherry, add some crushed fresh ginger. Crushed garlic goes with either, if you are in the mood (I'm always in the mood). Season with salt and pepper, and simmer, stirring occasionally, until the carrots are tender and the liquid has cooked down to a glaze that coats the carrots.

FOIL-ROASTED CARROTS

All root vegetables, rich as they are in natural sugars, develop a deeply caramelized flavour (and meltingly tender texture) after roasting. Eat them with a squeeze of lemon juice or purée them and use to enrich and thicken soups, stews and pan juices. Peel the carrots and enclose them in foil, shiny side in. Crimp well so that they are in a roomy, well-sealed pouch (several carrots can be wrapped together). Bake in the oven at 220°C, 425°F, Gas Mark 7 for about 1 hour or until the carrots are very tender, and their juices are caramelizing.

MARINATED CARROTS

MAKES 1 PINT (600 ML)

V ⊙

Steamed carrots are good, too, if they are then given a bit of personality with interesting seasonings. Here, they are steamed with garlic, and then marinated in a vinegar–spice mixture.

1 lb (450 g) carrots, peeled and cut into ¼ inch (0.5 cm) slices
3 garlic cloves, very coarsely chopped
4 fl oz (110 ml) wine vinegar
¼ teaspoon ground cumin

1–2 pinches cayenne pepper (or to taste)
1–2 pinches each of ground cinnamon and allspice
salt and freshly ground pepper
2 tablespoons chopped fresh parsley

1 Steam the carrots and garlic over boiling water for 5–10 minutes or until the carrots are crisp-tender. Cool under cold running water and drain well.

2 While the carrots are steaming, combine the vinegar with the ground spices and seasonings in a screw-topped jar, and shake well.

3 Toss together the carrots, vinegar mixture and parsley. Refrigerate until needed. Serve cold or at room temperature.

CAULIFLOWER

Stop and look, next time you dash madly through the greengrocery department – I mean really *look*, as if you were seeing things for the first time. It's like some sort of wild food fantasy: the greens, the purples, yellows, reds, all shades and hues, all shapes and sizes. Madly thrusting, furling and curling; the leaves, stalks, buds, bulbs and heads are a joy to see. Cauliflower is one of the most fantastic offerings of all. I never get tired of the sight of them, curving exuberantly out of their leaves like enormous edible bridal bouquets. Cauliflower is another member of the brassica family, with all the health benefits that implies; how nice to know, that in addition to its amazing appearance, and wonderful affinity for soaking up flavours, it contains a nice package of nutrients as well.

Steamed cauliflower florets (steamed until almost tender), work beautifully with the garlic and olive infusion (page viii) – simply stir-fry them with the infusion and a little extra stock, until the cauliflower is tender, and imbued with the flavour of the infusion. By the way, when you trim cauliflower and break it into florets, in preparation for steaming, cut the stem into chunks, steam the pieces along with the florets, and include in whatever dish you choose to make.

CAULIFLOWER CHINESE-STYLE

MAKES ABOUT 2 PINTS (1.1 LITRES)

V ☺

Give cauliflower a Chinese accent with hoisin sauce, that most useful of bottled condiments. This sauce would complement many other vegetables as well: steamed broccoli or brussels sprouts, shredded cabbage stir-fried in stock, sautéed whole button mushrooms.

6 spring onions, trimmed and thinly sliced
2 garlic cloves, crushed
1 thin slice of fresh root ginger, peeled and crushed
6 fl oz (175 ml) stock

2 tablespoons dry sherry
juice of ½ small orange
steamed florets from 1 cauliflower
2 tablespoons hoisin sauce
1 tablespoon chopped fresh coriander

1 Combine the onions, garlic, ginger, stock and sherry in a frying pan or non-stick wok. Simmer until the onions and garlic are tender, and the liquid almost gone.

2 Stir in the orange juice, then gently stir in the cauliflower. Stir and cook for a moment or two (being careful not to break up the cauliflower), then stir in the hoisin sauce. Stir and cook gently until hot and well combined. Sprinkle with coriander and serve.

CAULIFLOWER BRAISED IN SPICY TOMATO SAUCE

MAKES 1 ½ PINTS (900 ML)

V ⊙ ❊

As long as you don't cook it to mush, cauliflower is good almost any way at all. Bland, simple and unchallenging (cauliflower cheese, for instance, or just plainly steamed), it is delicious, but it also works with lively seasonings, as in this preparation spiked with chilli, rosemary and fennel.

3–4 sundried tomatoes, roughly diced with scissors (optional)
2–3 black olives in brine, drained and slivered off their stones
2 garlic cloves, crushed
1–2 generous pinches crushed dried chillies
½ teaspoon crumbled dried rosemary or 1½ teaspoons chopped fresh rosemary
1 teaspoon fennel seeds

1 pint (600 ml) stock
4–5 fl oz (110–150 ml) dry vermouth
1 red and 1 yellow pepper, peeled (page 48), deseeded and cut into 2 inch (5 cm) pieces
florets from 1 cauliflower, steamed until half cooked
2–3 tablespoons tomato purée
salt and freshly ground pepper
2 tablespoons chopped fresh parsley

1 Combine the sundried tomatoes (if using), olives, garlic, chillies, rosemary and fennel with half the stock, the vermouth and peppers in a large, heavy-bottomed frying pan or wok. Bring to the boil, then reduce the heat and simmer briskly, uncovered, for 10 minutes or until the peppers are tender and the liquid almost gone.

2 Stir in the cauliflower, the remaining stock and the tomato purée. Season with salt and pepper. Simmer, partially covered, for about 15 minutes, stirring occasionally, until the cauliflower is tender. Stir in the parsley.

LOW-FAT CAULIFLOWER CHEESE

Steamed cauliflower florets cry out for a creamy bath of cheese sauce. Fold the florets (steamed until tender), into any one of the warmed cheese sauces (page 94). Sprinkle with grated Parmesan, and flash under the grill until the cheese melts and the sauce bubbles.

CAULIFLOWER BRAISED IN GOAT'S CHEESE SAUCE

MAKES 1 ½ PINTS (900 ML)

V

Cauliflower florets, braised to tenderness in a sauce of creamy, medium-fat goat's cheese thinned with stock, soak up the flavour of the goat's cheese: it is a very successful marriage.

1 garlic clove, split
5 oz (150 g) medium-fat, soft goat's cheese
½ pint (300 ml) stock

1 cauliflower, trimmed and separated into
  florets
salt and freshly ground pepper

1 Preheat the oven to 220°C, 425°F, Gas Mark 7. Rub the inside of a gratin dish with garlic, then leave the garlic in the dish.

2 Put the cheese and stock in a blender and blend until smooth.

3 Spread the cauliflower out in the gratin dish and pour the blended mixture over it. Season with salt and pepper, cover tightly and bake in the oven for 20 minutes, then uncover and stir. Re-cover and bake for an additional 20 minutes or until the cauliflower is tender.

CORN
(Maize or Sweetcorn)

Fresh sweetcorn is one vegetable that does not travel well in time. As soon as it is picked, its sugars start to change to starch, and the bursting, milky sweetness that swells each kernel with goodness, begins to diminish. In Maine, where I used to spend part of my summers, farmers would post their harvest times every day. Hungry customers would put the water on to boil, speed down to the farm shop, grab an armful of ears directly from breathless farm workers, then – shucking with one hand, steering with the other, keeping in mind those sugars diminishing by the second – rush the corn straight back home into the waiting pan for a brief bath. Then: smother with butter, sprinkle salt, chomp, chomp, chomp. No wonder I eye those well-travelled supermarket ears with a baleful eye. They are just not the same – and it's not only the romance of the Maine farm-to-cooker run that is missing. Without that sweetness, the magic is gone.

Fortunately, sweetcorn freezes very well. Bags of kernels (especially those labelled 'bred for extra sweetness') resonate with flavour that is amazingly close to the fresh stuff. Corn kernels even survive the canning process quite well. So make the most of modern technology and keep a good supply of both the canned and frozen kernels on hand for a bit of summertime whenever you want it.

SWEETCORN AND MUSHROOM SAUTÉ

MAKES 12 FL OZ (350 ML)

V ⊙

This fresh-tasting, quick sauté looks beautiful served in steamed courgette boats (page 31). I love the simple, clear flavour of the basic recipe but, if you prefer it a bit jazzier, add some crushed ginger and a teaspoon of mild curry powder in step 1.

4 small button mushrooms (about 2 oz/50 g), sliced
3 spring onions, trimmed and sliced
3 fl oz (75 ml) stock

1 tablespoon dry sherry
1–2 dashes teriyaki or soy sauce
7 oz (200 g) can sweetcorn kernels, drained
1 tablespoon chopped fresh parsley

1 Combine the mushrooms, spring onions, stock, sherry and teriyaki in a small frying pan. Simmer for a few minutes or until the mushrooms are tender and the liquid almost absorbed.

2 Stir in the corn and parsley, and cook for 1–2 minutes longer or until hot through.

COURGETTES

Courgettes are very good to eat raw, cut into slices or sticks. It is never necessary to peel the tender skin, and as far as cooking is concerned, they can be grilled, stir-fried in stock, simmered in tomato sauce, or hollowed out and stuffed. If you are lucky enough to have a source of tiny new courgettes with their delicate yellow blossoms, then you will be able to stuff and steam those adorable blooms. Courgette blossoms can be filled with rice pilau-type mixtures, duxelles, the spinach mixture on page 38, or even with one of the meatball mixtures in the Meat chapter (pages 171–173). Steam the filled male blossoms, covered, on a plate set on a rack above boiling water for 10–20 minutes (depending on the filling). Serve as they are or set on a light tomato sauce (pages 85–86). (Don't blanket them with the sauce, or you will mask their beautiful colour.)

GRILLED COURGETTES

V ☙ ❄

Courgettes can be grilled, just like aubergine (page 4), either with a light spray of olive oil, or dredged in Fromage Frais 'Mayo' (page 97) and crumbs. Plainly grilled, they are tender and sweet – great for snacking as well as in recipes. Crumbed and grilled, stuff them into a crusty baguette, or bake, covered with tomato sauce and strips of mozzarella cheese or a shower of grated Parmesan. As with the Crumbed Grilled Aubergine (page 5), courgette slices can be trimmed into fish shapes and served with Spicy Oven-Fried Potatoes (page 52) and Green Pea Spread (page 74) for an alternative (vegetarian) version of fish and chips.

about 5 medium courgettes, slant-cut into ¼ *olive oil spray (page ix)*
  inch (0.5 cm) slices

1 Preheat the grill to high. Lightly mist a non-stick baking sheet with olive oil spray.

2 Spread out the courgette slices in one layer on the baking sheet. *Lightly* mist the slices with the spray, and grill, close to the heat, for 3–5 minutes or until tender and speckled with brown. Turn, mist *lightly* with spray, and grill for a moment or so on the second side.

STIR-FRIED COURGETTES

MAKES 1 PINT (600 ML)

V ⊙ ❄

For a simpler courgette stir-fry, cut the vegetables as described below, and stir-fry in a mixture of stock and lime or lemon juice. However, the addition of spring onions, garlic and fresh herbs complements them very well.

4 sundried tomatoes, chopped with scissors (optional)
6 spring onions, trimmed and thinly sliced
3 garlic cloves, crushed
½ pint (300 ml) stock

1 lb (450 g) courgettes, trimmed
juice of ½ lemon
salt and freshly ground pepper
2 tablespoons chopped fresh parsley
2 tablespoons shredded fresh basil leaves

1 Combine the sundried tomatoes (if using), spring onions and garlic with 4 fl oz (100 ml) stock in a heavy-bottomed frying pan. Cover and boil for 5 minutes. Uncover and cook briskly until the liquid is greatly reduced and syrupy.

2 Meanwhile, cut the courgettes into shapes measuring about 2 inches (5 cm) long and ½ inch (1 cm) wide.

3 Stir the courgettes into the tomato and onion mixture with the remaining stock and the lemon juice. Season with salt and pepper, and stir in the herbs. Cook, stirring, over a high heat, until the courgettes are tender (but not mushy) and the liquid almost gone.

COURGETTES STUFFED WITH SPINACH

MAKES 12 'BOATS'
V ❄

Two or three (or more!) of these spinach-filled, feta cheese-stuffed courgette boats make a delicious main course. Serve with couscous, bulghur or rice along with Cherry Tomato and Olive Salsa (page 81).

6 courgettes, each about 7 inches (18 cm) long and weighing 6–8 oz (175–225 g)
6 spring onions, trimmed and sliced
½ pint (300 ml) stock
juice of ½ large lemon
¼ teaspoon each of ground allspice and cumin
pinch each of ground cinnamon and cayenne pepper
2 tablespoons sultanas

2 black olives in brine, drained and slivered off their stones
8 oz (225 g) spinach, trimmed
2 tablespoons shredded fresh mint
2 tablespoons crumbled feta cheese
salt and freshly ground pepper
½ pint (300 ml) passata
1 tablespoon runny honey

1 Preheat the oven to 190°C, 375°F, Gas Mark 5.

2 Trim the courgettes and cut in half lengthways. With a teaspoon, scrape out the flesh, leaving a shell of about ¼ inch (0.5 cm) thick. Chop the flesh. Steam the shells over boiling water for 3–4 minutes or until partially tender. Refresh under cold running water and drain well.

3 In a heavy-bottomed wok or saucepan, combine the spring onions, stock, 1 tablespoon lemon juice, the spices, sultanas, olives and the chopped courgette pulp. Simmer briskly until the vegetables are tender and the liquid almost gone.

4 Rinse the spinach; do not dry it. Cram the spinach into the pan (it will greatly overfill it, but soon cook down). Clap on the lid, and allow to steam over a low heat for about 1 minute. Uncover, stir and cook for a few more minutes or until the spinach is cooked, but still bright green, and well combined with the other ingredients. Stir in the mint and crumbled feta cheese, and season with salt and pepper. Spoon this mixture into the courgette shells.

5 Combine the passata, remaining lemon juice and honey, and spread in the bottom of a baking dish large enough to hold the courgettes in one layer. Place the courgettes on the sauce. Cover with foil and bake in the oven for 15 minutes, then uncover and bake for about 15 minutes more or until the sauce is bubbly and the courgettes heated through.

VARIATIONS Once you have prepared courgette shells for stuffing, you'll want to try them again and again, filled with all manner of things. Particularly good in courgette shells are Keema Curry (page 161) and Lentil–Aubergine Bolognese Sauce (page 10).

FENNEL

If you love liquorice, you'll love fennel. It really is one of the most entrancing of vegetables. Shaped like bulbous celery, bearing feathery fronds, with a juicy crispness and a haunting anise flavour, it is a pleasure to eat either raw or cooked. A half pound (225 g) of fennel contains only about 50 calories, so – as with most vegetables – you can settle down for a 'therapeutic binge'. Fennel goes particularly well with fish, and it is very good with roasted chicken as well. In fact, puréed, cooked fennel, stirred into the de-greased pan juices of a roasted chicken (page 141) makes a mouthwatering gravy. Puréed cooked fennel also makes a fragrant addition to mashed potatoes.

PAN-BRAISED FENNEL

MAKES 4 PIECES

V ⊙ ❄

Some recipes advise blanching fennel first to mute its flavour. Balderdash! If you object to the anise flavour, eat celery instead.

2 bulbs fennel
stock

salt and freshly ground pepper

1 Trim the tough outer layers, and the stalks and leaves from the bulbs of fennel. (Save the trimmings for stock-making, and save the feathery fronds to use as a herb garnish.) Trim a little off the bottom, but leave the core intact – it keeps the fennel sections together.

2 Cut the fennel bulbs into halves or quarters. Put the fennel pieces, cut-sides down, in one layer in a heavy-bottomed frying pan. Pour in the stock and season with salt and pepper. Cover and simmer, stirring occasionally, until glazed and tender. If the liquid threatens to cook away, add a bit more. On the other hand, if the fennel is cooked, and quite a bit of liquid remains, remove the fennel and keep warm. Boil down the cooking juices, and pour them over the fennel.

FENNEL STIR-FRY

Fennel takes very well to the stock stir-fry method. Trim the halves or quarters and prepare as described for Pan-Braised Fennel (opposite), but cut crossways into strips. Stir-fry in stock alone for a very pure anise taste (to underline that taste, you could add a splash of Pernod, or a scattering of fennel seeds); stir-fry in the olive–garlic infusion (page viii). Or stir-fry in stock and a splash of orange juice, with a few halved, stoned black olives and – added towards the end – some coarsely diced fresh orange segments. Whichever version you try, finish the dish of tender fennel pieces with a scattering of the snipped feathery fronds.

OVEN-BRAISED FENNEL

SERVES 4

V ❊

Oven-Braised Fennel takes longer than Pan-Braised Fennel but involves no real work – simply bung it in and let it braise. If you like, turn it into a gratin by adding a shower of grated Parmesan in the last 15 minutes of baking.

2 bulbs fennel
4 fl oz (110 ml) stock
salt and freshly ground pepper

3 tablespoons freshly grated Parmesan cheese
(optional)

1 Preheat the oven to 180°C, 350°F, Gas Mark 4. Trim the tough outer layers off the fennel bulbs and remove the stalks and leaves. Trim a little off the bottom but leave the core intact. Cut each bulb in half lengthways, then cut the halves into wedges about ½ inch (1 cm) thick.

2 Arrange the fennel in one layer in a baking dish. Pour over the stock, and season with salt and pepper.

3 Bake, uncovered, in the oven for 45 minutes. Sprinkle Parmesan (if using) over the fennel during the last 15 minutes. The fennel will become meltingly tender and the stock will have cooked almost completely away, leaving a rich glaze. Serve at once.

FENNEL AND PEPPER SALAD

SERVES 4

V ⊙

Crisp, juicy raw fennel is a wonderful salad component. It combines well with mushrooms and colourful peppers. This salad is particularly good with fish.

1 medium fennel bulb
1 small red and 1 small yellow pepper, cut into
their natural sections, deseeded and peeled
(page 48)
4 oz (110 g) button mushrooms, cleaned and
thinly sliced

1 tablespoon capers, drained and rinsed
2 large garlic cloves
1 small bunch fresh parsley
one of the citrus dressings (pages 95–96)

1 Trim the tough outer layer off the fennel bulb and remove the stalk and leaves, reserving some of the leaves. Trim a little off the bottom but leave the core intact. Cut the fennel in half and slice across. Slice the pepper pieces into strips. Combine the fennel and pepper with the mushrooms and capers in a bowl.

2 Finely chop together the garlic and parsley. Snip the reserved feathery fennel leaves with scissors, and toss into the vegetables with the garlic and parsley. Toss in the dressing and serve.

GARLIC

From the beginning of recorded time, a bulb with a powerful taste and pervasive perfume – *Allium sativum* (garlic) – has been embraced as a kind of miracle drug. It has been reputed to cure a vast array of ailments from plague and hypertension to toothache and the common cold. And, today, there are many studies in contemporary medical literature implicating garlic as an agent in cholesterol and blood pressure control, and as an antibacterial, antifungal, and possibly anticarcinogenic agent. Do keep in mind, though, that not all of this work is definitive. And, according to much of the evidence, any beneficial qualities of garlic require it to be consumed in *large quantities*, and in its *natural form*, smell and all.

From my point of view, quantity is far from a problem. I am a passionate devotee of the stinking rose, and believe, wholeheartedly, in using it in quantity. Yes, garlic is a seasoning, and a clove or two, used with discretion here and there, adds a wonderful dimension to many dishes. But garlic is a vegetable as well and, used with abandon, will bring much pleasure. It will add fat-free richness and depth of flavour to your dishes without adding vulgarity. In fact, a whole bulb of garlic roasted gently in the oven or pan-braised (see opposite) is actually gentler and mellower than a single clove crushed in a garlic press and browned in oil!

Buy large, unblemished, heavy, unsprouting heads of garlic with no withered cloves. Don't store them in the fridge, or they will turn bitter and begin to sprout. Keep the bulbs, uncovered, in a cool, well-ventilated corner of the kitchen.

Be kind to garlic, and don't subject it to a garlic press; it turns garlic into an acrid mess. Instead, buy a wooden mallet and use it to crush garlic cloves in this manner: hit each clove lightly with the mallet to loosen the skin. Remove the skin, then crush the clove with the mallet. Alternatively, use the flat side of a wide knife. If you notice that the clove contains a green centre sprout, remove and discard the sprout (it tends to be bitter).

Sauté crushed garlic gently in stock, or a mixture of stock and wine instead of frying in oil (you won't be using oil anyway!) and the flavour will be mild, mellow and delicious. Try making a no-butter garlic 'butter' by baking whole bulbs of garlic gently in the oven:

ROASTED GARLIC PUREE

One bulb of roasted garlic will yield 1–2 tablespoons garlic purée.

large bulbs of firm, heavy, unblemished,
   unsprouting garlic

1 Preheat the oven to 190°C, 375°F, Gas Mark 5.

2 Remove the papery outer covering of the whole garlic bulbs, but do not separate the cloves or peel them. Place each whole bulb of garlic on a square of foil (shiny-side up). Fold up the foil and crimp so that the head is wrapped in a roomy but tightly sealed pouch.

3 Bake in the oven for about 1 hour (timing depends upon your oven and the size of the bulbs).

4 Remove from the oven, unwrap and cool for at least 5 minutes. Gently separate the cloves and squeeze each one over a fine-mesh sieve so that the softened garlic pops into the sieve.

5 With a rubber spatula or wooden spoon, rub the garlic through the sieve into a small container or bowl. If you are in a hurry, forget the sieve; simply squeeze the garlic into the bowl, and push it into a mound with a rubber spatula. Spread this magical purée on crusty bread, or stir it into soups, sauces and stews. (It can even be baked into bread, page 195.)

PAN-BRAISED GARLIC For a quicker way of obtaining soft, mellow cloves, peel any number of garlic cloves, but don't crush them. Put them, in one layer, in a heavy-bottomed frying pan and cover generously with stock. Cover tightly, and simmer for 10–15 minutes or until the garlic is meltingly tender and the stock greatly reduced. (Check and top up the stock if necessary as the cloves braise.) Drain (use any leftover stock in soups and sauces), and mash the cloves or push them through a fine-mesh sieve.

WHOLE ROASTED GARLIC

This is the most fun of all garlic methods, although you might give your friends and relatives a conniption fit as you bear the steaming, odorous platter of whole garlic heads to the table, and make it clear that you expect them to eat the damned things as a starter to their meal! But most people (except the dyed-in-the-wool, garlic-hating die-hards) love the sweet, mellow taste and mouthfilling texture, and gobble it all up with alacrity.

1 large, heavy, unwithered, unsprouting,
 exquisite head of garlic per person
olive oil spray (page ix)
2–3 fl oz (50–75 ml) stock
fresh thyme sprigs (optional)
freshly ground pepper

TO SERVE
crusty bread
no-fat fromage frais or medium-fat creamy
 goat's cheese (optional)

1 Preheat the oven to 150°C, 300°F, Gas Mark 2.

2 Remove the papery outer covering of the garlic bulbs, but do not separate or peel the cloves. With a sharp knife, slice the pointed end off each garlic bulb, so that the meat of the cloves is exposed.

3 Mist a baking dish with olive oil spray, and pour in the stock. Place the garlic, in one layer, cut ends up, in the dish, and spray the cut ends lightly with olive oil spray. Put a few sprigs of thyme (if you have them) in the dish, and grind on some pepper.

4 Cover tightly with foil (the foil should not touch the top of the garlic, but it should be well sealed all around) and bake in the oven for 1 hour or until the garlic meat within its skin is very tender. Serve each victim (excuse me, I mean *diner*) with a whole bulb of garlic and some crusty bread. A little no-fat fromage frais or medium-fat creamy goat's cheese would be nice as well. To eat, gently separate the cloves and squeeze over the bread so that the softened garlic pops out. Spread this gorgeous purée over the bread, along with the fromage frais or goat's cheese if you wish. Stunned (and appreciative) silence is the only proper response here!

GARLIC BREATH

Yes, you will smell afterwards. In fact, you will positively glow. You will breathe garlic from your lungs; you will exude it from your very pores. It is possible to sweeten the mouth with anise seeds, coffee beans, raw parsley, mint or even mouthwash, but this does nothing for the lungs and pores. To put it bluntly, you will breathe and sweat garlic. But when the garlic consumed was gently roasted or simmered, the smell is a fragrance rather than a stink; and not really offensive in the way it can be when the garlic consumed was raw, or browned in oil.

GREENS

Dark leafy greens are extremely low in calories and fat, yet they are powerhouses of vitamins (C, A and folic acid) and fibre. And minerals too; the darker the green, the more iron in the leaves, although the iron in vegetables (and the calcium) is not as well absorbed by the body as the iron and calcium in dairy products, meat and poultry. A diet rich in vitamin C will help make your body's absorption of vegetable iron and calcium more efficient.

Use greens lavishly in salads or steam them as you would spinach. The greens (tops) of young beetroot are delicious cooked this way, as are the leaves of young white turnips.

SPINACH

Spinach contains both iron and calcium, in addition to lovely vitamins. The problem with fresh spinach is the grit. Fill the sink with cold water, throw in the spinach, swish it around and let it float for a few minutes. Lift it out, shake it and drain away the water. The grit will have sunk to the bottom of the sink. Repeat one or two more times, then, finally, rinse under cold running water.

To cook fresh spinach, no liquid is needed other than the water clinging to it after washing. Cram into a large saucepan (never use uncoated aluminium or cast iron, or the leaves will darken and take on a horrible taste), cover and let steam until it starts to go limp. Stir until just cooked, but still bright green. The whole process takes 5 minutes at the most. Two to three pounds (900–1.4 kg) of raw spinach will collapse into a mere ¾ pint (450 ml) of cooked spinach.

CREAMED SPINACH PURÉE

MAKES ½ PINT (300 ML)

V ⊘

A gentle dish of creamed spinach is very nice with mashed potatoes and sautéed mushrooms – a perfect vegetable supper, or an accompaniment to simply grilled meat.

8 oz (225 g) young spinach
2 rounded tablespoons non-fat fromage frais
1 teaspoon mild mustard

pinch of sugar
salt and freshly ground pepper

1 Wash the spinach well but don't dry it. Put it into a large heavy-bottomed saucepan, cover and steam over a medium heat for 2–3 minutes. Uncover, and let cook, stirring, for another 1–2 minutes or until the spinach is cooked but still bright green. Remove from the heat.

2 Put the fromage frais, mustard and sugar in a blender or food processor, and process until well combined. Drain the juices from the spinach, and process in as well. Add the spinach and pulse the machine on and off until the spinach is finely chopped. Tip the purée back into the pan, season with salt and pepper, and heat gently, stirring. Don't boil or it will separate.

SPICED SPINACH

MAKES 1 PINT (600 ML)

V ☉

Frozen spinach is a very convenient product, and in a dish like this Middle-Eastern-inspired spiced spinach, no real compromise in flavour.

6 spring onions, trimmed and sliced
2 garlic cloves, crushed
2 tablespoons sultanas
pinch of cayenne pepper
¼ teaspoon ground cinnamon
½ teaspoon ground coriander

½ pint (300 ml) stock
juice and grated zest of ½ lemon
1 ½ lb (700 g) frozen chopped spinach, thawed, drained and squeezed dry
salt and freshly ground pepper

1 Combine the onions, garlic, sultanas, spices, stock, lemon juice and zest in a heavy-bottomed frying pan. Cover and boil for 5 minutes.

2 Stir in the spinach and season with salt and pepper. Cook and stir for a few minutes over a very low heat to thoroughly coat the spinach with the onion mixture, and to blend the flavours. Taste and adjust the seasonings, adding more salt, pepper, lemon juice or spices as needed.

WATERCRESS

Watercress is related to broccoli, cabbage, turnips and cauliflower, and shares their nutritional benefits. Bunches of the peppery greens are wonderful tucked in as a garnish in all sorts of places, but especially with grilled or roasted meats. The mingling of hot meat juices with the crisp, cold leaves is one of the greatest of culinary marriages, yet it is simplicity itself. And, of course, watercress is wonderful in salads.

ORANGE WATERCRESS SALAD

V ⊙

Beautiful to look at as well as delicious to eat and bursting with nutrients. About half an orange and a handful of watercress is enough for one serving.

juicy, seedless oranges
watercress, washed and shaken dry
very low-fat fromage frais

freshly ground pepper
½ teaspoon grated orange zest
pinch of ground cumin

1 On a chopping board, slice the oranges thinly. With a paring knife, neatly remove the peel and white pith from each slice. Do not wipe away the orange juice that collects on the board.

2 Overlap the orange slices on half of a clear glass plate. Fan out the watercress on the lower half. Stir the orange juice that has collected on the chopping board into the fromage frais along with the pepper, orange zest and cumin. Either serve the dressing in a clear glass jug along with the salad, or pour a thin stripe of dressing down the centre of each row of orange slices, and serve the rest separately.

VARIATION Coarsely chop a mild onion and a grilled and peeled (page 48) red pepper. Sliver a few black olives off their stones, cube the peeled oranges, and mix with the onion and pepper. Toss with one of the citrus dressings (pages 95–6) and serve on a bed of watercress.

MUSHROOMS

Mushrooms are high in flavour, very low in calories (125 Calories per *pound*!) and virtually fat-free. Traditionally, mushrooms are sautéed in some sort of fat or oil, adding 120 fat Calories per *single tablespoon* used, thereby destroying the wonderful low-fat, low-calorie profile of the fungi, and – to my mind – blunting the delicious mushroom flavour as well. Fortunately, mushrooms take very well indeed to no-fat cooking methods; if you sauté them in the 'trinity' of no-fat mushroom cookery – wine (especially sherry), teriyaki (or soy) sauce and stock – their flavour shines through. Any mushroom or combination of mushrooms can be cooked this way, from button mushrooms to the more flavourful brown caps (or chestnut mushrooms) through to delicate oyster mushrooms, and the intense and wild-tasting shiitake mushrooms.

Fresh mushrooms can be enhanced by combining with reconstituted dried mushrooms. Just 1 oz (25 g), or even a mere ½ oz (15 g) dried mushrooms reconstituted (see below) and cooked with a panful of fresh mushrooms results in an explosion of mushroom flavour. Small boxes of dried ceps (*porcini*) and shiitakes are available in many supermarkets.

SAUTÉED MUSHROOMS

Choose whole button mushrooms, or larger mushrooms cut into quarters or eighths, or sliced. A mixture of mushrooms – brown caps, shiitake (trim away the tough stems), white cultivated, oyster – gives very good results.

1–1½ lb (450–700 g) mushrooms (see above)
2–3 fl oz (50–75 ml) stock
2–3 fl oz (50–75 ml) sherry, dry red or white
  wine or vermouth

teriyaki or soy sauce
salt and freshly ground pepper

1 Put the mushrooms in a large wok or frying pan. Stir in the stock, sherry or wine and a few dashes of teriyaki or soy sauce, and simmer briskly until the mushrooms release a lot of liquid.

2 Reduce the heat a little and simmer until the liquid has been absorbed, and the mushrooms are gently 'frying' in their own juices. Season with salt and pepper.

VARIATION To increase the intensity of the sauté, add reconstituted dried mushrooms in step 1. To reconstitute them, rinse ½ oz (15 g) dried mushrooms under cold running water, then soak in plenty of hot water for 20–30 minutes. With your fingers, lift them out of the soaking water, rinse again and chop, trimming away any tough stems. Add these to the fresh mushrooms in step 1 above.

Strain the soaking water through a sieve lined with muslin or a double layer of coffee filters. Use 2–3 fl oz (50–75 ml) of this liquid in place of the stock in the recipe above. (Store the remaining liquid in the freezer and use for soups, stews and sauces.)

DUXELLES

MAKES 1 PINT (600 ML)

V ☉ ❄

This is a no-fat version of a very useful classic mixture; a sort of hash (almost a pâté or spread) of very finely chopped mushrooms. It can be tossed with cooked pasta, layered with lasagne, stirred by the spoonful into soups, stews or sauces, spread on toast, served in little tartlet shells (page 84), stuffed into vegetable cases or used to fill a reduced-yolk omelette. It is, essentially, concentrated mushrooms, and sheer joy for mushroom lovers. As for Sautéed Mushrooms, any mushrooms can be used, but dark mushrooms (brown caps, shiitakes or large, open mushrooms) give the deepest flavour and darkest (almost black) colour. Again, dried mushrooms can be included for depth of flavour.

1½ lb (700 g) mixed mushrooms, cleaned well　　　*teriyaki or soy sauce*
8 fl oz (225 ml) stock　　　*1 teaspoon dried tarragon, crumbled*
4 fl oz (110 ml) sherry　　　*salt and freshly ground pepper*

1 Chop the mushrooms very, very finely. This is best done in a food processor, if you have one. Quarter the mushrooms and put them into the food processor bowl. Pulse the machine on and off until the mushrooms are very finely chopped. You will need to do this in two or more batches.

2 Empty all the chopped mushrooms into a deep, heavy-bottomed frying pan. Add the stock, sherry, several dashes of teriyaki or soy sauce and the tarragon, and mix well. The mushrooms will be barely moistened, but it doesn't matter.

3 Cook over a moderate heat, stirring occasionally, until the mushrooms have rendered quite a lot of liquid. Turn the heat up a bit and simmer briskly, stirring occasionally, until the mushrooms are very dark, very thick and dry. Season with salt and pepper. Cool and store in the refrigerator until needed.

VARIATION To include dried mushrooms, use ½–1 oz (15–25 g), reconstituted as for Sautéed Mushrooms. Chop the rinsed soaked mushrooms with the fresh mushrooms in step 1, above, and replace the stock with an equivalent amount of the strained soaking water.

MUSHROOMS PAPRIKASH

MAKES 1¼ PINTS (750 ML)
V ☺

Cornflour can be used to 'stabilize' non-fat fromage frais so that it does not separate when simmered. The tender mushrooms, in their rosy sauce, would be perfect ladled over rice, or into a 'crater' that you have made in a mound of mashed potatoes.

10 spring onions, trimmed and sliced
1 tablespoon paprika
½ pint (300 ml) stock
2 fl oz (50 ml) white vermouth
1½ lb (700 g) small button mushrooms
salt and freshly ground pepper
3 tablespoons non-fat fromage frais

1 tablespoon tomato purée
Tabasco sauce
1 teaspoon mild mustard
1 tablespoon cornflour whisked into 2
 tablespoons water
snipped fresh dill or chives, to garnish
 (optional)

1 Combine the onions, paprika, stock, vermouth and mushrooms in a large, heavy-bottomed frying pan. Simmer, stirring occasionally, until the mushrooms are almost tender, and have rendered quite a bit of liquid. Simmer until the liquid has reduced by about one half. Season with salt and pepper, and remove from the heat.

2 Whisk together the fromage frais, tomato purée, a dash or two of Tabasco and the mustard until smooth. Whisk in 3 tablespoons of the mushroom liquid from the pan, then stir this mixture into the mushrooms. Return to a very low heat, and stir until just heated through.

3 Stir the cornflour mixture into the mushrooms and raise the heat a little. Simmer gently, stirring, for 2–3 minutes or until slightly thickened. Taste and adjust the seasonings before serving sprinkled with snipped fresh dill or chives, if desired.

GRILLED MUSHROOMS

Large flat mushrooms (sometimes they seem to be almost the size of Frisbees!) are just right for the grill. Remove the stems (save them for Duxelles, page 41), spray the mushrooms lightly on both sides with oil spray, and grill for a few minutes on each side. The idea is to grill to succulence, but not floppiness. Exact timing depends on your grill and the size of the mushrooms. These meaty beauties are wonderful in a sandwich; be sure to saturate the bread with any pan juices.

GRILLED MUSHROOM 'PIZZAS'

MAKES 4

V ⊙ ❋

Mushrooms form the bases of these 'pizzas' – one or two of them make a quick, interesting and filling meal. If you have no tomato sauce on hand, make a quick one with passata (page 86).

4 large flat mushrooms
2 fl oz (50 ml) dry red wine
2 fl oz (50 ml) stock
about ½ pint (300 ml) Basic Tomato Sauce
  (page 85)

1 tablespoon chopped fresh parsley
olive oil spray (page ix)
5 oz (125 g) package half-fat mozzarella cheese,
  drained, blotted dry and sliced
freshly ground pepper

1 Preheat the grill.

2 Remove the stems from the mushrooms, chop them and put them in a frying pan with the wine and stock. Simmer until the liquid has almost gone. Stir in the tomato sauce and parsley.

3 Line the grill pan with foil, shiny side up. Put the grill rack in the grill pan, and spray lightly with oil spray. Put the mushrooms, gill-side up, on the rack, spray lightly with the oil spray, and grill close to the heat, for 1–2 minutes. If the mushrooms are very large and thick, turn, spray lightly again, and grill for 1–2 minutes more. Turn the mushrooms gill-side up again. Tip any juices in the grill pan into the tomato sauce and stir in.

4 Spoon an equal amount of tomato mixture into each mushroom. Top with mozzarella slices and grind on some pepper. Grill for 2–4 minutes or until the cheese melts. Serve at once.

ONIONS

Life without onions would be hard to imagine. Sharp, strong and juicy when raw; sweet, mild and meltingly tender when cooked, they underpin savoury cooking like nothing else. Onions are believed to have many of the same therapeutic properties as garlic (page 34), so their appearance in quantity in many savoury recipes is health-enhancing as well as delicious. It is the sweetness of cooked onions that make them so satisfying to work with. As the onions cook, the sugars caramelize. An onion – just like garlic – may cause havoc with your digestion when raw, but becomes a sweet pussycat of a vegetable when cooked.

I occasionally use spring onions in the sauté base of certain dishes. Their delicacy and the speed with which they cook make them very useful. To prepare, trim off the roots, and then slice the white and green portions. Both white and green can be sautéed; alternatively, save some of the green to use raw as a garnish on the final dish.

CARAMELIZED ONIONS

V ⊘ ❄

If you have an enamelled cast-iron frying pan that has an enamelled interior (in other words, one that does *not* have a non-stick coating) you will be able to prepare these gorgeously sweet, amber brown onions. A Le Creuset buffet casserole, or something similar, is perfect. Use the onions as a garnish for meat, fish and poultry, or use as the flavour base for soups and stews. You can prepare up to six large onions at once this way (if your pan is big enough). The onions will keep in the refrigerator for about five days, or they can be frozen.

large Spanish onions, chopped, sliced or cut into wedges (with the pieces separated)

about ¾ pint (450 ml) stock
dry white vermouth (optional)

1 Combine the onion pieces and 10–12 fl oz (300–350 ml) stock in a heavy enamelled cast-iron frying pan. Cover, bring to the boil and boil for 5–10 minutes, stirring very occasionally.

2 Uncover, and reduce the heat a little. Simmer and stir until the onions are beginning to stick and brown. Pour in a splash of stock, or a splash of dry white vermouth, if using, stir and scrape the bottom of the pan to loosen all the browned bits. Continue cooking, stirring, for 1–2 minutes, adding a splash of stock or vermouth as necessary, until the onions are amber brown, meltingly tender and syrupy, and the liquid almost gone.

SAUTÉED ONIONS

V ⊙ ❄

This is the method to use if you have a non-stick frying pan, instead of an enamel-interior cast-iron one. The caramelization will not be as pronounced, because you will not be able to give them the 'sticking and burning' treatment that they receive in an enamelled pan, but the onion shreds will still be sweetly delicious.

*large Spanish onions, chopped, sliced or cut
into wedges (with the pieces separated)*

*about ¾ pint (450 ml) stock
dry white vermouth (optional)*

1 Combine the onions and ½ pint (300 ml) stock in a non-stick frying pan, cover and bring to the boil. Boil for 5–7 minutes.

2 Uncover, and reduce heat. Simmer, stirring, over medium heat, until the onions are very tender, a light amber, and syrupy, and the liquid is about gone. Add more stock or dry white vermouth, if using, during cooking, as needed.

SWEET AND SOUR ONIONS

MAKES ¾ PINT (450 ML)

V ⊙

Try a bit of Dijon mustard and balsamic vinegar along with a clove or two of garlic in a gently caramelized pan of onions. If your taste runs to a bit more of the 'sour', add a touch of lemon juice towards the end.

*6 large onions, halved and sliced into ½ inch
(1 cm) thick half moons
15–16 fl oz (450–475 ml) stock
½ teaspoon Dijon mustard*

*1½ tablespoons balsamic vinegar
1 tablespoon sugar
2 garlic cloves, crushed*

1 Place the onions in a frying pan with all the other ingredients.

2 Bring to the boil, then reduce the heat, cover and simmer for about 10 minutes, stirring occasionally.

3 Remove the cover and simmer, stirring, until the onions are amber brown and the liquid greatly reduced.

Onion 'Marmalade'

MAKES ABOUT ¾ PINT (450 ML)

V ❄

Add a little sugar to the basic caramelized onion recipe (page 44) to make a melting mass of onions that will transform a simple piece of grilled meat or chicken into a feast.

6 large onions, halved and sliced into thin half moons
about 16 fl oz (475 ml) stock

½ tablespoon sugar
dry white vermouth, dry red or white wine, dry sherry or balsamic vinegar

1 Combine the onions with 16 fl oz (475 ml) stock in a deep, 10 inch (25 cm), enamelled, cast-iron frying pan. Cover and bring to the boil, then reduce the heat a little and simmer for 10 minutes.

2 Stir in the sugar, and simmer, partially covered, for 35–40 minutes, stirring occasionally, until the onions are turning amber brown and the liquid is almost gone. Allow to cook for a few more minutes, stirring constantly. The onions will begin to stick just a bit. Keep cooking and stirring for about 10 minutes more or until the onions are just about dry and browned deposits are forming on the bottom of the pan. As you stir with your wooden spoon, keep scraping up the browned deposits.

3 Splash in 3–4 tablespoons dry vermouth, wine, sherry, balsamic vinegar or additional stock, and simmer until the liquid is absorbed. Immediately remove from the heat, and use a rubber spatula to scrape the mass of browned onions into a storage container. Use as a garnish for lean meats, as a base for stews, sauces and soups, or serve as a vegetable accompaniment.

PAN-FRIED ONIONS AND APPLES

MAKES 1 PINT (600 ML)

V ⊙ ❄

The apples in this recipe add a hint of tartness, and a texture contrast to the melting sautéed onions. Cider is used as part of the sauté liquid, to underline the apple flavour. Serve with mashed potatoes and pork sausages (page 171) for a heavenly version of sausage and mash.

1 large onion, halved and sliced into thin half
   moons
6 fl oz (175 ml) medium dry cider
4 tart eating apples, such as Granny Smith,

peeled, cored and sliced into ¼ inch (0.5 cm)
   wedges
about 4 fl oz (110 ml) stock
salt and freshly ground pepper

1 Combine the onion with the cider in a heavy-bottomed saucepan. Cover and boil until the onions are limp and the liquid almost gone.

2 Stir in the apples and stock, and season with salt and pepper. Cook briskly, stirring occasionally. Let the apples and onions begin to brown and stick. Pour in a little more stock, as needed, and stir and scrape up the browned bits from the bottom of the pan. When the apples are tender but not mushy, they are done.

ROASTED ONION

V ❄

A baked onion is sweeter than a baked apple. The outside of the onion blackens as it roasts, imparting its smoky flavour to the entire bulb. Use roasted onion as a vegetable or, puréed, as an enrichment for stews, soups and sauces.

large Spanish onions

freshly ground pepper and lemon juice or
   balsamic vinegar, to serve

1 Preheat the oven to 200°C, 400°F, Gas Mark 6.

2 Put the onions on a double sheet of foil, shiny side out, but do not wrap them. Bake in the oven for 1¼ hours or until very soft, almost collapsed.

3 With a sharp knife, cut off the stem and root ends of the onions. Remove and discard the blackened skin and first layer. Serve as is with freshly ground pepper and a sprinkling of lemon juice or balsamic vinegar, or purée the onions in a blender for use in other recipes.

PEPPERS

(Capsicums)

There are thousands of varieties of capsicums, of all shapes, sizes and colours, and of varying degrees of heat. Large sweet peppers are not hot at all; their flesh is ineffably sweet and juicy and their pure primary colours – green, red, yellow, orange, even purple – make them the jewels of the kitchen.

Peppers survive processing very well, so for cooks in a hurry, peeled canned or bottled red peppers are a great convenience. They can be used in virtually any recipe calling for peeled peppers. With capsicums, as with so many vegetables, nutrition goes hand in hand with good taste; peppers (sweet *and* hot) are a major source of vitamins C and A. And a large sweet pepper contains only about 20 Calories!

PEELING PEPPERS

To reach their full potential, sweet peppers must be peeled. Without peeling, the tough skins lessen the impact of the beautiful, juicy-when-raw, tender-when-cooked, texture of the pepper flesh. And pepper skins are not particularly digestible, and give many people intestinal grief. Peeling eliminates this problem and makes sweet capsicums much more universally acceptable.

Peeling is easily done in one of several ways. Peppers can be grilled until the skin wrinkles, blisters and blackens; then the skin slips off easily. This method renders the pepper flesh cooked, tender and subtly smoky. Alternatively, the peppers can be cut into their natural sections and peeled with an ordinary vegetable peeler. This results in a raw, crisp pepper – just right for salads, and for stir-frying or sautéeing. Finally, if you are using a quantity of peppers for a pepper sauce (pages 87–88), for example, chop them up without peeling, and simmer them in stock. When they are tender, purée them, then strain them in a fine sieve, pushing them through with a wooden spoon. The soft pepper flesh will pass through the sieve, while the tougher skins will remain in the sieve and can easily be discarded.

A FEW WORDS ABOUT CHILLI PEPPERS

There are thousands of different types of chillies, varying in shape, size, and shades of red, yellow and green. Lately, an interesting array of these feisty lovelies have been sighted in supermarkets and greengrocers' the length and breadth of the country. A general rule of thumb: the smaller the chilli, the hotter it will be, but do watch out; *all* chillies are hot – it is just a matter of degree. A red chilli is simply a riper chilli, not necessarily a hotter one. The heat of a chilli is contained in its seeds and inner membranes, so unless you are well inured to edible fire, remove the seeds and ribs before you proceed with a recipe. Do not touch your eyes or any other sensitive part of your body until you have washed your hands thoroughly in soap and water. Good heavens, man, *do not* use the loo, until you have washed those hands!

Some people have a sensitivity to the volatile oils in chillies, and find that their fingers burn after handling the fiery things. It's best in this case to leave chilli work to someone else, or to wear rubber gloves when handling them.

If you burn your mouth with a chilli-laden dish, don't gulp cold water – it will make matters worse. Eat a piece of bread, gulp a swallow of milk, or take a bite of banana, or a spoonful of sugar or honey.

GRILLED PEPPERS

V ☉ ❄

When grilling aubergines and courgettes (pages 4 and 29), the idea is to keep them under the grill until tender and just speckled with brown, but with peppers, the point is to *burn* them until they blacken and blister. The blackened skin slips off easily and the pepper flesh beneath is sweet, smoky, tender and supple, and the colour is still bright. Store the peppers on a plate in the fridge, covered with cling film. Any juices that collect on the plate are delicious, and should be used along with the peppers. Green peppers can be grilled as well as red and yellow ones, but the greens are not as sweet, and do not yield the same syrupy pan juices.

red and yellow peppers

1 If you have a gas hob, char the peppers by placing them directly on the flame. As the peppers blacken, turn them with tongs. Alternatively, cut them in half, 'break' them slightly (by bending) so they lie flat, and place under the grill, cut side down. Grill until they blacken and blister.

2 Put the hot black peppers in a plastic food bag and leave for at least 5–10 minutes (longer if necessary). Steam will form between the burnt skin and the flesh, making peeling a doddle. Strip off the skin and discard it. (Don't rinse the peppers in water or you will wash away the lovely smoky flavour.) Discard the cores, seeds and stems. Save any of the juices that have accumulated in the plastic bags, to use with the peppers.

STIR-FRIED PEPPERS

V ☉ ✳

Peeled red peppers, stir-fried in stock, make one of the most luscious low-fat vegetable dishes I know. It's utterly simple, yet the supple tender peppers, bathed in their 'buttery', rosy sauce, are quite magical. Use as a side vegetable, a garnish for meat, poultry or fish, a simple sauce to toss into freshly cooked pasta, a sandwich filling or an accompaniment to mashed or baked potatoes. The dish can be made in advance and re-warmed later or the next day.

6 red peppers
6 fl oz (175 ml) stock

freshly ground pepper

1 Cut the peppers in half lengthways. Remove the stems, the seeds and the ribs, and cut the halves into their natural sections. Peel each pepper piece with a swivel-bladed vegetable peeler. Cut each piece into strips about ½ inch (1 cm) wide.

2 Combine the peppers with the stock in a heavy-bottomed frying pan. Grind in some black pepper and bring to the boil. When boiling, use two wooden spoons to toss and turn the peppers in the hot stock until the liquid has cooked down considerably. Reduce the heat a little and 'fry' the peppers for a few minutes in their own juices, until they are very tender, and the pepper juices have formed a thick sauce. Serve with their delicious juices.

SHERRY PEPPERS

V ☉ ✳

Add some garlic to the peppers, and augment the stock with sherry for a very elegant version of Stir-Fried Peppers (above).

6–8 red peppers
4–5 garlic cloves, coarsely diced
4 fl oz (100 ml) stock

2 fl oz (50 ml) sherry
freshly ground pepper

1 Prepare the peppers as in step 1 above.

2 Combine the peppers with the remaining ingredients in a heavy-bottomed frying pan. Bring to the boil, and cook, stirring occasionally, until the peppers are tender and the liquid greatly reduced. Continue to stir and cook until the peppers are in a thick, syrupy sauce. Serve at once. They are also delicious eaten cold.

POTATOES

Potatoes are almost everyone's favourite vegetable: their starchy comfort, their exquisite nutrition, and their extraordinary versatility make it hard to imagine existence without them. But I do get cross when I hear someone say, 'No potatoes for me, please – I'm dieting.' It's not the potatoes that make you fat, it's the oily, buttery, creamy excesses committed upon them. A medium potato contains about 90 very low-fat Calories, and offers a good selection of vitamins, minerals and fibre. And spuds are satisfying and filling. A low-fat lifestyle means that you can dine on potatoes happily and guilt-free for the rest of your life.

CHIPS

V

Who says chips have to drown in oceans of oil? With a non-stick baking sheet and your trusty oil spray (page ix), you will be able to produce *really* gorgeous chips that are crunchy-brown on the outside, fluffy-tender on the inside; that are puffed up almost like *pommes soufflé*; and that fill your mouth with the taste of *potato*, not abused grease. They *vibrate* with flavour and texture.

baking potatoes   *salt, to serve (optional)*
oil spray (page ix)

1 Preheat the oven to 220°C, 425°F, Gas Mark 7.

2 Don't bother to peel the potatoes. Cut them crossways into ¼–½ inch (0.5–1 cm) slices. Cut each slice in half (or cut them into whatever size and shape you like for chips).

3 Mist one or two non-stick baking sheets with the oil spray. Spread the potatoes on the sheet(s) in one layer. Cook in the oven for 20–30 minutes, shaking to move them around once or twice.

4 Gently turn the potato slices with a spatula, then return them to the oven for another 10–20 minutes. (The timing depends on the size and shape of the slices, and on your oven.) They should be browned, crunchy on the outside and puffed. Serve at once, sprinkled with salt.

Opposite page 50: Sweetcorn and Pepper Soup Baked in Acorn Squash (page 111), Green Pea Spread (page 74) on a slice of Quicker Yeast Bread (page 198)

Opposite: Couscous-Orange Salad with Prawns and Smoked Fish (page 120), a green salad ready to be dressed with Pepper 'Mayo' (page 99)

OVEN-FRIED NEW POTATOES

V

Oven-fried, small new potatoes puff up like balloons in a hot oven. When you pop them into your mouth with your fingers and chomp down, they pop in a most satisfactory manner!

oil spray (page ix)
tiny new potatoes, scrubbed and dried

salt, to serve (optional)

1 Preheat the oven to its highest temperature.

2 Mist a non-stick baking sheet with oil spray. Halve the potatoes and spread them out, skin side down, in one layer on the sheet. Bake them in the oven for 25–40 minutes or until they are well browned, puffed up and cooked through, shaking occasionally. (The cooking time will depend on your oven and the size of the potatoes.) Tip the potatoes on to a serving platter, salt lightly if desired, and serve at once.

SPICY OVEN-FRIED POTATOES

SERVES 2–4
V

Cubed potatoes coated with a spice mixture and oven-fried on an oil-misted sheet make a wonderful snack, first course, or nibble to serve with drinks. It's hard to stop eating these – more-ish doesn't begin to describe them.

½ teaspoon each of ground turmeric and garam
  masala
¼ teaspoon ground cumin
a few drops of lemon juice

1 rounded tablespoon tomato purée
1 lb (450 g) all-purpose potatoes (such as Wilja),
  peeled and cut into ½ inch (1 cm) cubes
olive oil spray (page ix)

1 Preheat the oven to 220°C, 425°F, Gas Mark 7.

2 Whisk together the spices, lemon juice and tomato purée in a large bowl. Add the potatoes and, with two spoons, toss them in the spice mixture until very well coated.

3 Mist a non-stick baking sheet with oil spray. Spread the potatoes on the sheet and bake in the oven for 25–35 minutes or until they are browned, puffy and tender, turning once or twice.

OVEN-FRIED POTATOES WITH MUSTARD AND HERBS

SERVES 2–4

V

Amustard and herb coating does wonders for oven-fries, giving them a whole new character. These go particularly well with roasted meat.

1 rounded tablespoon Dijon mustard
a few drops of freshly squeezed orange juice
1 teaspoon each of chopped fresh rosemary and thyme leaves or ½ teaspoon each of dried rosemary and thyme

¼ teaspoon dried oregano, crumbled
1 lb (450 g) all-purpose potatoes (such as Wilja), peeled and cut into ½ inch (1 cm) cubes
oil spray (page ix)

1 Preheat the oven to 220°C, 425°F, Gas Mark 7.

2 Whisk together the mustard, orange juice and herbs in a large bowl. Add the potato cubes and, with two spoons, toss them in the mustard and herb mixture until well coated.

3 Mist a non-stick baking sheet with the oil spray. Place the potato cubes on the sheet in one layer, and not touching each other. (Place them on the sheet one at a time. If you tip them on to the sheet and then spread them out, and the mustard smears across the surface of the baking sheet, the smear may burn.) Bake in the oven for 25–35 minutes, loosening the potato cubes with a spatula and turning once or twice. When they are browned and puffed, crisp on the outside and tender on the inside, they are done.

SPICY OVEN-FRIED SWEET POTATOES

SERVES 2–4
V

Because of their higher sugar content, sweet potatoes must be oven-fried at a lower temperature than ordinary potatoes. When they are cooked, the cubes will be speckled with blackened caramelized bits; the taste of those bits is reminiscent of toasted marshmallows! The lime juice and spices balance the sweetness, so that each bite is a heady mixture of flavours.

1 rounded tablespoon tomato purée
a few drops of lime juice
½ teaspoon each of ground cumin and
 coriander
¼ teaspoon paprika

pinch of cayenne pepper
2 sweet potatoes, each weighing about 10 oz
 (275 g), peeled and cut into ½ inch (1 cm)
 cubes
oil spray (page ix)

1 Preheat the oven to 190°C, 375°F, Gas Mark 5.

2 In a large bowl, whisk together the tomato purée, lime juice and spices. Add the potato cubes and, with two spoons, toss them with the tomato–spice mixture until well combined.

3 Mist a non-stick baking sheet with the oil spray, and place the potatoes on the sheet so that they are in one layer, but not touching each other. Bake in the oven for 25–35 minutes, turning once or twice, until they are speckled with black on the outside and meltingly tender on the inside.

SWEET POTATOES

A sweet potato is not a potato at all. Potatoes belong to the nightshade family; sweet potatoes to the morning glory family. Sweet potatoes arrived in Europe from the New World, and were consumed with enthusiasm, long before ordinary potatoes were accepted as a wholesome food. The sweet potatoes available here now have a blushing, sunset-orange flesh, and a lightly honeyed sweetness that is never cloying or overwhelming.

A baked sweet potato makes a wonderful light meal. Pierce it in several places with a skewer and bake directly on the oven shelf for about 1 hour or until tender. Unlike an ordinary potato, the skin of a sweet potato does not crisp, so split the potato, and eat the flesh out of the skin.

POTATO PANCAKES

MAKES 15 PANCAKES

V ⊙

During the festival of Chanukah, Jewish families eat potato pancakes (latkes) fried in plenty of oil to commemorate the ancient miracle of the temple oil that lasted for many more nights than expected. Call me sacrilegious, but I feel quite happy to celebrate with a spritz of oil, instead of a splosh. The truth is, taste-wise, there is no compromise, in fact I think these pancakes are better than the traditional awash-in-oil version. No matter how assiduously the oily-method pancakes are blotted, they remain greasy. These oven-fried beauties are crisp on the outside, meltingly tender within, and never greasy. Serve them with fromage frais, either plain, or with some snipped fresh dill mixed in. Or, for a truly exquisite experience, top each hot pancake with a dollop of fromage frais and some shredded smoked salmon.

2 baking potatoes, each weighing about 12 oz
  (350 g)
1 large onion
2 egg whites

2 oz (50 g) plain flour
salt
olive oil spray (page ix)

1 Preheat the oven to 220°C, 425°F, Gas Mark 7.

2 Scrub the potatoes, but there is no need to peel them. Using the large-holed side of an old-fashioned square grater, or the large-hole grating disk of a food processor, grate the potatoes into long strips. Grate the onion into the potatoes (you will weep but it will be worth it!). Transfer the grated vegetables to a colander and leave to drain.

3 Lightly beat the egg whites in a large bowl. Stir in the flour and season with salt.

4 With your hands, squeeze the excess moisture out of the potato mixture, then stir the mixture into the egg white, combining it well.

5 Spray two non-stick baking sheets with oil spray. With a large spoon, scoop up dollops of the potato mixture and drop them on to the baking sheet. Flatten each dollop with the back of the spoon, and bake in the oven for 5 minutes.

6 Gently loosen each pancake with a spatula, then bake for 5 minutes more. Turn the pancakes and bake for 10–15 minutes more or until cooked through and speckled with brown. The centres will be tender, and the edges like crisp lace. Shake the baking sheets, move them around and reverse their position during the cooking time, and turn the pancakes once or twice more, if necessary.

BAKED JACKET POTATOES

v

A baked potato is one of the earth's greatest foods at its simplest and most satisfying. Oh, that glorious moment when you pierce the crisp skin, and then squeeze, so that the skin cracks, and the steaming, floury, tender flesh comes surging up through the cracks. (*Never* cut a freshly baked potato with a knife, or the flesh will be stodgy and dull. Perforate it with a fork, and then squeeze.) I have heard it said that most of the nutrients in a potato are contained in and just under the skin. This is *not* true; most of the nutrients are in the flesh. In fact, one recent study at Cornell University found that baking a potato in its jacket concentrates the nutrients in the fleshy centre of the spud.

large, unblemished baking potatoes   *salt and freshly ground pepper*

1 Preheat the oven to 220°C, 425°F, Gas Mark 7.

2 Scrub the potatoes and pierce them in several places with a thin skewer or the prongs of a fork. Never wrap the potatoes in foil, or they will steam rather than bake.

3 Bake directly on the oven shelf for about 1¼ hours or until the potatoes yield softly to a gentle squeeze. (Arm yourself with an oven glove before you squeeze!)

4 Split the potatoes by perforating them lengthways and crossways with the prongs of a fork, and squeezing, so that the tender potato flesh comes surging up. Sprinkle on a tiny bit of salt and a generous grinding of pepper.

BAKED POTATO EXTRAS

A perfect baked potato really needs nothing more than a bit of freshly ground pepper. Of course, a squeeze of lemon juice is good too. Or a shower of grated Parmesan. Or perhaps a dollop of Boursin Léger, or ... all right! Purist pretensions be damned! I admit that a well-filled jacket potato makes a fantastic meal, especially on those cruel winter days, when it gets dark far too early, and powerful comfort food is the order of the day. Look through the spreads, salsas, sauces and salad dressings sections for ideas for fillings. I particularly like the raitas (pages 100–101), the Pepper Relish (page 82), the salsas (pages 79–81, hot potato and cold salsa, what bliss!), and the pestos (page 76). Or try fromage frais, a small mound of Duxelles (page 41) a dab of Dijon mustard or one of the pan sautéed onion dishes (pages 45–47), or Mushroom Paprikash (page 42).

MASHED POTATOES

The best mashed potatoes (in my opinion) are made from baked potatoes. Prepare them as described on page 56, then scoop the flesh out of the skins into a large bowl (save the skins). Mash with an old-fashioned masher (or, if you want an airier and less homely effect, put through a ricer), then stir in a tablespoon or so of room-temperature fromage frais and, if you wish, a scattering of freshly grated Parmesan cheese or another medium-fat cheese. Season with salt and pepper and stir with a wooden spoon until the cheese melts into the potato. Eat with a large spoon in a quiet room, and all will be right with the world!

To use up the potato skins, crisp them under the grill and eat them like potato crisps (that's what they are) or top bite-sized strips with tomato sauce and half-fat mozzarella, grill until the cheese melts and eat like tiny pizzas.

Of course, baking potatoes can be boiled or steamed, and then mashed, if you don't want to take the time to bake them first. Just remember this: if you plan to enrich the potatoes with a spoonful or two of fromage frais, put the potatoes into a bowl before adding the fromage frais. If you add it to the potatoes while they are in a hot pan, the fromage frais might curdle (separate) – ugh! What a mess! Add it to the centre of the potatoes in the bowl, and immediately mash it in or stir it in with a wooden spoon. The potatoes will stabilize the fromage frais.

For a truly magical bowl of mashed potatoes, add some roasted garlic purée (page 35) or, if you are steaming or boiling the potatoes first, steam or boil some whole peeled garlic cloves along with the spuds, then mash everything together.

ENHANCED MASHED POTATOES

Potatoes are companionable, and love being paired with other roots. Combine mashed potatoes with equal amounts of mashed swedes, turnips, parsnips, carrots or celeriac (a starchy root with a celery flavour). Or try equal amounts of mashed pumpkin. Steam or foil-bake the roots, purée in a processor or mash with an old-fashioned masher and combine with the potatoes.

For a delectable mashed potato supper, mound the mash into a large bowl, make a well in the mound with the back of a large spoon, then fill the well with sautéed mushrooms or peppers or tomato sauce. Of course, the most delectable supper of all is sausages and mash. Choose any of the sausage recipes in the meat chapter (pages 171–173), lay them on a bed of mash that has been enriched with a little fromage frais, a grating of Parmesan cheese and a hint of roasted garlic, add one of the tomato sauces.... Isn't food wonderful?

Gratin of Potatoes, Onions and Garlic

SERVES 6

V

By far my favourite potato dish (and that's saying a lot, considering how I love spuds, particularly when cooked my way), this gratin is full of deep and mysterious flavour.

4 large baking potatoes, baked, scooped out of
their skins and mashed
1–2 large bulbs of garlic, roasted or pan-braised
and puréed (page 35)
2 large onions, roasted and puréed in a blender
(page 47)

salt and freshly ground pepper
2–3 tablespoons non-fat fromage frais
4–5 tablespoons freshly grated Parmesan cheese
2–3 tablespoons skimmed milk

1 Combine the potato, garlic and onion in a bowl, and season with salt and pepper. Beat with a wooden spoon, then beat in the fromage frais.

2 Scrape the mixture into a gratin dish. Smooth the top and sprinkle with the cheese. (If you wish the dish may be refrigerated, well covered, at this point. Bring to room temperature before continuing.)

3 If you have prepared the gratin ahead of time, sprinkle the milk evenly over the top and bake in the oven at 180°C, 350°F, Gas Mark 4 for 40 minutes or until browned, hot and bubbly. If, however, all the ingredients are hot and freshly put together, sprinkle with the milk and grill, not too close to the heat, until browned and bubbly.

Roasted Potatoes

V

Potatoes simply roasted in stock are uncomplicated and delectable. Roast them in good chicken stock and serve them alongside a roasted chicken. Or try them roasted in the juices from the Pâté with Chicken (page 176).

olive oil spray (page ix)
stock

small new potatoes or medium all-purpose
potatoes (such as Wilja), halved or quartered
salt and freshly ground pepper

1 Preheat the oven to 200°C, 400°F, Gas Mark 6.

2 Mist a shallow baking dish with oil spray. Pour stock into the dish to a depth of about ¼ inch (0.5 cm). Put the potatoes in the dish in one layer. Season with salt and pepper, and stir.

3 Bake, uncovered, in the oven for 40–50 minutes or until the potatoes are browned and tender, shaking the dish and stirring occasionally. (Pour a little more stock into the dish as necessary during cooking.)

ROASTED NEW POTATOES AND FENNEL

SERVES 4

V

Split new potatoes, roasted with an aromatic mixture of fennel and red wine, fill the kitchen with the most tantalising aroma. They take on a dusky colour, and the flavour of the wine, fennel and olives penetrates right to the heart of each potato.

10 new potatoes, each about the size of a golf ball
2 bulbs fennel, trimmed and cut into wedges
2–3 garlic cloves, lightly crushed
2–3 black olives in brine, drained and slivered off their stones

2–3 sundried tomatoes, chopped (use scissors)
4 fl oz (100 ml) dry red wine
4 fl oz (100 ml) stock
2–3 tablespoons chopped fresh parsley

1 Preheat the oven to 200°C, 400°F, Gas Mark 6.

2 With a kitchen mallet, gently hit each unpeeled potato once, so that they are partially split. Combine with all the other ingredients, except the parsley, in a heavy-bottomed roasting tin that holds them comfortably in one layer.

3 Roast, uncovered, in the oven for 40–50 minutes or until glazed and meltingly tender, stirring occasionally. By the end, most of the liquid will be gone. Should it begin to dry up before the potatoes and fennel are cooked, add a bit more wine and stock as needed, but don't swamp the potatoes.

4 Sprinkle with parsley, and serve.

SLICED POTATO GRATIN

SERVES 4
V

As the paper-thin slices of potato braise in the oven they absorb the flavourful liquid and become beautifully browned on top. All-purpose potatoes are just right; bakers are too starchy, boilers not starchy enough.

1 onion, chopped
1–2 garlic cloves, crushed
24 fl oz (670 ml) stock

1 lb (450 g) all-purpose potatoes (such as Wilja),
  scrubbed
salt and freshly ground pepper
4–6 tablespoons freshly grated Parmesan cheese

1 Preheat the oven to 200°C, 400°F, Gas Mark 6.

2 Combine the onion, garlic and 4 fl oz (100 ml) stock in a flameproof casserole, cover and simmer briskly until the onion is tender and the liquid almost gone.

3 While the onions are simmering, slice the unpeeled potatoes as thinly as possible using the slicing blade on an old-fashioned grater, the slicing disk of a food processor, or a mandoline. Stir the potato slices into the onions, pour in the remaining stock, season with salt and pepper and sprinkle on the cheese. Stir together and spread out in the casserole.

4 Bake, uncovered, in the oven for about 40 minutes or until the potatoes are tender, the top browned, and the stock absorbed.

VARIATIONS *Potato Mushroom Gratin* Add another 4 fl oz (100 ml) stock, and 8 oz (225 g) thinly sliced mushroom to the casserole at the end of step 2 (after the onions are tender) and sauté until tender and the additional stock almost gone. Omit the cheese.
Goat's Cheese and Potato Gratin In a blender, blend 5 oz (150 g) medium-fat creamy goat's cheese with 1 pint (600 ml) stock until very smooth. Combine with 1 lb (450 g) all-purpose potatoes, scrubbed and sliced paper-thin. Season with salt and pepper and spread out in a gratin dish. Bake, uncovered in the oven, at 200°C, 400°F, Gas Mark 6 for 50–60 minutes or until the creamy sauce is absorbed, the casserole is bubbling at the edges, and the top is browned. (This variation also works with Boursin Léger, and is good cold, too.)

GARLIC POTATOES WITH PARMESAN

MAKES 1½ PINTS (900 ML)
V ⊙

Garlic potatoes can be made with chicken or vegetable stock, but chicken stock gives a deeper flavour and beautifully syrupy pan juices. As a change, other medium-fat cheeses can be substituted for the Parmesan. Fontina, if you can find it, elevates this dish to ambrosia!

*2 large all-purpose potatoes (such as Wilja),
  scrubbed*
4–6 large garlic cloves, crushed

about ¾ pint (450 ml) stock
salt and freshly ground pepper
2–3 tablespoons freshly grated Parmesan cheese

1 Cut the potatoes into slices ¼ inch (0.5 cm) thick, then halve each slice crossways. Toss them in a large frying pan with the garlic, one third of the stock and salt and pepper to taste. Bring to the boil, then immediately reduce the heat, cover and simmer for 15–20 minutes or until the potatoes are almost tender, stirring occasionally. Add more stock as needed.

2 Uncover the pan and continue to cook, adding more stock as needed to prevent burning, until the potatoes are tender. Spread the potatoes out evenly in the pan, sprinkle with cheese, cover and let sit for 5 minutes on the *lowest* heat, to melt the cheese. Serve at once.

PAN-BRAISED NEW POTATOES WITH PEPPERS

MAKES 1½ PINTS (900 ML)
V ⊙

The luscious pepper juices meld with the syrupy balsamic to glaze the potatoes.

*10 oz (275 g) new potatoes, each about the size
  of a golf ball, quartered*
*3 red peppers, peeled (page 48), deseeded and
  cut into strips*
7 spring onions, trimmed and sliced
3–4 sundried tomatoes, chopped (use scissors)

*3–4 black olives in brine, drained and slivered
  off their stones*
pinch of crushed dried chilli flakes
4 fl oz (100 ml) stock
2 tablespoons balsamic vinegar
2–3 tablespoons chopped fresh parsley

Combine all the ingredients, except the parsley, in a heavy-bottomed frying pan. Cover and simmer, stirring occasionally, until the potatoes are very tender and glazed, and the liquid almost gone. Scatter on the parsley and serve.

ROOTS

Although roots have a reputation for stodginess, and are perceived as the most unglamorous of vegetables, they are – in reality – extraordinarily useful, comforting and dependable.

Swedes and turnips are low in calories and fat; swedes are an excellent source of minerals and vitamin A; turnips a good source of minerals; and both are a good source of fibre. Young white spring turnips have a delicate, crisp, peppery sweetness that makes them scintillate grated in salads, or sliced as part of an array of crudités. Both roots can be steamed or, best of all, roasted in foil so that their sweetness is emphasized as their juices begin to caramelize. And swedes are perfectly gorgeous peeled, chunked and roasted in an open baking dish in fat-free chicken stock or meat juices. Roast these beauties at high heat (220°C, 425°F, Gas Mark 7), turning them in the juices occasionally, until they are crusty on the outside, and melting within.

Parsnips are subtle, sweet and exquisitely creamy when cooked, and make a fine addition to stews, soups (especially creamy purées) and gratins. They are also splendid when foil-roasted or steamed, or roasted in meat or poultry juices. The parsnip is a paler, whiskery relative of the carrot, another ineffably sweet root. In fact, parsnips and carrots are sometimes referred to as 'garden candy' or 'underground honey'. Parsnips are an excellent source of vitamin A, and potassium, as well as a good source of iron and vitamin C.

FOIL-ROASTED ROOTS

This method is suitable for parsnips, swedes and turnips, as well as for chunks of winter squash – especially pumpkin and acorn squash (page 66). Peel swedes and cut into large chunks; peel turnips and parsnips and cut in half (or leave whole if they are small). Enclose in foil, shiny side in, so that the vegetables are in a roomy but well-sealed pouch. Cook in a hot oven (220°C, 425°F, Gas Mark 7) for 1–1¼ hours or until the vegetables are very tender and beginning to caramelize around the edges. Foil-roasted roots can be refrigerated (out of their foil package) and used when needed.

MASHED ROOTS

Foil-roasted roots can be eaten, piping hot, as they are, with a squeeze of lemon or lime juice or a sprinkling of balsamic vinegar. Even better, purée them (with an old-fashioned potato masher or in a food processor), beat in a tablespoon or two of fromage frais to make them even creamier than they already are, and add, if you like, some grated Parmesan. Combinations of roots are delicious this way, or combine puréed roots with mashed potatoes (page 57), or with puréed roasted winter squash.

ROOT GRATINS

Try combinations of puréed foil-roasted roots flavoured with roasted garlic purée (page 35), lightened with a little fromage frais and baked into a heart-warming gratin. The gratins can be frozen, to be reheated at a later time in the microwave or the conventional oven. To save time, cut the roots into small chunks and steam rather than foil-roast them. The deep caramelized flavour will be missing, but there will still be plenty of good root sweetness. These gratins make a fine supper served with sautéed mushrooms and a creamy vegetable, such as Creamed Spinach Purée (page 37), or cauliflower, brussels sprouts or broccoli in cheese sauce. Or serve the gratins to accompany Beef Stew with Rosemary (page 180), Beef with Mushrooms and Caramelized Onions (page 178) or meatballs or sausages in tomato sauce.

GRATIN OF FOIL-ROASTED VEGETABLES

SERVES 4

V ✲

This simple gratin of roots is seasoned with salt and pepper alone; the natural sweetness of the roots shines through.

5 foil-roasted white turnips (opposite)
6 foil-roasted medium carrots (page 23)
½ foil-roasted swede (opposite)
1 bulb of garlic, roasted or pan-braised and puréed (page 35)

2–3 tablespoons fromage frais
salt and freshly ground pepper
4 tablespoons freshly grated Parmesan cheese
2–3 tablespoons skimmed milk

1 Put the turnips, carrots and swede in the bowl of a food processor. Add the garlic purée, and process the vegetables until they are smooth. Add the fromage frais and process until blended. Season with salt and pepper.

2 Scrape the mixture into a gratin dish or shallow baking dish. Smooth the top and sprinkle with Parmesan. (The dish may be prepared ahead of time to this point. Refrigerate, well covered, for up to 2 days. Bring to room temperature before proceeding.)

3 Preheat the oven to 180°C, 350°F, Gas Mark 4. Sprinkle the top of the gratin with the milk, and bake, uncovered, for 30–45 minutes or until golden brown on top, bubbly and thoroughly hot.

SPICY GRATIN OF ROASTED ROOTS

SERVES 4

V ❄

A gratin of roasted roots can be seasoned any way you wish. The olive–garlic infusion (page viii) lends a Mediterranean note to the wintry vegetables. Serve the gratin with stir-fried peppers and Stir-Fried Roman Broccoli (page 17).

2–3 sundried tomatoes, coarsely chopped (use scissors)
pinch of crushed dried chillies
pinch of dried oregano, crumbled
6 spring onions, trimmed and sliced
½ pint (300 ml) stock
6 foil-roasted carrots (page 23)

3 foil-roasted small white turnips (page 62)
½ foil-roasted small swede (page 62)
1 bulb of garlic, roasted and puréed (page 35)
3 tablespoons very low-fat fromage frais
salt and freshly ground pepper
2 tablespoons freshly grated Parmesan cheese
a few tablespoons of skimmed milk

1 Preheat the oven to 220°C, 425°F, Gas Mark 7.

2 Put the sundried tomatoes in a heavy-bottomed frying pan with the chillies, oregano, spring onions and stock. Cover and boil for 5–7 minutes, then uncover and simmer until the onion is tender and the liquid about gone.

3 Transfer the mixture to a food processor and add the foil-roasted vegetables, the garlic and fromage frais. Process to a purée and season with salt and pepper.

4 Spread the mixture in a gratin dish, sprinkle with Parmesan cheese and pour a thin drizzle of milk evenly over the top of the gratin. Bake in the oven for 30–45 minutes or until bubbly, puffy and browned on the top. (To save time, warm through in the microwave and then flash under the grill to brown.)

CURRIED GRATIN OF FOIL-ROASTED ROOTS

SERVES 4

V ❄

If you don't feel like mixing your own spice mixture from the long list given for this recipe, then use a good curry powder or garam masala. Serve the curried gratin with a raita (pages 100–101) and Stir-Fried Cabbage (page 21)

1 onion, chopped

½ teaspoon each of ground coriander, ground cumin, mild chilli powder, paprika and ground ginger

¼ teaspoon each of ground turmeric and allspice

pinch of cayenne pepper (or to taste)

½ pint (300 ml) stock

salt and freshly ground pepper

2 foil-roasted small white turnips, puréed or mashed (page 62)

1 bulb of garlic, roasted and puréed (page 35)

2 foil-roasted carrots, puréed or mashed (page 23)

3 foil-roasted small parsnips, puréed or mashed (page 62)

½ foil-roasted small swede, puréed or mashed (page 62)

2–3 tablespoons buttermilk or fromage frais

2–3 tablespoons skimmed milk

1 Preheat the oven to 200°C, 400°F, Gas Mark 6.

2 Combine the onion, spices and stock in a heavy-bottomed frying pan. Season with salt and pepper, cover and boil for 5–7 minutes, then uncover and simmer until the onion is tender and the liquid almost gone.

3 Combine the onion and spice mixture with the puréed vegetables in a food processor or bowl. Process or beat in the buttermilk or fromage frais. Spread the mixture in a gratin dish.

4 Pour a thin drizzle of milk evenly over the top of the gratin, and bake in the oven for 30–45 minutes or until bubbly, puffy and browned on top. (If you wish, to save time, heat through in the microwave, and flash under the grill to brown.)

SQUASH

Exotic produce has a way of slowly creeping into general use and becoming almost 'ordinary'. After all, aubergines, red and yellow peppers, mangos and even bananas(!) were once foreign exoticisms, but now overflow from supermarket shelves all around the country. The newest class of vegetable to pass from exotic to almost ordinary seems to be hard-shelled squash, sometimes called winter squash, in particular acorn squash, butternut squash and pumpkins. Squash are native to the Americas – in fact the wonderful name 'squash' comes from the Narragansett Indians.

Hard-shelled squash are extremely low in calories (½ pint/300 ml cooked squash flesh contains about 35 Calories and virtually no fat) and provide valuable vitamins and fibre. Although their hard shells look quite impenetrable, they are easy to hack into, easy to cook, and provide sweet, mouthfilling taste and texture. Uncut squash will keep for a month in a cool, well-ventilated spot. Once cut, it will keep for at least a week in the fridge, covered well with cling film. Cooked squash freezes well.

Butternut squash has a butterscotch-coloured shell, and is shaped like a gourd; acorn squash is round, ribbed and usually green with orange highlights (although I have seen bright orange ones). A pumpkin, of course, is that round, glowing orange, most folkloric of vegetables, evocative of autumn, Hallowe'en and harvest festivals. To cut into any one of these well-protected beauties, put a sharp cleaver or large, sharp knife against the shell, and tap gently with a wooden kitchen mallet, until you have cut right through. Scrape out the seeds and fibres with a spoon and a small, dull knife. Once cut and cleaned, the squash can be baked in their shells and then stuffed with a savoury filling, or they can be pared (with a knife or an ordinary vegetable peeler) and steamed, braised in stock, wrapped in foil and oven roasted as described for roots (page 62) or cubed and cooked in stews and soups.

Cooked, puréed squash is delicious combined with mashed potatoes and/or mashed roasted roots. Here are some ideas to get you started in the squash game. The beauty of these vegetables, their ease of preparation and their delicious sweet taste and melting texture (similar, in fact, to more familiar roots such as swede, parsnip and turnip) may turn you into a regular user.

BAKED SQUASH FOR FILLING

Choose acorn squash or butternut squash. Preheat the oven to 200°C, 400°F, Gas Mark 6. Halve the squash from stem to stern and scrape out the seeds and fibres as described above. Place the squash halves, cavity up, on a baking sheet, and mist lightly with oil spray (page ix). Bake in the oven for 35–45 minutes (the timing depends on the size of the squash). The idea is to bake them long enough for the flesh to become very tender, but not long enough for the shells to collapse. Fill the cavities with a savoury mixture – Rice Pilau (page 115) or Wild Rice Pilaf with Cherries (page 118), for example, or Sautéed Mushrooms (page 40) or lentil or beef bolognese (pages 10 and 159).

GLAZED ACORN SQUASH

MAKES 1 PINT (600 ML)

V ❄

An acorn squash is a beautiful object. A group of them will casually decorate a kitchen the way designer doodads, however chic and trendy, can never do. They keep well, so you can admire them as décor for a while, then – with great pleasure – cook and eat them.

4 acorn squash, each weighing about
  8 oz (225 g)
juice of 1 lime
1 tablespoon honey
1 teaspoon dried tarragon, crumbled
¼ teaspoon each of ground cumin and
  cinnamon

a few dashes of Tabasco sauce
dash of teriyaki or soy sauce
¼ pint (150 ml) stock
salt and freshly ground pepper

1 Preheat the oven to 200°C, 400°F, Gas Mark 6.

2 Halve the squash and scrape out the seeds and fibres. Cut the squash into wedges and peel.

3 Mix together all the remaining ingredients, except the salt and pepper. Combine with the squash in a baking dish that will hold the squash in one layer. Bake, uncovered, in the oven for 40–45 minutes or until the squash is tender, stirring occasionally.

4 Scrape the squash into a serving dish. Tip the pan juices into a small frying pan, and boil down until thick and syrupy. Season with salt and pepper. Scrape and pour the juices over the squash and turn with two spoons to coat the squash with the mixture.

Opposite page 66: Salmon and Mushrooms Cooked in a Bag (page 129), Oven-fried New Potatoes (page 52), Fennel and Pepper Salad (page 34)

Opposite: Festive Fish and Shellfish Stew (page 140), served with Potato Bread (page 196) and Pumpkin Lime 'Butter' (page 75)

TOMATOES

The perfect tomato *can* be hard to find. Some supermarket tomatoes are objects of derision, something more like pale pink tennis balls than tomatoes, and certainly no match for truly ruby-red, juicy-ripe summertime beauties. But things are slowly changing. Someone, somewhere has tumbled to the fact that people value real flavour, not pallid imitations, and tomatoes bred for tomato flavour (what an innovative idea!) lurk here and there among the tennis balls. Still, you'll have to plan ahead. Buy flavour tomatoes several days before you plan to use them, and keep them, uncovered, in a cool part of the kitchen. In a few days (or a week, depending on how unripe they were) their flavour will have developed. Don't refrigerate them, or the flavour will never arrive. Cherry tomatoes and vine-ripened tomatoes are almost always a good bet, with their excellent true-tomato flavour, but they also benefit from a few days of ripening in the kitchen.

TO PEEL AND DESEED TOMATOES

To peel a fresh tomato, immerse it in boiling water for 10 seconds, then cut out the stem and slip off the skin. The seeds may be removed with your finger. Alternatively, spear the tomato on a long handled fork and hold it over a gas flame (if you have a gas cooker). In a few seconds you will hear a high-pitched 'zingg' and the skin will split. Immediately remove from the flame, and slip off the skin.

TOMATO AND BASIL SALAD

V ⊙

The best way to eat a home-grown, vine-ripened tomato, still warm from the sun, is in the garden, straight off the vine, in great slurping bites. When that palls (actually it never palls, but if you grow your own, you'll have plenty of tomatoes to play with), there are plenty of splendid salads that bring out their best. This one hardly needs a recipe, but when the tomatoes are ripe, and the basil plentiful, there is no better combination. Tomato and Basil Salad and its variations look beautiful served on a bed of dark leafy greens.

ripe tomatoes
salt and freshly ground pepper

basil leaves, torn into shreds
balsamic vinegar

1 Neatly cut the stems out of the tomatoes. Slice them from stem to stern and arrange the slices on a plate. Sprinkle lightly with salt and pepper.

2 Scatter the shredded basil over the tomatoes, and sprinkle on a modest amount of vinegar. Allow to stand for 10 minutes before serving.

VARIATIONS *Tomato and Peach Salad* Remove the stems and slice the tomatoes as above. Halve and stone some ripe peaches (working over a bowl to catch the juices), and cut into slices the same thickness as the tomato slices. Overlap the peach and tomato slices on a pretty plate. Scatter over shredded basil or mint leaves, grind some pepper over them, and sprinkle with balsamic vinegar and the reserved peach juices. Serve at once.

TOMATO AND MANGO SALAD

SERVES 4

V ⊙

Ripe tomatoes cosy up to ripe mangoes almost as well as they do to peaches.

1 ripe mango
6 small ripe tomatoes, sliced

Mango 'Mayo' (page 99)

1 With a sharp knife, slice straight down the length of the mango, cutting it through, but missing the large flat centre stone to which quite a bit of mango flesh clings. Repeat on the other side of the stone.

2 Carefully peel the skin from both halves. Slice each half thinly to produce long strips of mango, and set aside.

3 Peel the skin from the mango flesh around the stone. Cut the flesh away from the stone and put it in a small bowl along with any juices. Set aside to use in the dressing.

4 Arrange the tomato slices in two rows around the perimeter of a pretty dish. Fill the centre with overlapping mango slices. Serve the dressing separately.

VEGETABLE STEWS

If you are a vegetarian, or if you eat a vegetarian meal several times a week, as so many do these days (or if you simply love vegetables), a collection of vegetable stews is a valuable addition to your repertoire. As you know, the health benefits are incalculable, but beyond that, vegetable stews provide bowlfuls of exhilarating colour, flavour and texture. Served with a grain and a salsa, or with green salad and raita, they give low-fat satisfaction along with their overflow of fibre, vitamins and minerals.

BRAISED VEGETABLES

MAKES 2 PINTS (1.1 LITRES)

V ⊙ ❄

As the peppers and the mushrooms braise in the stock, they help form the delicious sauce that will bathe the cauliflower. Serve with rice, or toss with pasta shapes.

2 medium or 1 large cauliflower, trimmed and
  broken into large florets
2 red and 2 yellow peppers, cored, deseeded,
  peeled (page 48), and cut into 1 inch (2.5 cm)
  wide strips

8 oz (225 g) mushrooms, thickly sliced
2 garlic cloves, crushed
½ pint (300 ml) stock
salt and freshly ground pepper
4 tablespoons chopped fresh parsley

I Combine the vegetables and garlic in a heavy-bottomed frying pan. Pour in the stock and season with salt and pepper. Cover and simmer for 5–7 minutes.

2 Uncover the pan and cook over a high heat, stirring occasionally, until the liquid is cooked away, the vegetables are tender, and the cauliflower is beginning to brown. Stir in the parsley and serve at once.

RATATOUILLE

MAKES 2 PINTS (1.1 LITRES)

V ☉ ❄

There are many ways to make non-fat ratatouille. This one uses the olive oil spray (page ix) in addition to black olives in the flavour infusion (page viii). For another version, add chopped grilled peppers, aubergine and courgettes to the Basic Tomato Sauce on page 85 and simmer for a few minutes.

olive oil spray (page ix)
1 large onion, cut into wedges
4 red peppers, deseeded, cut into natural sections and peeled (page 48)
½ pint (300 ml) stock
1–2 garlic cloves, crushed
2 black olives in brine, drained and slivered off their stones
3 sundried tomatoes, chopped (use scissors)

1 aubergine, weighing about 14 oz (400 g), peeled, trimmed, halved lengthways and cut crossways into ½ inch (1 cm) thick slices
2 courgettes, each weighing about 6 oz (175 g), trimmed and cut into ½ inch (1 cm) slices
5–6 ripe tomatoes, peeled, deseeded and cut into quarters or eighths
3 tablespoons chopped fresh parsley
1–2 tablespoons shredded fresh basil leaves
salt and freshly ground pepper

1 Spray a heavy-bottomed frying pan with the oil spray and heat. Separate the onion layers and spread them in the pan. Cook, stirring for a minute or so until they begin to soften. Add the peppers, and cook, stirring for another moment or so. Stir in the stock, garlic, olives and sundried tomatoes, and bubble, stirring, for another few moments. Stir in the aubergine and courgettes, and cook, stirring, for 2–3 minutes.

2 Stir in the tomatoes, parsley and basil, season with salt and pepper, and simmer, uncovered, for 10–15 minutes or until the vegetables are tender and bathed in a thickened and savoury sauce.

VEGETABLE STEW FOR COUSCOUS

MAKES 3 PINTS (1.7 LITRES)

V ⊙ ❄

Loosely based on the wonderful curried vegetable stews served with couscous in North Africa, this symphony of gently spiced roots and pumpkin makes a colourful and warming meal. Serve it as it is with couscous, or add the Moroccan-Style Meatballs on page 173, or the sweet and sour version of the Roasted Spicy Chicken on page 142.

3 carrots
3 parsnips
3 white turnips
½ swede
1 small pumpkin, halved, seeds and fibre
  scraped out (page 66)
2 onions, chopped
2 garlic cloves, crushed
1 teaspoon each of ground paprika, cumin and
  coriander

½ teaspoon ground cinnamon
pinch of cayenne pepper
1 pint (600 ml) stock
salt and freshly ground pepper
3 ripe, flavourful tomatoes, peeled, deseeded
  and cut into strips
4 tablespoons raisins or sultanas

1 Peel the carrots, parsnips, turnips, swede and pumpkin. Cut into 1 inch (2.5 cm) chunks.

2 Combine the onions and garlic with the spices and ½ pint (300 ml) stock in a large frying pan. Cover and boil for 5 minutes, then uncover and simmer briskly, stirring occasionally, until the onions are tender and the liquid considerably cooked down. The onions, garlic (and spices) should be gently 'frying' in their own juices.

3 Stir in all the vegetables (except the tomatoes) and the remaining stock. Season with salt and pepper, cover and simmer for 5 minutes.

4 Stir in the tomatoes and raisins or sultanas, taste and add more salt and pepper if necessary, and simmer for 10–15 minutes more or until the vegetables are tender and the tomatoes have cooked down to a sauce. Taste and adjust the seasoning again. Serve with couscous (page 119).

SPREADS AND DIPS

'**W**hat do I spread on my bread?' This is the question that perplexes many of the people who write to me, and whom I meet when I put my show on the road. The prospect of no butter, no marge, not even the currently fashionable option of a little pot of olive oil into which to dip a crust of bread, leaves many people, new to the low-fat lifestyle, wondering how to cope with naked slices of bread. The truth is, a naked slice of bread is not the most terrible thing in the world, especially if the bread is of excellent quality. But there are other options as well. No-fat fromage frais or quark make beautiful spreads for bread, on their own or mixed with a little honey or marmalade (or mix in some mashed, raw fresh fruit – bananas and pears are particularly good this way). For a savoury spread, mix fromage frais or quark with chopped fresh herbs, roasted or pan-braised garlic (page 35) or chopped spring onions.

Many interesting spreads can be made with vegetables, beans and pulses, canned fish and the like – they can serve as sandwich fillings, snacks, dips, light meals, first courses – and they need no added fat to speak of at all.

APRICOT SPREAD

MAKES ½ PINT (300 ML)

V ⊙

A slightly creamy, sunny-orange spread for morning toast, or for fresh-baked fruit scones (page 203).

one 9 oz (250 g) package ready-to-eat dried apricots
7 oz (200 g) carton quark

2 tablespoons orange marmalade

1 Put the apricots in a food processor, and process until chopped.

2 Scrape in the quark and marmalade, and process to a rough purée. Store in the fridge until needed.

CHICKEN LIVER PATE

MAKES 1½ PINTS (900 ML)

Aliver pâté with no cream, no butter and no chicken fat! Prunes, brandy and no-fat fromage frais will make your pâté as unctuous, silken and wicked-tasting as a high-fat one.

about 6 fl oz (175 ml) stock
1¼ lb (550 g) chicken livers, trimmed
1 onion, chopped
3 tablespoons brandy
30 stoned prunes, soaked in water for 1 hour
   and drained

juice and grated zest of 1–2 large lemons
14 fl oz (400 ml) very low-fat fromage frais
1–2 pinches ground allspice
salt and freshly ground pepper

1 Film a non-stick frying pan with a tiny bit of stock. Add the chicken livers in one layer and sauté until they are just cooked through, using tongs to turn them. Remove from the pan and set aside. Pour the liquid out of the pan and discard.

2 Put the onion in the pan with the brandy and 4 fl oz (100 ml) stock. Boil for 1 minute, stirring and scraping the browned bits off the bottom of the frying pan. Reduce the heat, cover and simmer briskly until the onions are very tender and amber brown. Add more stock, if needed, but there should be no liquid left when the onions are done.

3 Scrape the onions into a food processor, add the livers, prunes, juice and zest from 1 lemon, fromage frais and a pinch of allspice. Season with salt and pepper, and blend until very smooth. Taste and add more spice, seasonings, lemon juice and zest, if desired, and blend again. Pour into ceramic pots, cover and leave overnight in the fridge to set, and for the flavours to blend.

GREEN PEA SPREAD

MAKES 1 PINT (600 ML)
V ☉

Pea purées are my speciality; I make several versions, and serve them as a first course, or as an accompaniment to spicy dishes of all kinds. I love the bright green colour, and the vibrant fresh taste. Vary it by using mint or chervil in place of coriander, and chives or spring onions in place of red onion. It is a glorious accompaniment to Crumbed Grilled Aubergine (page 5) or courgettes (page 29), beans and rice (or other grains), roast pork and oven-fried potatoes, or just used as a dip or spread on to fresh, crusty bread.

1½ tablespoons roughly chopped fresh parsley
2 tablespoons fresh coriander leaves (optional)
juice of 1 lime
1 fresh chilli, deseeded and coarsely diced
  (optional)

1½ lb (700 g) frozen peas, thawed
salt
½ small red onion, roughly diced

1 Put all the ingredients, except the onion, in a blender or food processor, and process to a rough purée.

2 Add the onion and pulse the blender or processor on and off a few times to chop and mix in the onion.

PUMPKIN LIME 'BUTTER'

MAKES ½ PINT (300 ML)
V ☺

Pumpkin is a stunning vegetable that can be prepared in countless ways (pages 66–67). It makes a velvet-textured spread perfect for serving as you would butter, in little pots, with crusty bread, as a snack or as a dinner accompaniment.

12 oz (350 g) pumpkin, cleaned of seeds and
  fibres, cut into wedges, peeled and cubed
3 tablespoons very low-fat fromage frais

a few drops of lime juice
salt and freshly ground pepper

1 Steam the pumpkin cubes for about 15 minutes or until very tender. Refresh under cold running water, drain well, and cool thoroughly.

2 Put the pumpkin, fromage frais and lime juice in a food processor or blender. Season with salt and pepper, and purée until very smooth. Taste and add more lime, salt and pepper to taste.

VARIATION *Pumpkin Garlic 'Butter'* Follow the above recipe, but steam 1 garlic clove, cut into chunks, with the pumpkin, and omit the lime juice.

CREAMY PESTO

MAKES 12 FL OZ (350 ML)

V ⊘

Pesto sauces are among the few recipes in this collection that call for nuts – a high-fat (albeit nutritious) food. Those who must drastically curtail their fat levels (and who are on a weight *loss* régime) should give the pesto sauces a miss. The substitution of quark (non-fat curd cheese) for oil makes a creamy smooth pesto that clings to pasta very well, but it is also good spread on bread. Make little pizzas with pita bread or split bagels: spread with pesto, top with mozzarella, and grill. With pasta, toss it in alone, or add some tomato sauce as well. Use a measuring jug to measure the herbs.

¾ pint (450 ml) torn fresh basil leaves
½ pint (300 ml) roughly chopped fresh parsley
5 tablespoons freshly grated Parmesan cheese
1 oz (25 g) pine nuts

7 oz (200 g) carton quark or very low-fat
*   fromage frais*
roasted or pan-braised garlic (pages 35–36)
salt and freshly ground pepper

1 Combine all the ingredients in a food processor, adding garlic, salt and pepper to taste. Process to a thick paste.

2 Scrape the pesto into a bowl and refrigerate. If the quark is fresh, pesto will keep in the fridge for up to a week.

WHITE PESTO

MAKES ½ PINT (300 ML)

V ⊘

White pesto is a perfect garlic spread for crusty bread (either spread on to the bread and eaten as is, or grilled briefly). It also serves as an alluringly creamy garlic sauce to toss into freshly cooked pasta. An entire bulb of garlic (I mean a bulb, not a clove) is not excessive – roasted garlic is sweet, mellow and inoffensive.

7 oz (200 g) carton quark
1 oz (25 g) pine nuts
5 tablespoons freshly grated Parmesan cheese

1 bulb of garlic, roasted or pan-braised and
*   puréed (pages 35–36)*

Put all the ingredients in a blender or food processor, and process until smooth. Scrape the pesto into a bowl and store in the fridge.

AUBERGINE AND GARLIC SPREAD

MAKES ½ PINT (300 ML)

V ⊙ ❄

Here, aubergine forms a glorious alliance with garlic, olives and wine. The resulting purée bursts with flavour. Spread it on crusty bread, use it to fill lightly grilled or poached button mushroom caps or pizza, or use it in a meatball or sausage mix in place of roasted aubergine (page 157).

2 aubergines, each weighing about
* 12 oz (350 g), trimmed, peeled and diced*
2–3 garlic cloves, crushed
3 sundried tomatoes, chopped (use scissors)
1–2 pinches crushed dried chilli flakes
* (optional)*

3 black olives in brine, drained and sliced off
* their stones*
½ pint (300 ml) stock
2 fl oz (50 ml) dry red wine
salt and freshly ground pepper

1 Put all the ingredients in a heavy-bottomed frying pan, season with salt and pepper, and simmer, uncovered, stirring occasionally, until the aubergine is very tender and the liquid has been absorbed. Taste and adjust the seasonings, then leave to cool.

2 Process to a rough purée in a food processor.

SMOKED SALMON AND HERB SPREAD

MAKES ¾ PINT (450 ML)

⊙

Simple, elegant, and a lovely way to wrap a little smoked salmon around your tongue. I love this best spread on to a lightly toasted split bagel, topped with a slice of ripe tomato.

two 7 oz (200 g) cartons quark or very low-fat
* fromage frais*
1 tablespoon chopped fresh parsley
1 tablespoon snipped fresh dill

1 tablespoon snipped fresh chives
4 oz (110 g) smoked salmon, shredded
freshly ground pepper

Put all the ingredients in a bowl, season with pepper, and fold together gently but thoroughly with a wooden spoon or rubber spatula. Refrigerate until needed. If the mixture 'weeps' a little as it sits in the fridge, drain away the liquid before serving. Serve spread on toast, bagels or non-fat savoury biscuits.

PIQUANT TUNA SPREAD

MAKES ½ PINT (300 ML)

⊙

The most wonderful lime-chilli pickle (Geeta brand) is available now in many supermarkets. It is *very hot* (to quote a line from the film, *My Favourite Year*, 'One bite and your tongue dials the fire department'), and – for those who love edible fire – it is irresistible. Chilli fanatics (I know you are out there) will love what it does to a can of tuna. Those who prefer tamer tuna will enjoy the fillip that mango-lime chutney provides.

7 oz (200 g) can tuna in water or brine, well
drained
4–5 tablespoons mango-lime chutney or lime-
chilli pickle

2–3 oz (50–75 g) quark

1 Put all the ingredients in a food processor, and blend until the mixture is well combined and smooth.

2 Serve as a sandwich filling, a spread, or a dip.

TUNA SPREAD

MAKES ½ PINT (300 ML)

A bit more refined and mainstream than the preceding rambunctious tuna spread, this one is gently flavoured with chives and a few capers.

7 oz (200 g) can tuna in brine or water, drained
1 tablespoon drained capers
4–6 tablespoons quark
1 bunch chives, snipped

1 tablespoon chopped fresh parsley
juice of ¼ lemon
freshly ground pepper

1 Put all the ingredients together in a food processor, season with pepper, and process to a rough purée.

2 Pour into a sieve lined with muslin set over a bowl, and leave to drain for at least 1 hour. Serve chilled, as a spread, dip or sandwich filling.

SALSAS AND DIPPERS

Salsas are part-salad, part-relish, part-chutney, simply made from very fresh ingredients. They originate with the table salsas of Mexico, and can be as simple as a tumble of diced fresh tomato (ripe and bursting with flavour), roughly chopped fresh coriander and bits of fiery chilli. (If you have ever eaten in a Mexican-style restaurant, you will have sampled a simple salsa, served in a bowl with tortilla chips for dipping.)

As you will see from the following eclectic salsa collection, salsas can be quite elegant, and although always lively (and colourful) they don't have to aggressively assault your digestive system. Salsas work beautifully with oven-poached fish fillets as well as grilled or oven-fried fish fillets and chicken breasts, or with slices of roasted pork tenderloin. A salsa can also be used as a soup garnish: float a table-spoon of cold salsa on the surface of a bowl of thick soup. For a many-splendoured vegetarian meal, serve Butter Bean Sausages (page 12) with Tomato and Grilled Pepper Salsa (below), rice, Green Pea Spread (page 74) and fromage frais mixed with chopped coriander and parsley. Provide tortillas or pita breads for wrapping it all up, and plenty of paper napkins.

TOMATO AND GRILLED PEPPER SALSA

MAKES 3 PINTS (1.7 LITRES)

V ☉

This is the salsa that I make more than any other. It is delicious freshly made, but it seems to get better and better (and soupier) as it sits in the fridge. For cooks in a hurry, canned or bottled red peppers can be substituted for the fresh grilled peppers, and extra drained and diced, canned tomatoes can stand in for the fresh ones (although the resulting salsa will not be nearly as vibrant). It's heavenly (and messy) scooped up with tortilla chips (page 83) and as a garnish for almost anything, but I like to eat it in large quantities, with a spoon!

two 14 oz (400 g) cans Italian tomatoes
6 fresh, ripe, flavourful tomatoes, peeled and
  deseeded
1 chilli, finely chopped, or to taste
2 fl oz (50 ml) balsamic vinegar

1–2 garlic cloves, crushed
2 tablespoons chopped fresh parsley
2 tablespoons shredded fresh mint or basil
4 red peppers (or 2 red and 2 yellow peppers),
  grilled (see page 49) and coarsely chopped

1 Drain the canned tomatoes. Chop the canned and fresh tomatoes.

2 Combine all the ingredients in a non-reactive bowl. Chill thoroughly before serving.

CUCUMBER AND FENNEL SALSA

MAKES 1 PINT (600 ML)
V ⊙

Cucumber, fennel and orange make a refreshing salsa with an exhilarating combination of textures and flavours. This salsa is particularly good with simply cooked fish.

2 oranges
½ long cucumber, peeled, halved, deseeded and
   diced
1 bulb fennel, trimmed and diced
1 tablespoon each of chopped fresh parsley,
   coriander and mint

1 chilli, deseeded and finely chopped (optional)
juice of 1 orange and 1 lime
1 tablespoon balsamic vinegar
salt and freshly ground pepper

1 Peel the oranges, trimming away all skin and pith. Segment the oranges over a bowl, so that you catch all the juices. Dice the segments and add to the juices in the bowl.

2 Add the remaining ingredients, season with salt and pepper, and refrigerate until needed.

PEPPER SALSA

MAKES 2 PINTS (1.1 LITRES)
V ⊙

The multi-coloured peppers make this salsa look jewelled. It is particularly good as a soup garnish: float the cold, crisp salsa by the teaspoon on the surface of a thick steamy bowlful of one of the puréed vegetable soups (pages 104–108).

6 large peppers (a mixture of colours)
1 chilli, deseeded and diced
4 thin spring onions, trimmed and thinly sliced
2 tablespoons chopped fresh parsley

1 tablespoon chopped fresh coriander
juice of 1½ limes
salt
½ teaspoon sugar

1 Cut the peppers in half lengthways. Remove the stems, the seeds and the ribs, and cut the halves into their natural sections. Peel each pepper piece with a vegetable peeler, then dice.

2 Combine all the ingredients in a bowl, and mix well with two spoons. Add salt to taste.

3 Allow to stand for at least 30 minutes before serving.

CHERRY TOMATO AND OLIVE SALSA

MAKES 2 PINTS (1.1 LITRES)
V ⊙

Those with medical conditions that preclude the consumption of even small amounts of fat, and those who are seriously trying to lose weight, should avoid all but the odd sliver of olive, but for the rest of us low-fat foodies, a few olives here and there are pure delight. With all its succulent goodness still encased in its delicious pulp, an olive delivers flavour and a nice, controlled dose of essential fatty acids without greasing the skids to oily over-indulgence the way that olive oil, splashing out of its bottle at 120 fat Calories per tablespoon, does. The partnership of olives and cherry tomatoes, sparked with herbs and chilli, makes an extremely pleasing salsa.

18 oz (500 g) firm, ripe cherry tomatoes, stemmed and quartered (use half red, half yellow cherry tomatoes, if available)
5 green olives in brine, drained and slivered off their stones
5 black olives in brine, drained and slivered off their stones
2 teaspoons olive brine
1 chilli, finely chopped
1½ tablespoons drained capers

1½ tablespoons balsamic vinegar
1–3 garlic cloves, crushed
juice of ½ lemon
3 spring onions, trimmed and thinly sliced
2 tablespoons chopped fresh parsley (flat-leaf if possible)
2 tablespoons shredded fresh mint or basil
freshly ground pepper

Put all the ingredients together in a bowl, season with pepper and mix. Leave to stand at room temperature until needed, stirring occasionally. To keep for more than a few hours, store in the refrigerator.

PEPPER RELISH

MAKES ABOUT 24 FL OZ (670 ML)
V

This vibrant (in colour *and* taste) relish may be prepared with canned or bottled peppers, if you don't feel like messing about with the grill. The relish is splendid with cold meats, roasted pork tenderloin, steamed vegetables (especially asparagus or artichoke), butter bean sausages, hamburgers and sausages, or any of the dippers below and opposite. Use red peppers for a red relish; yellow for a yellow relish.

1 large red onion, coarsely chopped
1–2 garlic cloves, crushed
2 teaspoons caster sugar
½ teaspoon each of ground turmeric and
  coriander

2 tablespoons balsamic vinegar
6–8 red or yellow peppers, grilled and peeled
  (page 49)
1–2 tablespoons each of chopped fresh mint
  and parsley (optional)

1 Combine all the ingredients, except the peppers and fresh herbs. Stir to dissolve the sugar, and leave to stand for 1 hour.

2 Purée the peppers in a blender or food processor. Combine the pepper purée with the onion mixture, and stir in the chopped herbs, if using.

DIPPERS

VEGETABLE DIPPERS

I am a devotee of crudités (raw vegetables cut into bite-sized pieces), especially when they are used as dippers for savoury spreads, dips and salsas. Carrots, celery, cauliflower florets, fennel, halved brussels sprouts, radishes, white turnip, sugar snap peas and mangetout, courgettes, cucumber, baby sweetcorn cobs and snap beans are all brilliant for dabbling into various savoury mixtures. If you need to go into serious dieting mode, to drop a few pounds in a hurry, prepare loads of crudités, and your favourite dips and salsas from this chapter and live off them for a few days. You'll be astonished at how quickly you start to lose weight.

Endive leaves, peppers cut into little 'boats' and button mushrooms caps make attractive and good-tasting containers for a variety of dips and spreads. For parties, I like to prepare a varied multi-coloured platter to titillate the palates and the eyes of the guests.

TORTILLAS

In Spain, a tortilla is an omelette, but in Mexico, a tortilla is a wonderfully useful flat maize or flour pancake. I learned to make maize tortillas in an Aztec farmhouse. Actually, it was in a stone-walled enclosure just outside the farmhouse, next to the pigpen. I learned the ancient way, kneeling on a cold, hard floor, patting the lime-treated *masa* (maize flour) by hand, and cooking the tortillas on a clay griddle set over blazing corn cobs. Believe me, it was a sobering experience for a woman with two food processors, a microwave and a dishwasher. I think I still – fifteen years later – have bruises on my knees! These days, I buy my tortillas at the supermarket. Use tortillas to wrap bean dishes or ragouts, garnished with salsas and Green Pea Spread (page 91), or use them to make tortilla chips – perfect for dips.

TORTILLA CHIPS

V ☙

corn (maize) tortillas

1 Preheat the oven to 150°C, 300°F, Gas Mark 2.

2 Bake the tortillas directly on the oven shelf for 15–20 minutes, turning once, until crisp right through (they will break with a clean 'snap'). Break into quarters or eighths and store in an airtight tin.

VARIATION *Microwave Tortilla Chips* Put a double layer of kitchen paper on the microwave turntable. Arrange five tortillas around the edge of the towel. They should not quite touch each other. Microwave at full power for 2–2½ minutes. If the towels are damp, replace them. Turn the tortillas over, and microwave at full power for 2½ minutes. Remove the tortilla chips to a wire cooling rack, and allow to rest for 5 minutes. Break into quarters or eighths.

PITA CRISPS

V ☙

white or wholemeal pita breads

1 Preheat the oven to 150°C, 300° F, Gas Mark 2.

2 With scissors, cut the pita bread into quarters or eighths, then separate each piece into two. Bake, in one layer, on a non-stick baking sheet for 10–15 minutes or until dried out and crisp.

CRISPS

If you have a microwave, you can buy a simple gadget that turns raw potato slices into fat-free crisps. It looks like a mini toast rack (I've seen a circular version and a rectangular version), and it really works. Lakeland Plastics (page 242) has a version, as do the cooking departments of some department stores. The gadget is not very expensive, and is extraordinarily useful. It makes pita, tortilla and bagel crisps as well. Just follow the directions that come with the gadget.

TARTLET SHELLS

MAKES 12 SHELLS

V ⊙

Ordinary bread slices, moulded into bun tins and baked until dried through, make adorable 'pastry' cases that are perfect for filling with dips and spreads of all kinds. The idea is to bake them so they dry right through, without browning. You might find it necessary to reduce the oven temperature a bit as they bake – only *you* know your own oven! In the cooking departments of some department stores, you may find special bun tins with tiny depressions, perfect for making little pastry cases for party finger food (use a liqueur glass as a cutter).

12 slices top-quality bakery bread, white or brown

1 Preheat the oven to 150°C, 300°F, Gas Mark 2.

2 With a 3 inch (7.5 cm) cutter or drinking glass, cut a circle out of the centre of each slice of bread. Flatten each circle with a rolling pin. (Save all the trimmings for breadcrumbs, etc.)

3 Press a round of bread into each depression in a 12-section bun tin. With your fingers, press it down and mould it up the sides.

4 Bake in the oven for 15 minutes, then remove from the bun tin, and bake directly on the oven shelf for 10 minutes more, until totally dried right through. Turn once or twice during this time. Cool on a cooling rack, then store in an airtight tin. (They keep for weeks.)

SAUCES

The conventional vision of very low-fat meals is of austerity: steamed vegetables, plain grilled fish or chicken breast, a small lonely potato or two, and maybe a piece of fruit to finish. No sauces – oh no indeed! Sauces pile on the fat, don't they? *Not necessarily.* I'm happy to say that there is a whole world of low-fat sauces, made from tomatoes, or vegetable purées, or skimmed-milk products. These sauces will not only dress up your meals, but add their own valuable measure of good nutrition as well. And your meals will never be austere.

BASIC TOMATO SAUCE

MAKES 1½ PINTS (900 ML)

V ☙ ❄

Basic Tomato Sauce is a low-fat staple that you will find yourself using again and again. Tomato sauces can sauce pasta or other grains for a quick, satisfying non-meat meal, as well as quick-cooking fish and chicken fillets. This recipe and the ones that follow form a collection of tomato sauces that are simple to prepare and wonderful to eat any number of ways. And all of them can be doubled or tripled. They freeze very well; if you're going to make a batch, it might as well be a large one. Freeze in small containers for future use. Most can be made in a heavy-bottomed or non-stick flameproof casserole or frying pan, or even in a non-stick wok.

1 red or yellow onion, finely diced
2 garlic cloves, crushed
1–2 carrots, peeled and finely diced
pinch of crushed dried chillies (optional)
2–3 black olives in brine, drained and slivered off their stones (optional)
2–3 sundried tomatoes, chopped with scissors (optional)
6 fl oz (175 ml) stock

6 fl oz (175 ml) dry red wine
¼ teaspoon dried basil, crumbled, or 1 tablespoon shredded fresh basil
¼ teaspoon dried oregano, crumbled, or 1 tablespoon chopped fresh oregano
three 14 oz (400 g) cans chopped tomatoes
salt and freshly ground pepper
1–2 tablespoons tomato purée
1–2 tablespoons chopped fresh parsley

1 Combine the onion, garlic, carrot and chillies, olives and sundried tomatoes (if using), stock, wine and dried herbs (if using) in a heavy-bottomed frying pan. Cover and bring to the boil, then reduce the heat and simmer until the carrots are tender and the liquid almost gone.

2 Stir in the canned tomatoes and season with salt and pepper. Simmer, partially covered, for 15–20 minutes. Stir in the tomato purée, parsley and other fresh herbs (if using), taste, and add more salt and pepper if needed. Simmer for 5–10 minutes more. Serve the sauce as it is or, if you prefer a smoother sauce, purée in batches in a blender.

PICADILLO TOMATO SAUCE

MAKES 1½ PINTS (900 ML)

V ⊙ ❋

Capers, raisins, cumin and chilli put a Latin-American spin on basic tomato sauce. While delicious on pasta, it would really come into its own with a can or two of drained, rinsed beans stirred in, with one of the meatball recipes (pages 170–173) or with fish.

1 red onion, chopped
2 small inner stalks of celery with leaves,
  chopped
2 tablespoons drained capers
2 tablespoons raisins
1 chilli, deseeded and chopped
½ teaspoon ground cumin

½ pint (300 ml) stock
three 14 oz (400 g) cans chopped tomatoes
salt and freshly ground pepper
2 tablespoons tomato purée
1 tablespoon chopped fresh parsley
2 tablespoons chopped fresh coriander

1 Combine the onion, celery, capers, raisins, chilli, cumin and stock in a heavy-bottomed frying pan. Cover and bring to the boil, then reduce the heat and simmer until the onion and celery are tender and the liquid almost gone.

2 Stir in the tomatoes and season with salt and pepper. Simmer, partially covered, for 15–20 minutes. Stir in the tomato purée and fresh herbs, taste, and add more salt and pepper if needed. Simmer for 5–10 minutes more.

FAST TOMATO SAUCE

MAKES 18 FL OZ (525 ML)

V ⊙ ❋

This passata-based sauce is ready in a paltry 15 minutes. Vary it by adding slivered black olives and drained capers, or replace the seasonings with a teaspoon or so of good curry powder for a quick tomato-curry sauce.

5–6 spring onions, trimmed and sliced
3–4 sundried tomatoes, chopped (use scissors)
1–2 garlic cloves, finely chopped
1–2 pinches crushed dried chillies

1–2 pinches dried oregano
6–8 fl oz (175–225 ml) stock
16 fl oz (475 ml) passata
freshly ground pepper

I Combine the onions, sundried tomatoes, garlic, chilli, oregano and stock in a non-reactive frying pan. Cover, bring to the boil, and boil for 3–4 minutes, then uncover and simmer until the onions and garlic are tender and the liquid has cooked down considerably and become syrupy.

2 Stir in the passata and grind in some pepper. Simmer for about 10 minutes.

RED PEPPER SAUCE

MAKES 1½ PINTS (900 ML)

V ❄

Red or yellow peppers are intoxicating: their colour, along with their sweet succulence and a mighty dose of vitamins, makes them very hard to resist. When simmered in stock, then puréed and strained (pepper sauces are always strained before serving to eliminate the tough skins), they make clinging, velvety sauces that go with almost anything: pasta, fish, chicken fillets, meatballs and sausages, and all sorts of vegetables. Sauces made from puréed peppers can be varied in many ways by experimenting with different herbs and seasonings. For a beautiful presentation, try positioning a poached or grilled chicken breast or fish fillet on a plate that has been coated with red pepper sauce on one side of the plate, yellow on the other.

10 red peppers, deseeded and coarsely chopped
6 spring onions, trimmed and sliced
1 red chilli, deseeded and diced (optional)
½ tablespoon paprika
½ pint (300 ml) stock
salt and freshly ground pepper

I Combine all the ingredients in a deep, heavy-bottomed frying pan. Bring to the boil, then reduce the heat and simmer for 20–30 minutes or until tender. Season with salt and pepper, and leave to cool slightly.

2 Purée the mixture in batches in a blender or food processor. Strain through a sieve or strainer, rubbing it through with a rubber spatula or wooden spoon. The skins, which are tough, will be left behind. Discard them.

3 Return the sauce to a saucepan and bring to a simmer. Taste and adjust the seasonings before serving.

YELLOW PEPPER SAUCE

MAKES 1½ PINTS (900 ML)

V ❄

I can't say which is the most exciting feature of pepper purée sauces: the vivid colour, the splendid nutrition, or the pure and intense taste. Vegetable purée-based sauces are so much more satisfying than old-fashioned fat-based sauces that are clogged up with butter or margarine, oils, cream, or egg yolk emulsions.

10 large yellow peppers, deseeded and coarsely
   diced
½ pint (300 ml) stock
½ teaspoon dried tarragon, crumbled

pinch of cayenne pepper
4 spring onions, trimmed and sliced
salt and freshly ground pepper

1 Combine all the ingredients in a deep, heavy-bottomed frying pan. Bring to the boil, then reduce the heat and simmer for 20–30 minutes or until the peppers are tender and the liquid greatly reduced. Season with salt and pepper, and leave to cool slightly.

2 Purée the mixture in batches in a blender or food processor. Strain through a sieve or strainer, rubbing it through with a rubber spatula or wooden spoon. Discard the debris.

3 Return the sauce to a saucepan and bring to a simmer. Taste and adjust the seasonings.

MANGO SAUCE

MAKES 1 PINT (600 ML)

V ◔

You will want to fall into this sauce and wallow; you'll want to polish it off all by itself (and by yourself) with a big spoon; you'll want to lavish it over everything in sight. It turns poached fish fillets into an elegant dish (serve the sauce in a wide strip on the plate *alongside* the fish, not blanketed on top); it can be poured on top of skinned chicken drumsticks and roasted, or it can be served with a grilled or poached chicken breast.

2 large onions, halved and sliced into thin half
   moons
¾ pint (450 ml) chicken stock
2 mangoes, peeled (page 69) and cubed
4 tablespoons mango chutney

juice of 1 lime
grated zest of ½ lime
pinch of freshly grated nutmeg
salt and freshly ground pepper

1 Combine the onions and ½ pint (300 ml) stock in a heavy-bottomed frying pan. Cover, bring to the boil, and boil for 5–7 minutes, then uncover and simmer for a few minutes until tender.

2 Stir in the mango cubes, mango chutney, lime juice and zest, and grated nutmeg. Season with salt and pepper and add the remaining stock. Simmer for 7–10 minutes or until the mixture is thickened and savoury, and the mango is cooked. Cool slightly, then purée in batches in a food processor or blender. Reheat and serve.

RED PEPPER TOMATO SAUCE

MAKES 1½ PINTS (900 ML)
V ❄

Any of the red pepper purée sauces can be combined with any of the tomato sauces for a double-whammy of colour, taste and nutrients. For a ridiculously easy, yet impressively good pepper sauce, simply purée a can or jar of drained pimientos (red peppers) in brine and combine with a carton of passata. Here, canned chopped tomatoes and fresh peppers are gently seasoned with paprika, another form of pepper. To make a paprikash sauce to serve with steamed cauliflower, sautéed whole button mushrooms, pan-sautéed chicken breasts, or stir-fried strips of lean beef or pork tenderloin, stir a tablespoon of this sauce into a few tablespoons of room temperature fromage frais, then stir it back into the sauce. Heat gently, but don't boil, or the sauce will separate.

1 pint (600 ml) stock
1 large mild onion, chopped
1 garlic clove, crushed
1 tablespoon paprika

6 red peppers, deseeded and coarsely chopped
14 oz (400 g) can chopped tomatoes
salt and freshly ground pepper

1 Combine half the stock with the onion, garlic and paprika in a heavy-bottomed frying pan. Cover, bring to the boil, and boil for 5–7 minutes, then uncover, reduce the heat and cook, stirring occasionally, until the onions are almost tender and the liquid almost gone.

2 Stir in the peppers and the remaining stock, and simmer, uncovered, over a moderate heat for a few minutes or until the peppers are tender and the liquid greatly reduced.

3 Add the canned tomatoes and season with salt and pepper. Simmer, uncovered, for 15–20 minutes or until thick and savoury. Cool slightly.

4 Purée in small batches in a blender or food processor, then push through a sieve to remove the pepper skins. Taste and adjust the seasonings before serving.

PUMPKIN AND SWEET POTATO SAUCE

MAKES 1½ PINTS (900 ML)

V ☉

Pumpkin and sweet potato form the basis of this very special sauce. The hint of spiciness, the seductive creamy-velvety texture, and the glowing sunset colour will knock your socks off. Fold steamed cauliflower, broccoli florets or steamed brussels sprouts into the sauce, sprinkle with a bit more Parmesan cheese and grill until the cheese melts, or thin the sauce with stock, for a soul-satisfying soup.

1½ lb (700 g) pumpkin
1 sweet potato weighing about 14 oz (400 g)
6 spring onions, trimmed and sliced
2 garlic cloves, crushed
½ teaspoon each of ground paprika, cumin, coriander

pinch of cayenne pepper
½ pint (300 ml) stock
salt and freshly ground pepper
3 tablespoons freshly grated Parmesan cheese

1 Cut the pumpkin into wedges, scrape off the seeds and fibres, peel and cube the flesh. Peel the sweet potato and cube it.

2 Steam the pumpkin and sweet potato together for about 15 minutes or until very tender. Refresh under cold running water and drain well.

3 Combine the onions, garlic, spices and ¼ pint (150 ml) stock in a frying pan, and simmer until the onions and garlic are tender, and the liquid is greatly reduced.

4 Put the pumpkin and sweet potato in a food processor or blender, scrape in the onion and spice mixture, pour in the remaining stock, season with salt and pepper and process until smooth. Sprinkle in the Parmesan, and process until very smooth. Taste and adjust the seasonings and reheat before serving.

CURRY SAUCE

MAKES 1½ PINTS (900 ML)

V ⊙ ❄

Sauces made from vegetable purées are silky and clinging, and they provide health-enhancing nutrition along with their gorgeous colour and texture. This burnished golden sauce of puréed parsnips, small white turnips, and carrots will sauce steamed vegetables, poached or grilled chicken breasts or fish, or pan-sautéed pork cutlets.

1 large onion, chopped
2 garlic cloves, crushed
1 tablespoon mild Korma curry powder
about 1¾ pints (1 litre) stock
2 white turnips, each weighing about 3 oz (75 g), peeled and roughly chopped

4 parsnips, each weighing about 6 oz (175 g), peeled, cored and roughly chopped
2 carrots, each weighing about 3 oz (75 g), peeled and roughly chopped
salt and freshly ground pepper

1 Combine the onion, garlic, curry powder and ½ pint (300 ml) stock in a heavy-bottomed frying pan or wok. Cover and simmer for 10–12 minutes or until the onions are very tender and the liquid is almost gone. Don't let it scorch.

2 Stir in the vegetables and an additional ¾ pint (450 ml) stock. Season with salt and pepper, cover and simmer until the vegetables are *very* tender and the liquid greatly reduced. Cool slightly.

3 Purée the mixture in batches in a blender, adding a little more stock if necessary to ease the blending. Return to the pan, and stir in ½–¾ pint (300–450 ml) additional stock, so that the consistency is that of a silky sauce. Heat gently, then taste and adjust the seasonings before serving.

REDCURRANT AND VERMOUTH SAUCE

MAKES 12 FL OZ (350 ML)

V ⊙

This is a variation of the classic Cumberland sauce, and is perfect with the pâté on page 176 and poultry and game. It will keep, well covered, in the fridge for a couple of weeks.

1 orange
1 lemon
1½ tablespoons cornflour
¼ pint (150 ml) red vermouth

1 tablespoon finely chopped spring onions
8 oz (225 g) redcurrant jelly
pinch of cayenne pepper

1 With a zester, pare the zest from the orange and lemon, being careful to leave the bitter white pith behind. Sliver, then parboil in water to cover for 2 minutes, then drain and set aside.

2 Squeeze the juice from the orange and the lemon. Stir in the cornflour until it dissolves.

3 Put the vermouth in a saucepan and bring to the boil. Add the spring onions and simmer for 1 minute. Add the jelly and stir until thoroughly dissolved. Add the citrus zests.

4 Stir the cornflour mixture into the sauce, and bring to the boil, stirring constantly. When it thickens nicely, remove from the heat and season with cayenne. Cool, then refrigerate.

ORANGE MANGO SAUCE

MAKES 1 PINT (600 ML)

V ⊙

Adapted from a colourful cookbook called *Nuevo Cubano* by Sue Mullin, this sweet/spicy sauce serves as a cold dipping sauce for crusty Butter Bean Sausages (page 12) or for meatballs (pages 170–173).

9 oz (250 g) mango chutney
9 oz (250 g) orange marmalade

1 tablespoon Dijon mustard
a few drops of lemon or lime juice

Chop up the mango pieces in the chutney by briefly whirling in a blender or processor, or by snipping them with kitchen scissors. Put the chutney in a bowl. Whisk the marmalade and mustard into the chutney, taste, and whisk in a few drops of lemon or lime juice to your taste.

WHITE SAUCES

Low-fat white sauces, made from skimmed milk that has been enriched with skimmed milk powder, sound so boring, but – if properly seasoned – can be surprisingly good. Unfortunately, making a no-fat white sauce in a saucepan, even a heavy-bottomed, non-stick pan, is difficult to do: skimmed milk scorches in the blink of an eye and when the milk is scorched, the sauce is inedible. If you have a microwave (and I recommend one highly) there will be no problem: the blessed machine scalds and boils milk, even skimmed, with no danger of scorching and burning.

It is very important, when making milky sauces in the microwave, to whisk the mixture very well first to aerate it, and then to whisk it once or twice more during the cooking process. Because a microwave heats unevenly, hot pockets can form in the milky liquid, causing occasional geyser-like eruptions which can be very dangerous: whisking well helps alleviate such a possibility. Before you remove the cling film to stir the sauce, pierce the film to release the steam, and always step back and avert your face. Have the roll of cling film on hand so that you can quickly re-cover the sauce and continue the cooking. (You could use a plate to cover the container, instead of cling film.) Since microwaves can vary considerably, you will have to work out the timing for your particular machine. The first time through should be a test run. Jot down the timing so that you will know it for all subsequent occasions. The result to aim for is a silky, creamy sauce that is not too thick and pasty, but will nicely coat a dish of cauliflower florets, macaroni, or the like.

BASIC WHITE SAUCE

MAKES 1 PINT (600 ML)

V ⊙

This is the very basic sauce. Do be sure to season it well.

6 tablespoons skimmed milk powder
3 tablespoons cornflour

salt and freshly ground pepper
about 18 fl oz (500 ml) skimmed milk

1 Spoon the milk powder and cornflour into a 3½ pint (2 litre) capacity, 7 inch (18 cm) top diameter, opaque white plastic measuring jug. Alternatively, use a 7½ inch (19 cm) top diameter clear glass Pyrex jug. Season with salt and pepper.

2 Using a wire whisk, whisk the milk into the dry ingredients. Whisk well – you don't want lumps, and vigorous whisking helps reduce the chance of volcanic eruptions. Cover the jug tightly with cling film (or use a plate). *[continues overleaf]*

3 Microwave on full power for 3 minutes. Carefully pierce the cling film (avert your face, be careful, the steam is hot) to release the steam, then uncover (begin with the side *away* from you) and whisk thoroughly. Re-cover tightly with a fresh piece of cling film, and microwave for another 2 minutes. Carefully pierce the film, uncover, whisk, re-cover tightly and microwave for a final 1½–2 minutes or until boiled, thickened and smooth.

4 Uncover and whisk again, then leave to stand for 3–4 minutes. Taste and adjust the seasonings, if necessary. Serve at once, or store in the refrigerator with a sheet of microwave cling film directly on the surface of the sauce.

5 When reheating, if the sauce has thickened too much overnight in the refrigerator, whisk in some skimmed milk to thin it to the desired consistency. Cover the jug with cling film and microwave in 30-second bursts, stopping to whisk well (be careful of steam) between bursts, until the sauce is warm and smooth. It is important to follow these directions because a cornflour-bound sauce, if overheated, may break down.

VARIATIONS *Cheese Sauce* With a rubber spatula, fold 3–4 tablespoons freshly grated Parmesan cheese into the warm sauce.
Feta Cheese Sauce Instead of Parmesan, whisk in 4–5 oz (110–125 g) crumbled, medium-fat feta cheese, stirring until the cheese melts into the sauce. A little freshly grated nutmeg would not be amiss stirred in here. Use this feta cheese sauce for Moussaka (page 166).
Goat's Cheese Sauce Whisk the contents of one of those little pots (4 oz/125 g) of creamy medium-fat goat's cheese (Chevroux, Chevrette, etc.) into the warm sauce, and stir until it melts right through.
Mustard Sauce Stir in 2 rounded tablespoons Dijon mustard after you've whisked in the milk in step 2.
Garlic Sauce After the sauce is made, stir in sieved garlic purée from a bulb of Roasted or Pan-Braised Garlic (page 35). Remember, garlic cooked this way is sweet and mellow, and will give the sauce a wonderful dimension. This Garlic Sauce, along with Parmesan, would be perfect on the Aubergine Gratin (page 6).
Olive and Sundried Tomato Sauce When the sauce is done, stir in the olive infusion with sundried tomatoes (page viii). This, with Parmesan or feta, is glorious with steamed cauliflower or broccoli (or a mixture).
Parsley Sauce At the very last minute, stir in a good handful of chopped fresh parsley.
Tarragon Sauce Combine four sliced spring onions, 4 fl oz (100 ml) dry white vermouth, ½ pint (300 ml) stock, ½ teaspoon dried tarragon and a pinch of ground allspice in a small saucepan or frying pan, and simmer until the onions are tender and the liquid greatly reduced and syrupy. Stir this mixture into the freshly made white sauce. If you have some fresh tarragon leaves, snip them up and stir them in. This sauce is lovely with fish.

SALAD DRESSINGS

At first it seems impossible – to dress a salad without benefit of oil and without mayonnaise. But oil (at 120 fat Calories per tablespoon) and mayonnaise (an emulsion of egg yolk and oil – in other words, pure fat) undermine quite a bit of the low-fat, low-calorie, high-nutrition goodness of salad. And once your palate has adjusted to the low-fat way of life, oil and mayonnaise spoil a salad's taste and texture, clogging up its crisp fresh-ness. But a naked salad lacks pizzazz, and lack of pizzazz is something to be avoided at all costs. The trick is to dress the salad well without resorting to oceans of oil, or fatty dressings. First, some simple methods:

1 A good squeeze of lemon or lime juice can be very effective on a green salad.

2 Balsamic vinegar has a thick, treacly, sweet and sour quality that makes it perfect for salads all by itself. Even the inexpensive supermarket brands make salads sing.

3 If you are a die-hard vinaigrette fan, and can afford a soupçon of oil now and then, make yourself a vinaigrette spray. Buy a small atomizer bottle (just like the one you have for your oil and water spray, page ix). In a small jug, whisk together 1 teaspoon Dijon mustard and 1 tablespoon extra-virgin olive oil. Whisk in approximately 4 fl oz (100 ml) balsamic vinegar. Pour this mixture into your spray bottle, and top up with a little more balsamic (don't fill the bottle to the tippy-top, or the dressing will not shake up properly). To dress your salad, shake and spritz. It can be even simpler, if you wish: just fill the bottle seven-eighths full with balsamic, one-eighth with extra-virgin olive oil. The following dressings keep for 2–3 days in the fridge.

OLIVE–CHILLI–CITRUS DRESSING

MAKES 4 FL OZ (100 ML)

V ⊙

1 garlic clove
3–4 black olives in brine, drained and slivered
  off their stones
½ red onion, finely diced

1 chilli, deseeded and finely diced
2 tablespoons balsamic vinegar
juice of ½ lime and 1 large lemon

Crush the garlic and olives together. Scrape into a screw-top jar and add the remaining ingredients. Put the top on and shake well. Refrigerate until needed. Shake again before serving.

SPICY CITRUS DRESSING

MAKES ¼ PINT (150 ML)

⊙

4 tablespoons balsamic vinegar
4 tablespoons lime juice
4 tablespoons orange juice
2 teaspoons teriyaki or soy sauce

several dashes Tabasco sauce
several dashes Worcestershire sauce
1 garlic clove, crushed

Put all the ingredients in a screw-top jar, put the lid on, and shake well. Refrigerate until needed. Shake again before serving.

SWEET AND SOUR CITRUS DRESSING

MAKES ½ PINT (300 ML)

V ⊙

juice of 3 large oranges
juice of 3 limes
3 tablespoons teriyaki sauce
2 tablespoons balsamic vinegar

1 tablespoon sugar
½ inch (1 cm) piece of fresh root ginger, peeled
 and crushed
1 garlic clove, crushed

Put all the ingredients together in a screw-top jar, put the lid on and shake well. Refrigerate until needed. Shake again before serving.

BUTTERMILK DRESSING

MAKES ½ PINT (300 ML)

½ pint (300 ml) cultured buttermilk
1 tablespoon Dijon mustard

1 teaspoon granulated sugar
1 tablespoon balsamic vinegar

Whisk together the buttermilk and mustard, then whisk in the sugar and vinegar. Store in the fridge until needed. Whisk again before serving.

CREAMY GARLIC DRESSING

MAKES ½ PINT (300 ML)

2 garlic cloves, crushed
1½ teaspoons white wine vinegar

½ pint (300 ml) very low-fat fromage frais
salt and freshly ground pepper

Combine the garlic and wine vinegar, and leave to marinate for 15 minutes. Whisk the garlic vinegar into the fromage frais. Season with salt and pepper, and refrigerate until needed.

FROMAGE FRAIS 'MAYO'

MAKES ¾ PINT (450 ML)
V ☺

In place of mayonnaise, try fromage frais flavoured with Dijon mustard and balsamic vinegar. Mayonnaise is an emulsion of egg yolk and oil – pure fat. This not-mayo is virtually fat-free but it spreads on bread for sandwiches, dresses salads and acts as a dip for steamed and raw vegetables in much the same way as the real thing. Although it doesn't taste exactly like mayonnaise, it is a very creditable healthy stand-in, and very delicious in its own right. These mixtures may 'weep' as they sit in the fridge; simply pour off any excess liquid before using them.

17 oz (500 g) carton very low-fat fromage frais
1 tablespoon balsamic vinegar

1 teaspoon Dijon mustard
salt and freshly ground pepper

Place all ingredients in a bowl and whisk well to combine. Refrigerate until needed.

VARIATIONS The basic fromage frais 'mayo' can be varied in many different ways. The most obvious is to stir in spice mixtures (a tandoori or tikka spice mixture will pep it up wonderfully), but there are less obvious choices as well. The velvety texture and glowing orange hue of steamed pumpkin, for instance, makes a magnificent 'mayo' addition, and roasted garlic purée can be used to make a sort of low-fat äoli (garlic mayonnaise) to serve with boiled potatoes, steamed vegetables, fish and shellfish. A puréed grilled red pepper or two will give the 'mayo' a delicious sweet/smoky dimension and a beautiful rosy blush. As for the amazing Mango 'Mayo', words fail me – just try it with the Tomato and Mango Salad on page 69, and you will see what I mean!

PUMPKIN 'MAYO'

MAKES ½ PINT (300 ML)
V ⊙

12 oz (350 g) pumpkin, peeled and cubed
  (page 66)
6 tablespoons very low-fat fromage frais

salt and freshly ground pepper

1 Steam the pumpkin cubes for about 15 minutes or until very tender. Refresh under cold running water, drain well, and cool thoroughly.

2 Put the pumpkin in a food processor or blender with the fromage frais, season with salt and pepper, and purée until very smooth. Store in the fridge until needed.

GARLIC 'MAYO'

MAKES ½ PINT (300 ML)
V ⊙

sieved purée from 1 bulb of Roasted or Pan-
  Braised Garlic (page 35)
1 teaspoon Dijon mustard

½ tablespoon balsamic vinegar
½ pint (300 ml) very low-fat fromage frais

Whisk the garlic, mustard and vinegar into the fromage frais. Store in the fridge until needed.

Opposite, clockwise from top: Sliced Potato Gratin (page 60), Grilled Chicken Parcels filled with Creamy Garlic Cheese (page 149), Sautéed French Beans (page 13), Cherry Tomato and Olive Salsa (page 81)

PEPPER 'MAYO'

MAKES ½ PINT (300 ML)

V ☉

2 large red peppers, grilled and peeled (page 49), or use bottled or canned peppers
3 tablespoons very low-fat fromage frais

1 tablespoon balsamic vinegar
salt and freshly ground pepper

Put all the ingredients (including the juices from the grilled pepper) in the blender and purée. Store in the fridge until needed.

MANGO 'MAYO'

MAKES ½ PINT (300 ML)

☉

1 whole, ripe mango, cubed (page 69)
3 tablespoons very low-fat fromage frais
2 tablespoons balsamic vinegar

dash of Worcestershire sauce
pinch of mustard powder
1–2 pinches brown sugar

Put the mango flesh in a blender. Whisk together the remaining ingredients, except the sugar, and add to the mango. Blend until perfectly smooth, then taste and blend in some sugar, if necessary. Refrigerate until needed.

Opposite, clockwise from top left: Chicken-Berry Salad (page 155), Mango 'Mayo' (page 99), Roasted New Potatoes and Fennel (page 59), Roasted Asparagus (page 3)

RAITAS

DRAINED YOGHURT

Raitas (creamy yoghurt dips, salads or sauces) don't work with non-fat yoghurts straight out of the carton; such yoghurts are too thin, watery and sour. That's why I usually opt for non-fat fromage frais when preparing raitas; it is thick, creamy, and a low-fat-food-lover's salvation. But non-fat yoghurt can be drained to give it a thick, Greek-yoghurt-like consistency. It will still be quite sour, but yoghurt-lovers won't mind. Fold some garlic purée (page 35) or chopped herbs into the drained yoghurt (it is usually referred to as 'yoghurt cheese') or fold in marmalade for a sweet spread. Spread it on toast or bagels. If you drain it for 2–3 hours, it can be used, unflavoured, as the base of any of the raita-like mixtures that follow, instead of fromage frais.

very low-fat natural yoghurt

1 Line a sieve with a double layer of muslin or a jelly bag, and place over a large bowl. Pour the yoghurt into the sieve, fold the cloth over the top and refrigerate overnight. (If you are draining the yoghurt for use in a raita, refrigerate for 2–3 hours only.)

2 The next day, drain the liquid from the bowl (it can be used as part of the liquid in bread baking), and rinse and dry the bowl. Scrape the drained yoghurt into the bowl.

CREAMY HERB RAITA

V ☺

Raitas don't only go with Indian meals. Depending on their seasonings, they can go with almost anything. This basic and useful creamy herb sauce goes with virtually everything. I use it time after time to top beans and vegetable ragouts, and to float on the top of thick soups. Vary the herbs to your taste and to the season; good combinations are mint and coriander, mint and dill, chives and parsley, thyme and tarragon, or oregano and basil. Or try one herb at a time.

very low-fat fromage frais   *shredded or snipped fresh herbs (see above)*

Whisk the fromage frais with a generous amount of fresh herbs. Refrigerate until needed.

MINT AND CORIANDER RAITA

MAKES ½ PINT (300 ML)
V ☉

This is perfect for curries and other spicy stews and ragouts. Or try a small bowlful as a dip for any of the oven-fried potatoes, particularly the spicy versions (pages 52–54).

½ pint (300 ml) very low-fat fromage frais
4 spring onions, trimmed and sliced
1 green chilli, deseeded and chopped (optional)
4 tablespoons shredded fresh mint leaves

6 tablespoons chopped fresh coriander
½ inch (1 cm) piece of fresh root ginger, peeled and crushed

Combine all the ingredients, including the ginger. Refrigerate until needed.

TZATZIKI

MAKES 24 FL OZ (725 ML)
V

Tzatziki makes a terrific topping for hamburgers or sausages (try them stuffed into a pita pocket with a dollop of tzatziki on top), a great dip or spread, or an accompaniment to grilled meat. The idea is to serve the creamy mixture on the plate with the (slightly rare) meat, so that the warm meat juices mingle with the cold cucumber sauce. Exquisite!

2 large cucumbers
salt and freshly ground pepper
2 large garlic cloves, finely chopped

1½ teaspoons white wine vinegar
1¾ pints (1 litre) very low-fat fromage frais

1 Peel the cucumbers, cut them in half lengthways, and use a teaspoon to scrape out and discard the seeds. Grate the cucumbers into a non-reactive colander, sprinkle with salt, and leave to drain for 30 minutes.

2 Place the garlic and vinegar in a small bowl and leave to marinate while the cucumbers are draining.

3 Rinse the drained cucumbers, squeeze them as dry as possible and wrap in a tea-towel to dry. Place in the bowl with the garlic and vinegar. Add the fromage frais and a few grindings of fresh pepper, and stir. Serve at once or store in the refrigerator (it will keep for days, and improve in flavour each day).

SOUPS

Soups are a marvellous way to eat quantities of lovely vegetables in the most delicious and comforting manner imaginable. I particularly like big, satisfying soups that can serve as a complete meal, with some crusty bread and a nice pudding to follow. Low-fat soups never have to taste thin and anaemic because the vegetables they contain provide body and wonderful flavour. It is not necessary to resort to the traditional enrichments of butter, cream, olive oil, and so on.

It's convenient and time-saving to make a big pot of soup that will last for more than one meal. And, of course, many soups can be frozen.

SOUP SAVVY

1 Sauté the flavouring vegetables using one of the basic stock sauté methods (page viii): it is never necessary to resort to oil or fat of any kind.

2 Skimmed milk can be used, with great effect, to 'cream' a soup, if you stir some skimmed milk powder into it first. The powder makes the milk seem richer and less watery, without, of course, making it fatty. And the milk powder adds valuable nutrients (calcium, protein, vitamins A and D) to the soup.

3 Soups can also be 'creamed' without using any dairy products at all, with a can of flageolet beans. Drain the beans, purée them in a blender or food processor, and stir into the soup. The purée will add a remarkable creaminess, and round out the soup beautifully.

4 The vegetables used to make some soups add enough of a creamy texture in themselves, so that nothing else is really needed. Root vegetables, in particular, have this ability. A sweet potato, a parsnip, or even an all-purpose potato, can thicken, give body, and 'cream' a soup most effectively. The entire soup can be puréed to a smooth creaminess, or half the soup can be puréed, then added to the unpuréed portion for a chunkier texture. Either way, the soup will be delicious and soothing.

5 For a low- (rather than no-) fat method of making a 'creamy' soup, a tub of Boursin Léger (low-fat Boursin, a herb and garlic flavoured French cheese spread) can be puréed with the soup, adding garlic and herb flavour, along with a creamy texture. However, if you are trying to *lose* weight, or have a medical problem that negates the use of *any* added dietary fat, give this method a miss.

BLENDER SAFETY
Many soups are puréed in the blender, after they are cooked. Remember these rules:

1 Cool slightly before blending.

2 Always fill the blender container less than half full. Overfill it and the liquid will surge up and blow off the cover. Just to make sure, hold down the cover and avert your face as you turn on the blender.

'INSTANT' SOUP
With stock in the freezer or vegetable bouillon powder in the cupboard, and a nice supply of frozen (or leftover) vegetables, instant soup gratification is yours. Simmer a good handful of frozen (or leftover) vegetables in enough stock to cover until tender and warm. Put in a blender with a spoonful or two of Boursin Léger or medium-fat creamy goat's cheese, and blend until very smooth and creamy. Return

to the saucepan and stir in warm stock until you achieve a nice soup consistency. Simmer gently for a few minutes, season to taste, and pour into a sturdy pottery mug. Sip and slurp to your heart's content.

SOUP GARNISHES

A nice sloppy, solitary serving of soup, spooned or sipped from a sturdy pottery mug, with a big napkin tied around your neck, makes a lovely meal after a hard day's work (especially if you made the soup the day before), but sometimes soup is served more formally, at the table, in bowls or shallow soup plates, and shared with others. This is the time to garnish the soup. Garnishes dress up a bowl of soup, and supply textural contrast; always a pleasure during any part of the meal. The garnish can be a shoal of crisp croûtons, a spoonful of cooked rice, couscous or bulghur, a floating island of herbed fromage frais, a jewelled cluster of salsa, a small shower of grated medium-fat cheese, or even a scattering of freshly made air-popped popcorn.

GARLIC CROUTONS

Dry slices of day-old bread in the oven (directly on the oven shelf) at 150°C, 300°F, Gas Mark 2, turning occasionally. When they are dry and crisp right through (but not browned), remove them from the oven and rub each thoroughly with the cut side of a halved garlic clove. Cut or break the slices into ¼–½ inch (0.5–1 cm) cubes.

CHEESE CROUTONS

Make the croûtons as above, but sprinkle the bread with grated Parmesan (or other medium-fat cheese) before you put it in the oven, and don't turn them as they dry out. Omit the garlic rub.

RED PEPPER PUREE

Puréed grilled peppers (page 49) or bottled peppers seasoned with a dab of honey and a dash of Tabasco sauce, swirled on to the surface of a serving of a vegetable purée soup makes a spectacular garnish.

CREAMY BROCCOLI SOUP

MAKES 4 PINTS (2.3 LITRES)

V ⊙ ✳

This soup uses the florets of the broccoli only, and is seasoned with curry powder (use mild or medium, to your taste, but use a good brand). The creamy texture is provided by the addition of a can of drained and puréed flageolet beans. For heaven's sake, don't throw the broccoli stalks away. See page 17 for suggestions on how to prepare the crisp and succulent stalks.

6 spring onions, trimmed and sliced
1–2 garlic cloves, crushed
1 tablespoon mild or medium Madras curry powder
3 ¾ pints (2.2 litres) stock
florets from 2 heads of broccoli (about 4 pints/2.3 litres florets)

4 oz (110 g) all-purpose potato (such as Wilja), peeled and cubed
15 oz (425 g) can flageolet beans, drained and rinsed
salt and freshly ground pepper

1 Put the onions, garlic and curry powder in a large saucepan with ¼ pint (150 ml) of the stock, and simmer until the onions and garlic are tender and the liquid greatly reduced. Add all the remaining ingredients, except the beans. Season with salt and pepper and simmer, partially covered, for 20–25 minutes or until the potato and broccoli are tender. Cool slightly.

2 Purée the soup in a blender, in small batches, returning each batch to a clean saucepan. Put the beans in the blender with a ladleful of the soup, and purée. Stir into the soup.

3 Bring the soup back to a simmer, taste and adjust the seasonings before serving.

SWEET POTATO AND CHICK PEA SOUP

MAKES 2½ PINTS (1.4 LITRES)

V ⊙ ❄

A sweet potato is a lovely thing, with its hint of sweetness and its voluptuous texture. Put it into a soup with sesame seeds and chick peas: the flavour will be reminiscent of hummous and the texture will be velvety.

2 tablespoons sesame seeds
2 pints (1.1 litres) stock
juice of 1 lime
1–2 garlic cloves, crushed
1 onion, chopped

12 oz (350 g) sweet potato, peeled and cut into
*   rough chunks*
15 oz (425 g) can chick peas, drained and rinsed
salt and freshly ground pepper

1 Put the sesame seeds in a large heavy-bottomed saucepan and heat gently, stirring constantly, for 30–60 seconds or until toasted (be careful not to scorch them).

2 Stir in ½ pint (300 ml) of the stock, half the lime juice, the garlic and onion. Cover and simmer for 5–7 minutes, then uncover and simmer briskly until the onions and garlic are tender, and are gently 'frying' in their own juices.

3 Add the sweet potato pieces and stir for a few moments. Add the remaining stock and simmer, partially covered, for about 15 minutes or until the sweet potatoes are almost tender.

4 Stir in the chick peas and remaining lime juice, and season with salt and pepper. Simmer, partially covered, for about 10 minutes or until the potatoes are tender. Cool slightly.

5 Purée the soup, in small batches, in a blender until smooth and velvety. Return to a saucepan and heat through, taste, and adjust the seasonings before serving.

PUREE OF PEA SOUP

MAKES 2 ¾ PINTS (1.6 LITRES)
V ⊙

This soup bursts with garden flavour, even though the peas are frozen. The seasonings are kept simple, so that the vegetable flavour shines through.

12 spring onions, trimmed and sliced
1 ½ pints (900 ml) stock
1 ¼ lb (550 g) frozen peas
2–3 tablespoons shredded fresh mint

½ pint (300 ml) skimmed milk mixed with 3
  tablespoons skimmed milk powder
salt and freshly ground pepper

1 Combine the onions, ½ pint (300 ml) stock and the peas in a large saucepan, and simmer for a few minutes or until the peas are tender. Don't overcook; they should retain their lovely green colour. Cool slightly, then purée in small batches in a blender. Return the soup to a saucepan.

2 Stir in the mint and remaining stock, and simmer for 5 minutes, then stir in the milk and simmer for 2–3 minutes more. Season with salt and pepper.

CREAM OF CAULIFLOWER CHEESE SOUP

MAKES 2 ½ PINTS (1.4 LITRES)
V ⊙

In this suave brew of cauliflower and potatoes, Boursin Léger (low-fat French cheese spread) provides the 'cream' plus a delicious hint of garlic and herbs.

1 medium cauliflower, trimmed, cored and
  separated into florets
4 oz (110 g) all-purpose potato (such as Wilja),
  peeled and cubed

1 ½ pints (900 ml) stock
salt and freshly ground pepper
5 oz (125 g) tub Boursin Léger

1 Combine the cauliflower, potato and stock in a large saucepan and season with salt and pepper. Simmer, partially covered, for 20 minutes or until the vegetables are tender. Cool slightly.

2 Purée the soup in small batches in a blender, returning the purée to a saucepan. Put the Boursin in the blender, add a ladleful or two of soup, and purée. Stir into the soup.

3 Bring the soup to a simmer, taste and adjust the seasonings before serving.

CARROT AND AUBERGINE SOUP

MAKES 2½ PINTS (1.4 LITRES)
V ❋

Carrots and aubergines may sound like strange soup-fellows, but they do – along with potatoes, celery, and a panoply of interesting flavourings – make a gorgeous soup. Soup-eating is about comfort, and this soup is about as comforting as they come.

*2 aubergines, each weighing about
   8 oz (225 g), peeled and coarsely chopped
2 onions, chopped
2 garlic cloves, crushed
3 celery stalks, destrung and thinly sliced
2–3 sundried tomatoes, chopped (use scissors)
1–2 pinches crushed dried chillies
1½ teaspoons ground coriander
1 teaspoon paprika
½ teaspoon ground cumin*

*4 fl oz (100 ml) red wine
juice of ½ orange
juice of ½ lemon
2½ pints (1.4 litres) stock
1½ lb (700 g) carrots, peeled and chopped
6 oz (175 g) all-purpose potatoes (such as
   Wilja), peeled and chopped
two 14 oz (400 g) cans chopped tomatoes
1 tablespoon tomato purée
salt and freshly ground pepper*

1 Combine the aubergines, onions, garlic, celery, sundried tomatoes, spices, wine, fruit juices and ½ pint (300 ml) stock in a large heavy-bottomed saucepan. Cover and simmer for 5–7 minutes, then uncover and simmer until the vegetables are very tender, and most of the liquid is absorbed.

2 Stir in the carrots and potatoes and a splash more stock. Stir and cook for 1–2 minutes. Stir in the canned tomatoes, the tomato purée and the remaining stock, and season with salt and pepper. Simmer, uncovered, until the vegetables are very tender. Cool slightly.

3 Purée the soup in small batches in a blender, returning the puréed soup to a saucepan. Bring back to a simmer, and taste and adjust the seasonings before serving.

WILD MUSHROOM SOUP

MAKES 2½ PINTS (1.4 LITRES)

V ❄

The 'wildness' is provided by reconstituted dried mushrooms (page 40). 'The best I've ever had,' said one well-travelled gourmet at my table, gazing in ecstasy into his soup bowl. I didn't bother to tell him how extremely low in fat it was, but I was very pleased with myself. It's the 'holy trinity' of low-fat mushroom cookery that makes it so good: stock, sherry and teriyaki.

1 oz (25 g) dried porcini (ceps)
½ oz (15 g) dried shiitakes
*2 lb (900 g) fresh mushrooms, cleaned and
    quartered*
about ½ pint (300 ml) medium sherry
1–2 dashes teriyaki or soy sauce

2½ pints (1.4 litres) stock
8 spring onions, trimmed and sliced
1 teaspoon dried tarragon, crumbled
2 garlic cloves, crushed
salt and freshly ground pepper

1 Rinse the dried mushrooms well under cold running water. Put them in a bowl and cover them generously with hot water. Leave to soak for 20 minutes.

2 In a large, heavy, non-stick frying pan or wok, combine the fresh mushrooms with the sherry, teriyaki, 4 fl oz (100 ml) stock, the spring onions, tarragon and garlic. (If your frying pan is too small, do this initial 'frying' in several batches.) Simmer briskly until the mixture is almost dry. Stir frequently and do not let the ingredients scorch or brown. Scrape the mixture into a large saucepan.

3 Lift the dried mushrooms out of their soaking water and rinse under cold running water. Strain the soaking water through a sieve lined with muslin or a double layer of coffee filters to eliminate grit and sand. Discard any tough stems and chop the mushrooms coarsely (scissors are good for this). Add the soaked mushrooms and their filtered water to the fresh mushrooms in the pan.

4 Add the remaining stock to the pan, and season with a little salt and pepper. Bring to the boil, then reduce the heat and simmer, partially covered, for 1 hour. Taste, and add more salt and pepper, if necessary. Cool slightly.

5 In batches, put the soup in a blender, and flick the motor on and off once or twice. (You want a rough chopped effect, *not* a smooth purée.) Return to a saucepan to reheat, and serve piping hot.

MINESTRONE WITH SAUSAGE BALLS

MAKES ABOUT 3 ½ PINTS (2 LITRES)

❀

One of my most satisfying culinary achievements has been to slim down my favourite (beloved!) Italian recipes. The cult of olive oil has reached absurd proportions; surely it is time for the oily tide to turn. The truth is, it is highly questionable that olive oil is healthier than any other unsaturated oil, and olive oil, as all oils, has virtually the same (fattening) calories as butter, margarine and other hydrogenated vegetable oils, lard, or any other fat that you care to name. The olive, sundried tomato and garlic infusion gives this main dish its Italian soul; there is no need to mourn the absence of oil, whether extra-virgin or totally debauched. Without the sausage balls, the soup makes a sumptuous vegetarian feast.

2 onions, coarsely chopped

1 small carrot, peeled and diced

3 sundried tomatoes, chopped (use scissors)

3 garlic cloves, crushed

4 black olives in brine, drained and slivered off their stones

pinch of crushed dried chillies (optional)

2 ½ pints (1.4 litres) stock

two 14 oz (400 g) cans tomatoes, drained and mashed

12 fl oz (350 ml) dry red wine

1 small red pepper, cut into its natural sections, deseeded, peeled and coarsely diced

3 small courgettes, trimmed and cut into ½ inch (1 cm) slices

2 ½ oz (60 g) tiny dried pasta shells

salt and freshly ground pepper

2–3 tablespoons shredded fresh basil

1 tablespoon chopped fresh oregano

2–3 tablespoons chopped fresh parsley

15 oz (425 g) can borlotti beans, drained and rinsed

Italian Sausage Balls, grilled (page 172)

freshly grated Parmesan cheese, to serve

1 Combine the onions, carrot, sundried tomatoes, garlic, olives, chillies (if using) and ½ pint (300 ml) stock in a large, heavy-bottomed saucepan. Cover and simmer for 7–10 minutes, then uncover and simmer, stirring, until the onions and carrot are tender and the liquid almost gone. Stir in the canned tomatoes, wine and remaining stock, and simmer briskly, uncovered, for 15 minutes, stirring occasionally.

2 Add the red pepper, courgettes and pasta. Season with salt and pepper, cover, and simmer for 10 minutes or until the pasta and vegetables are tender, stirring occasionally.

3 Add the herbs, beans and sausage balls. Heat through and serve piping hot, with Parmesan cheese.

SWEET AND SOUR CABBAGE SOUP

MAKES 4 PINTS (2.3 LITRES)

V ❄

Another soup to eat with or without meatballs as a sturdy main course, this cabbage soup has an Eastern European profile. It is based on the comforting and hearty stuffed cabbage dishes of my childhood. To make the meal perfect, serve with slices of Rye Bread (page 197).

2 medium onions, halved and sliced into thin
* half moons*
2 pints (1.1 litres) stock
1–2 garlic cloves, crushed
1 tablespoon paprika
2 lb (900 g) cabbage, trimmed of tough outer
* leaves, halved, cored and shredded*
8 oz (225 g) all-purpose potatoes (such as
* Wilja), peeled and cut into 1 inch (2.5 cm)*
* cubes*

two 14 oz (400 g) cans chopped tomatoes
juice of 1 large lemon
6 tablespoons sultanas
1 tablespoon mild runny honey
salt and freshly ground pepper
TO SERVE (OPTIONAL)
Paprika Meatballs (page 171)
fromage frais
snipped fresh dill

1 Combine the onions, ½ pint (300 ml) stock, the garlic and paprika in a large, heavy-bottomed saucepan. Cover and simmer briskly for 5–7 minutes, then uncover and simmer briskly until the onions are tender and the liquid greatly reduced. Add the cabbage, and stir until the cabbage wilts.

2 Stir in the remaining ingredients, including the remaining stock, season with salt and pepper, and simmer, partially covered, until the potatoes are tender. Taste and adjust the seasonings.

3 Serve as is, or with a few Meatballs nestled in each bowl. If you wish, garnish each bowl with a dollop of fromage frais mixed with snipped fresh dill.

SWEETCORN AND PEPPER SOUP BAKED IN ACORN SQUASH

SERVES 4
V

This is a wonderful way to serve acorn squash – filled with an aromatic, flavourful soup. The soup is actually baked in the whole squash, so as you spoon out the soup, you also spoon out some of the sweet, tender flesh of the squash. It's beautiful, delicious, and amusing: who could ask for anything more?

10 oz (275 g) frozen sweetcorn kernels
  (preferably 'bred for extra sweetness')
4 red peppers, grilled and peeled (page 49) or
  use canned or bottled peppers
½ chilli, deseeded and chopped
1–2 garlic cloves, crushed

8 spring onions, trimmed and thinly sliced
1½ pints (900 ml) stock
salt and freshly ground pepper
4 acorn squash (page 66), of about equal size
oil spray (page ix)

1 Preheat the oven to 200°C, 400°F, Gas Mark 6.

2 Thaw the corn and cook until just tender (3–5 minutes in the microwave with no added liquid will thaw and cook it perfectly). Put the corn in a blender with the peppers.

3 Sauté the chilli, garlic and onions in ½ pint (300 ml) stock until the garlic is tender and the liquid almost gone. Cool slightly, then scrape into the blender. Pour in ¼ pint (150 ml) additional stock, and purée.

4 Tip the purée into a saucepan and stir in the remaining stock. Season with salt and pepper, and simmer, partially covered, for 10 minutes.

5 If necessary, cut a very thin slice off the bottom of each squash so that they will sit on a level bottom. Be careful – there must be no leaks in the squash, and the bottom must remain thick. Cut a 'cap' off the top of the squash and scrape out the seeds and fibres, taking care not to pierce through the bottom of the squash. (Should you accidently pierce the bottom of the squash, take the 'cap' that you have cut from the top of the squash, and insert it, pointed side down, into the hole. It will act as a plug, and prevent leaks.) Season the inside of the squash with salt and pepper. Put the kettle on to boil.

6 Pour about ½ pint (300 ml) of the corn soup into each squash. Spray the top edges of the squash lightly with oil spray, and put the 'caps' back on. Set each squash in an ovenproof glass or ceramic soup bowl or small soufflé dish that fits it nicely, and put these in a large baking dish. Put the baking dish in the oven, and pour in boiling water to come halfway up the sides. Bake for 45 minutes to 1 hour or until the squash flesh is tender and the soup is simmering. Serve one squash, set in its bowl, per person.

GRAINS AND PASTA

Although not as colourful, grains are almost as exciting as vegetables. It's easy to get into a rut and depend on the same grains, time after time (white rice with everything), but there are wonderful lesser-known grains out there. Try organically grown short-grain brown rice instead of the usual long-grain white; try wheaty bulghur; dark and smoky wild rice; tender couscous. Each grain has its own character, a good measure of valuable nutrients, and an excellent ability to team up with colourful vegetables and soak up flavourful sauces. Check the supermarket shelves next time you go shopping; the array of international grains on offer will fascinate you.

BROWN RICE

Organically grown short-grain brown rice is one of the most delicious and useful grains there is (find it in wholefood and health food shops). If your image of brown rice is of a stodgy, dowdy, depressingly earnest grain, you will be pleasantly surprised. The rice is firm and slightly chewy without being hard, with a slightly nutty flavour, and can be used to make a number of delightful risotto-like dishes. A true risotto is made with arborio (Italian white short-grain rice) and is painstakingly prepared, adding a bit of stock, stirring and cooking the rice until the stock is absorbed, adding a little more, stirring and cooking, and so on until the dish is ready. And a traditional risotto is usually quite buttery as well, so in no way are these brown rice dishes *real* risottos. But the cooked brown rice, sautéed in seasoned stock with vegetables (mushrooms and asparagus tips are notable examples), with some Parmesan cheese melted in, gives the same kind of gentle comfort a risotto does, and – eaten in bowls, with a little Creamy Herb Raita (page 100) on the side, and perhaps a cherry tomato or a bean salsa – makes a most pleasing meal.

TO COOK SHORT-GRAIN BROWN RICE

Measure the uncooked rice by pouring it into a measuring jug – ½ pint (300 ml) raw rice will yield 1½ pints (900 ml) cooked rice. Choose a heavy-bottomed saucepan that can be covered tightly and is large enough to allow for the rice's expansion. Measure the rice first, then rinse in a sieve under cold running water. Pour the rice into the pan, then measure out twice the volume of the rice in stock or water, and pour it in. In other words, for ½ pint (300 ml) raw rice, add 1 pint (600 ml) liquid. Add some salt and a bay leaf, and bring to the boil. Stir once (if you overstir, the rice will become gummy), cover tightly, reduce the heat, and simmer over the lowest possible heat for 35–40 minutes. (The exact timing depends on the rice, your cooker, and the thickness of the pan.) Remove from the heat, uncover, fluff up the rice with a fork, drape with a tea-towel, re-cover over the tea-towel and leave to stand, off the heat, for 10 minutes or until the rice is tender and fluffy, and the liquid absorbed.

RICE WITH ASPARAGUS TIPS

MAKES ABOUT 1 PINT (600 ML)

V

This is good made with the packages of asparagus tips (usually from Kenya or New Zealand) available from supermarkets virtually all year round. Seasonal, locally grown asparagus is best steamed and served as it is (page 2); separating the tips from the stalks would be a massacre.

4 oz (110 g) asparagus tips
8 fl oz (225 ml) stock
juice of 1 lime

1 pint (600 ml) well-seasoned cooked short-grain brown rice (opposite)
2–3 tablespoons freshly grated Parmesan cheese

1 Trim off any tough woody parts at the base of each asparagus stem. Wash the asparagus and shake dry. Put into a heavy-bottomed frying pan or non-stick wok with 6 fl oz (175 ml) stock and half the lime juice. Stir-fry for 3–4 minutes or until tender (but not at all mushy) and bright green. The stock will have cooked down to about 1 tablespoon and become quite syrupy. (If it cooks down too much, add just a little more during the stir-frying.)

2 Stir in the remaining stock and lime juice. Bring to the boil, and stir in the rice. Cook, stirring, until the rice is very hot, then fold in the grated cheese and remove from the heat. Serve at once.

VARIATION *Rice with Mushrooms* Sauté chopped or sliced mushrooms in the low-fat trinity of sherry, teriyaki or soy sauce, and stock (page 40). Cook until the mushrooms are tender, but there is still a little liquid in the pan. Add brown rice, stir and cook until the rice has absorbed the pan juices and is thoroughly hot.

CASSEROLE OF BROWN RICE WITH ARTICHOKES AND AUBERGINE

MAKES 4 PINTS (2.3 LITRES); SERVES 6–8

V

This festive and colourful paella-like main dish of vegetable-studded rice is served topped with overlapped grilled aubergine slices, and a sprinkling of grated cheese. Serve with one of the meatball or sausage recipes (pages 170–174), if you wish, or add shredded, cooked chicken (or turkey, if it is post-Christmas) in step 2. All the components can be prepared ahead of time, then warmed, put together and grilled at the last moment.

6 spring onions, trimmed and sliced

4 sundried tomatoes, chopped (use scissors)

4 black olives in brine, drained and slivered off their stones

4 green olives in brine, drained and slivered off their stones

1 tablespoon drained capers

1 tablespoon paprika

2 garlic cloves, crushed

2 peppers (1 red, 1 yellow), deseeded, peeled (page 49) and coarsely chopped

1 chilli, deseeded and finely chopped

2 courgettes, each weighing about 6 oz (175 g), chopped

1 pint (600 ml) stock

2 fl oz (50 ml) vermouth

salt and freshly ground pepper

a few tablespoons chopped fresh herbs (such as parsley or chives)

1½ pints (900 ml) cooked short-grain brown rice

14 oz (400 g) can artichoke hearts, drained and cut into eighths

15 oz (425 g) can chick peas, drained and rinsed

1 lb (450 g) aubergine, sliced and grilled (page 4)

4–6 tablespoons freshly grated Parmesan cheese

1 Combine the onions, sundried tomatoes, olives, capers, paprika, garlic, peppers, chilli, courgettes, ½ pint (300 ml) stock and the vermouth in a heavy-bottomed saucepan. Simmer briskly, stirring occasionally, until the vegetables are tender, and the liquid about gone.

2 Add ½ pint (300 ml) additional stock and season with salt and pepper. Add the herbs and the rice, and stir to combine and to break up any clumps of rice. Stir in the artichoke hearts and chick peas, and cook, stirring, until the mixture is heated through, and the rice has absorbed the stock. Preheat the grill to high.

3 Put the rice mixture into a shallow, round baking dish or casserole. Overlap the grilled aubergine slices around the perimeter of the casserole. Sprinkle with grated cheese and grill until the cheese melts.

WHITE RICE

White rice doesn't pack as much of a nutrient/fibre punch as brown, but those who eat a good mixed diet of fruit, vegetables, lean meats, poultry, fish and other grains, need have no qualms about using it. Long-grain white rice is excellent in pilau-type dishes; short-grain white rice is perfect for rice puddings (page 212).

Long-grain white rice is cooked in the same manner and with the same measurements as short-grain brown rice (page 112), but it needs less time (20–25 minutes). I find white rice bland compared to the nutty-flavoured organic short-grained brown – therefore the white takes very well to preparations involving lively seasonings and flavourful liquids. Stock is always preferable to water; part stock, part dried mushroom soaking water will add woodland depths. Sometimes citrus juice or tomato juice can be added as part of the liquid, but you'll need to add a little extra liquid, and cook the rice a little longer, since acidic ingredients can impair rice's ability to absorb liquid.

RICE PILAU

MAKES 1½ PINTS (900 ML)

V ☉

This is a basic recipe that you can play around with endlessly, changing the seasonings, and adding vegetables to your heart's content.

6 spring onions, trimmed and sliced
½ inch (1 cm) piece of fresh root ginger, peeled and crushed
1 garlic clove, crushed
pinch each of ground allspice and cayenne
¼ teaspoon each of ground turmeric, paprika, coriander and cumin

1¼ pints (750 ml) stock
½ pint (300 ml) white long-grain rice
salt and freshly ground pepper
chopped fresh herbs (such as coriander, parsley or mint), to serve

1 Combine the onions, ginger, garlic, spices and ¼ pint (150 ml) stock in a heavy-bottomed saucepan with a tightly fitting lid. Simmer until the onions are tender and the liquid almost gone. Add the rice, and stir so that the rice grains are thoroughly coated with the spices.

2 Add the remaining stock, and season with salt and pepper. Bring to the boil, stir once, clap on the lid, and turn the heat down to the lowest point. Leave for about 20 minutes.

3 Uncover the rice and remove from the heat. Fluff with a fork, then drape a clean, dry tea-towel over the pan and re-cover over the towel. Leave to stand for 10 minutes.

4 To serve, spread the rice on a platter and sprinkle with chopped fresh herbs, or pack into small ramekins or a larger bowl, then unmould (it will shake out easily) on to a plate. Surround with herbs, or Stir-Fried Peppers (page 50), or Sautéed Mushrooms (page 40), or whatever will look devastatingly attractive.

WILD RICE

Names are deceiving. Wild rice is not rice, and is not necessarily wild. The seed of a wild grass from North America, once it only grew wild, and was harvested and processed by native Americans. The processing included toasting the seeds over an open fire, then stamping on them in moccasined feet to separate the seeds from the husks. Finally, the seeds were flung up and down in baskets so the wind could blow off the chaff. Wild rice is still grown and processed this way in a few places in America and Canada, but it is now cultivated as well, and so it is not nearly as expensive as it used to be, and has become much easier to find. Look for it in boxes in supermarkets, and in cellophane bags in wholefood shops.

Wild rice looks like thin black rice, and cooks so that some grains puff open tenderly while some stay closed and *al dente*. Because it is a very special food, a meal of wild rice is an event. Don't overcook it – a plateful of fluffy stuff is not what wild rice is all about.

BASIC METHOD FOR COOKING WILD RICE

MAKES ABOUT 1 ½ PINTS (900 ML)

v

When cooked, wild rice expands to about three times its raw volume.

8 oz (225 g) or 12 fl oz (350 ml) wild rice　　　　*salt*
3 pints (1.7 litres) stock

I Place the rice in a sieve, and rinse briefly under cold running water. Tip the rice into a deep saucepan, pour in the stock and season. Bring to the boil, uncovered, stirring frequently.

2 Reduce the heat, cover, and simmer for 40–60 minutes or until most of the grains are tender (some will remain *al dente*), stirring occasionally. The cooking time will vary with the wild rice, so taste as it cooks.

3 Drain the wild rice and return it to the pan. Drape a clean tea-towel over the pan, cover with the lid, and leave it to stand, off the heat, until ready to serve or use in a recipe. Wild rice prepared in this manner is delicious tossed with Sautéed Mushrooms (page 40), spring onions, toasted pine nuts, cubes of ham, smoked chicken or turkey, or prawns. Don't season it too aggressively; the lovely natural taste of the grain should shine through. Cooked wild rice will keep in the fridge for several days.

WILD RICE WITH WILD MUSHROOMS

MAKES ABOUT 1 PINT (600 ML)

V

One wild thing deserves another. Actually, the mushrooms – reconstituted dried shiitakes – aren't quite wild, but they do impart a strong wild mushroom taste to the grains. If you wish, add some flaked smoked trout, or some tiny cooked prawns.

1 oz (25 g) dried shiitake mushrooms
2 fl oz (50 ml) chicken stock
6 spring onions, trimmed and sliced
1 thin slice of fresh root ginger, peeled and crushed
1 tablespoon dry sherry

1½ teaspoons sugar
2 tablespoons teriyaki or soy sauce
¾ pint (450 ml) cooked wild rice (opposite)
8 oz (225 g) can water chestnuts, diced
salt and freshly ground pepper

1 Rinse the dried mushrooms under cold running water. Put them in a bowl, cover them with hot water and leave to soak for 30 minutes. Lift them out of the water and squeeze dry. Trim off tough stems, and chop the mushrooms coarsely with scissors. Strain the soaking water through a sieve lined with muslin or a double layer of coffee filters.

2 Put the stock and 2 fl oz (50 ml) of the mushroom soaking water into a frying pan or wok. Add the spring onions, ginger and mushrooms, and simmer for a few minutes.

3 Combine the sherry, sugar and teriyaki, and pour over the mushroom mixture. Simmer until the liquid is almost all absorbed.

4 Stir in the wild rice and water chestnuts, and cook, stirring, for a few moments to heat through. Season with salt and pepper before serving.

RICE FRITTERS

If you have some leftover cooked rice or wild rice on hand, make rice fritters. For every ½ pint (300 ml) cooked rice or ¾ pint (450 ml) cooked wild rice, lightly beat two egg whites. Stir the rice into the egg and season with salt and pepper. Drop the mixture, by the rounded tablespoon, on to a heated, oil-misted, non-stick frying pan, and flatten with a spatula. Pan-fry on one side until set, loosen, turn and pan-fry on the second side. Serve for breakfast with maple syrup (you have to taste it to believe it – words fail me) or with a bean stew, or Sautéed Mushrooms (page 40) along with raita and salsa for a wonderful supper.

WILD RICE PILAF WITH DRIED CHERRIES

MAKES 1½ PINTS (900 ML)

V

If you can't find dried cherries, use dried cranberries (cutely named 'craisins' by some marketing type). If you can't find craisins, use small raisins. This wild rice pilaf would be a spectacular addition to Christmas dinner; wild rice is a natural partner to that other New World native, the turkey. (Believe it or not, Benjamin Franklin wanted to make the turkey the American national bird – somehow the eagle ended up with the job.)

2 carrots, peeled and finely chopped
1 celery stalk, destrung and finely chopped
5–6 spring onions, trimmed and thinly sliced
  (green and white parts)
28 fl oz (800 ml) chicken stock
juice of 1 orange

6 oz (175 g) wild rice, rinsed
4 tablespoons dried cherries or cranberries
  (craisins)
¼ teaspoon fresh thyme or a pinch of dried
salt and freshly ground pepper
3–4 tablespoons toasted pine nuts (see note)

1 Preheat the oven to 180°C, 350°F, Gas Mark 4.

2 Combine the vegetables, 8 fl oz (225 ml) stock and half the orange juice in a large flameproof casserole. Cover, bring to the boil, and boil for 5 minutes. Uncover, and sauté until the vegetables are tender and the stock has evaporated. Add the wild rice and 2 tablespoons cherries, and stir so that the vegetables and rice are well combined. Add the remaining stock and the herbs, and season with salt and pepper. Bring to the boil, cover and bake in the oven for approximately one hour or until all the liquid is absorbed and the wild rice is cooked. (Some of the grains will remain somewhat crunchy.)

3 Stir in the remaining orange juice, drape a clean tea-towel over the casserole, re-cover over the tea-towel, and leave to stand, off heat, for about 5 minutes.

4 Fluff up with a fork, and tip on to a platter or into a bowl. Scatter on the remaining cherries and the pine nuts.

Note To toast pine nuts, stir them, over medium heat, in a heavy-bottomed frying pan, for 20–40 seconds. Take care not to scorch them.

COUSCOUS

Couscous is made up of tiny grains of semolina (pasta is made from semolina as well); when soaked in hot liquid, the grains swell and become tender. Couscous is a staple of North African cookery, where it is prepared and served with spicy stews. The traditional manner of cooking couscous requires several steamings and is a bit of a production. The couscous available to us these days (you will find it in the supermarket in cellophane packages) is pre-cooked, and needs only a brief soaking – it is a most convenient grain to work with. If you enjoy rice and pasta, then you will enjoy couscous as well. Serve it with sauces, stews and ragouts.

To prepare couscous, combine in a bowl with boiling well-seasoned stock. Leave to soak for 10–15 minutes or until the liquid is absorbed, and the grains are tender, then fluff with a fork. To make 2 pints (1.1 litres) cooked couscous you will need 12 oz (350 g) couscous, and 16 fl oz (475 ml) stock.

COUSCOUS SALAD WITH BLACK-EYED BEANS

MAKES 2½ PINTS (1.4 LITRES)

V ⊙

Couscous salads make wonderful warm-weather main dishes, and they look terrific as part of a buffet. The various textures and colours of the vegetables against the tender beige of the grains are a treat for the eye and the palate.

4 black olives in brine, drained and slivered off their stones
½ red onion, finely diced
1 garlic clove, crushed
1 chilli, deseeded and finely diced
2 tablespoons balsamic vinegar
juice of 1 lime and ½ lemon
15 oz (425 g) can black-eyed beans, drained and rinsed
9 oz (250 g) cherry tomatoes, quartered
1 yellow pepper, peeled (page 49), deseeded and diced
1 small inner stalk of celery with leaves, diced
1 small carrot, peeled and diced
6 oz (175 g) couscous
½ pint (300 ml) boiling well-seasoned stock
1 tablespoon each of chopped fresh parsley and shredded fresh mint

1 Put the olives, onion, garlic, chilli, vinegar and citrus juices in a bowl, mix and leave to marinate for a few minutes.

2 Combine the beans, tomatoes, pepper, celery and carrot, then toss with the vinegar mixture.

3 Put the couscous in a bowl, pour over the boiling stock, cover and leave to stand for 10–15 minutes. Uncover and fluff with a fork, then – with two spoons – thoroughly combine with the tomato–bean mixture. Toss in the herbs.

Couscous–Orange Salad with Prawns and Smoked Fish

MAKES 2 PINTS (1.1 LITRES)

⊙

The strong taste of smoked mackerel against the juicy sweet tartness of diced orange works very well with couscous. The softer taste of smoked salmon (or smoked trout) would do nicely too. Mackerel and salmon are oily fish – those who must avoid fat altogether should prepare the salad minus the fish. For the rest of us, oily fish are an excellent source of a group of particularly heart-healthy essential fatty acids, so enjoy without worry.

COUSCOUS
juice and finely grated zest of ½ lime
juice and finely grated zest of ½ orange
about 6 fl oz (175 ml) boiling well-seasoned
    stock
6 oz (175 g) couscous
salt and freshly ground pepper (optional)
DRESSING
2 tablespoons balsamic vinegar
2 tablespoons lime juice
2 tablespoons orange juice
1 teaspoon soy sauce
several dashes each of Tabasco and
    Worcestershire sauce

1 garlic clove, crushed (optional)
SALAD
1 large seedless orange, peeled of all skin and
    pith, and diced
4 oz (110 g) smoked mackerel fillet, flaked, or
    4 oz (110 g) shredded smoked salmon
3 oz (75 g) tiny cooked peeled prawns
2 tablespoons chopped fresh parsley
4 spring onions, trimmed and sliced
2 tablespoons shredded fresh mint
GARNISH
halved cherry tomatoes
small wedges of lemon, lime and orange

1 For the couscous, combine the lime juice, orange juice and grated zests in a saucepan with enough stock to make the mixture up to 8 fl oz (225 ml). Bring to the boil.

2 Put the couscous in a bowl, pour over the hot liquid, and season with salt and pepper if it needs it. Leave to soak for 10–15 minutes or until the liquid is absorbed and the grains are tender. Fluff with a fork.

3 Put all the dressing ingredients in a screw-top jar and shake well. Combine all the salad ingredients in a large bowl, and toss with half the dressing. Add the couscous and toss everything together with the remaining dressing. Pile on to a platter and surround with the garnishes.

BULGHUR

Bulghur is pre-cooked grains of cracked wheat, produced by steaming and drying wheat berries, then cracking them into grains. Wholefood shops and almost all supermarkets stock bulghur. It is very easy to cook: because the grains are pre-cooked, they can be prepared by soaking, in either cold or hot water. The cold water soak takes several hours and results in a chewy (*very chewy* – your teeth may bounce if you don't leave it to soak long enough) texture; boiling water results in a softer grain. Bulghur can also be prepared, like rice, by the absorption method; the texture will be quite tender. The method you choose depends on your attitude towards *al dente* textures. I used to prefer the toothsome quality of the cold-water-soak method – now, as middle age creeps ever onward, I prefer the tender mercies of the hot-soak or absorption methods. Whichever method you choose, bulghur makes a delicious and delicate wheat pilaf or salad, to serve either as a main course, or as an accompaniment.

SIMPLE WHEAT PILAF

MAKES 1½ PINTS (900 ML)

V ☉

This gently spiced, wheaty pilaf goes beautifully with the vegetable stews on pages 70–71. This particular combination of aromatic spices brings out the grain's wheaty best, but the seasonings can be varied endlessly, depending on your taste and your mood.

1 pint (600 ml) stock
6 spring onions, trimmed and sliced
½ teaspoon each of ground coriander and
* cumin*

¼ teaspoon ground cinnamon
6 oz (175 g) bulghur
salt and freshly ground pepper

1 Combine 4 fl oz (100 ml) stock with the onions and spices in a flameproof casserole or a heavy-bottomed frying pan that can be covered. Cover and simmer until the onions are tender and the liquid almost gone. While the onions are cooking, bring the remaining stock to the boil.

2 Stir the bulghur into the onions, then stir in the boiling stock. Season with salt and pepper, cover tightly, reduce the heat to its lowest point and leave for 20–25 minutes or until the bulghur is tender and the liquid absorbed. Fluff with a fork, remove from the heat, and drape a clean tea-towel over the open pan, then re-cover over the towel. Leave to stand for 5–10 minutes before serving.

Bulghur Salad

MAKES 2 PINTS (1.1 LITRES)
V ⊘

Bulghur has a pleasant wheaty, rather nutty taste that is quite different from the neutral flavour of couscous. It soaks up flavours as efficiently as couscous does, but the taste of the bulghur shines through as well.

8 oz (225 g) bulghur
1 garlic clove, crushed
6 spring onions, trimmed and thinly sliced
juice of 1 lemon and ½ orange
1 courgette, weighing about 4 oz (110 g),
   trimmed and diced

4 red radishes, trimmed and diced
4 tablespoons chopped fresh parsley
3 small inner stalks of celery with leaves,
   chopped
salt and freshly ground pepper

1 Put the bulghur in a bowl and cover generously with boiling water. Cover and leave to stand for 30 minutes.

2 Meanwhile, combine the garlic, onions and citrus juices in a bowl and allow to marinate.

3 When the wheat is tender, drain it through a sieve, and press with the back of a large spoon to squeeze out excess liquid. Tip into a clean bowl, then add the garlic and onion mixture, and all the remaining ingredients. Season with salt and pepper, mix well with two spoons, and serve at room temperature.

PASTA

Pasta is fast, nourishing and comforting, and is equally good as a solitary meal, a family feast, or an elegant offering for guests. Pasta can be cooked in so many different ways; it is a food that you might find yourself turning to day after day. Pasta has a reputation for being fattening, but it is not: it's all the creamy, oily, buttery sauces lavished on pasta that bump up the fat calorie levels. Is it possible to prepare soul-satisfying pasta dishes *without* the fat dimension? I think you can guess the answer.

TO COOK PASTA

Cook it, uncovered, in plenty of rapidly boiling salted water, stirring every once in a while to keep it from clumping together. Use the timing instructions on the package as a guide, but start fishing out strands or pieces a bit before the time suggested, and taste; you want to catch it at the exact moment of doneness. Pasta is at its best when it is *al dente*, that is when the pasta is tender, but not at all mushy – a bit of resistance 'to the tooth' (*al dente*) remains.

Have a colander ready in the sink. With oven gloves, grab the pan, haul it over to the sink and tip the contents into the colander. If the drained pasta sits around, it turns gummy, so put it into a large warm bowl, pour the sauce over it, mix well with two large spoons and serve.

A general (*very* general) rule of thumb is that 2 oz (50 g) uncooked pasta constitutes a serving as a first course or side dish when cooked; 4 oz (110 g) is a main dish.

SAUCES FOR PASTA

Any of the tomato or pepper sauces in the sauce chapter (pages 85–89) would sauce pasta very well – whether long thin spaghetti or macaroni (pasta shapes). See also the pestos (page 76), Bolognese Sauce with Roasted Aubergine (page 159) and Lentil-Aubergine Bolognese Sauce (page 10). Several others follow and I'm sure that you will come up with plenty of varieties of your own.

The following sauces will sauce up to 1 lb (450 g) pasta (uncooked weight). Exactly what the proportions should be of sauce to pasta is a matter of individual taste. In Italy, pasta is not served swamped in sauce; rather it is lightly dressed in the sauce. But in Italy, sauces are made with olive oil or butter, so the sauce/pasta dynamic is quite different – the 'cling factor' of the sauces works differently – from these no-fat sauces. Personally, I like plenty of sauce – and the more sauce, the more nutrition the dish delivers. Extra sauce will keep in the fridge for several days or can be frozen. It can also be simmered with a can of beans to make a quick bean stew, or thinned with stock and heated with a little grated Parmesan to make a comforting soup.

CREAMY CHEESE PASTA

To make a lovely melted cheesy, creamy pasta dish, whisk freshly grated Parmesan cheese into room temperature fromage frais, then – with two big spoons – fold it into freshly cooked drained pasta shapes. Season with freshly ground pepper and serve at once.

To make Macaroni Cheese, fold the freshly cooked pasta shapes into one of the quickly made cheese sauces on page 94, sprinkle the top with 2–3 tablespoons freshly grated Parmesan and grill until golden and bubbly.

COURGETTE AND PEPPER SAUCE FOR PASTA

MAKES 1 ½ PINTS (900 ML)

V ☺ ❄

Peeled red peppers added to a sauce always increase the 'cling factor'. As the peppers sauté in stock they release delicious syrupy juices that coat the pasta strands beautifully.

½ pint (300 ml) stock
1 red onion, coarsely chopped
3 peppers (1 red, 1 yellow, 1 green), deseeded,
   peeled (page 49) and coarsely chopped
2 medium courgettes, coarsely chopped
3 black olives in brine, drained and slivered off
   their stones

3–4 sundried tomatoes, chopped (use scissors)
2–3 garlic cloves, crushed
14 oz (400 g) can chopped tomatoes
4 fl oz (100 ml) passata
3–4 tablespoons chopped fresh herbs (such as
   oregano, basil and parsley)

1 Combine the stock, vegetables, olives, sundried tomatoes and garlic in a heavy-bottomed frying pan. Cover, bring to the boil, and boil for 5–7 minutes, then uncover and simmer briskly until the vegetables are tender and the liquid about gone.

2 Stir in all the remaining ingredients and simmer, uncovered, for 10–15 minutes.

BROCCOLI SAUCE FOR PASTA

MAKES 1 ¾ PINTS (1 LITRE)

V ☺ ❄

This sauce uses only the stalks of the broccoli. You can use the leftover florets for Creamy Broccoli Soup (page 104).

broccoli stalks from 1 lb (450 g) broccoli
2 leeks, trimmed, halved lengthways and sliced
8 oz (225 g) fresh shiitake or brown cap
   mushrooms, trimmed of tough stems and
   thickly sliced
3 black olives in brine, drained and slivered off
   their stones
3 sundried tomatoes, chopped (use scissors)
2 garlic cloves, crushed

1–2 pinches crushed dried chillies
4 fl oz (100 ml) each of red wine and stock
dash of teriyaki sauce
14 oz (400 g) can chopped tomatoes
16 fl oz (475 ml) passata
1 tablespoon tomato purée
salt and freshly ground pepper
3 tablespoons chopped fresh parsley
3 tablespoons freshly grated Parmesan cheese

1 Peel the broccoli stalks, and cut into ¼ inch (0.5 cm) thick slices. Put in a heavy-bottomed frying pan with the leeks, mushrooms, olives, sundried tomatoes, garlic, chillies, wine, stock and teriyaki. Simmer until the broccoli slices are almost tender, and the liquid greatly reduced and syrupy.

2 Stir in the canned tomatoes and the passata. Simmer for 10–15 minutes or until thickened and savoury, then stir in the tomato purée and season with salt and pepper. Simmer for 5 minutes more. Stir in the parsley and Parmesan cheese.

MUSHROOM AND SMOKED CHICKEN SAUCE FOR PASTA

MAKES 1 ¼ PINTS (750 ML)

☙ ❄

Smoked chicken or turkey, purchased unsliced from the deli section of the supermarket, gives its haunting smokiness to a plate of pasta – how delightful it is! Vegetarians who crave a bit of that smoky haunting will get very good results with some cubed smoked tofu standing in for the chicken or turkey.

3 large garlic cloves, crushed
1 pint (600 ml) stock
4 fl oz (100 ml) dry white vermouth
3–4 sundried tomatoes, coarsely diced with scissors (optional)
3–4 black olives in brine, drained and slivered off their stones
1–2 pinches crushed dried chillies

1 yellow and 1 red pepper, deseeded, peeled (page 49) and cut into large squares
6 oz (175 g) mushrooms, quartered
dash of soy sauce
2 tablespoons tomato purée
freshly ground pepper
8 oz (225 g) unsliced smoked chicken or turkey, diced

1 Combine the garlic, half the stock, the vermouth, sundried tomatoes (if using), olives and chillies in a heavy-bottomed frying pan. Bring to the boil and boil, uncovered, stirring occasionally, until the garlic is tender and the liquid is reduced to about half.

2 Stir in the peppers, and cook on moderate heat, stirring, until they are almost tender. Add the mushrooms and soy sauce, and a little more stock, if needed. Cook, stirring occasionally, until the mushrooms are tender.

3 Add the remaining stock, and boil until reduced by half. Stir in the tomato purée and cook for a few more minutes. Season with pepper. Add the diced chicken or turkey and stir to heat through.

FISH

Fish is splendid health food, especially for devotees of a low-fat lifestyle. Many fish varieties are extremely low in fat, and the fat they do contain is very low in saturates. Even the fattiest fish is relatively low in calories, and 'leaner' than fatty meat or poultry. Perhaps you are familiar with the so-called 'Eskimo diet', which, not so long ago, drew attention to the Omega-3 fatty acids present in fish fat. Omega-3s are believed to be heart-protective, so, unless you are trying to *lose* weight, or you have been warned by your doctor to keep the fats and oils to a drastic minimum, a serving of fatty fish (salmon, herring, mackerel, and so on) every once in a while would be far from a problem.

Fish is one of the fastest of foods to cook, and accommodates itself well to many different combinations of ingredients. For best results, buy truly fresh fish.

This chapter takes you through the various low-fat methods of cooking fish. One type of fish can easily be substituted for another, for instance hake or haddock for cod, lemon sole or brill for plaice, and so on. When preparing the fillets, trim away the scales and any bones.

As far as cooking times are concerned, the quicker fish is cooked the better. Fish is already tender, so it needs to be cooked only long enough to coagulate ('set') the protein. If fish cooks too long it becomes dry and unpalatable; it is cooked when it is opaque right through. A general rule of thumb is to cook fish at high heat for 9–10 minutes per 1 inch (2.5 cm) of thickness, but always check for doneness just to make sure.

FISH IN A BAG

Fish *en papillote* is a wonderful way to preserve all the moist succulence of a piece of fish, and to infuse it with the flavours of herbs, spices and seasonings. *En papillote* essentially means 'in a bag', and the 'bag' can be made from either foil or greaseproof paper. The easiest is foil – it is always on hand, and it is much easier to seal foil to make a leak-proof parcel than to seal paper. The fish, with its seasonings and vegetables, 'steam-roasts' within the foil, so that the flavours infuse the fish, and the fish remains moist. Part of the excitement of this technique is the wonderful fragrance that is released as you slash open the foil, and the steam wafts up.

When cooking fish *en papillote*, cook at high heat for about 10 minutes per inch (2.5 cm) thickness of the fish, plus an extra minute to allow for the foil. Adjust the timing for your particular oven, and your taste. The following recipes each make one packet of fish, to serve one. Prepare as many packets as you need. They can be made early in the day and kept in the fridge, but bring to room temperature before baking.

FISH AND VEGETABLES IN A BAG

SERVES 1

⊙

For the simplest fish *en papillote*, enclose a fish fillet in an oil-spray-misted foil envelope with just a sprinkling of lemon juice, dry vermouth and stock. Season with salt and pepper and seal the parcels. Bake in a preheated oven at 220°C, 425°F, Gas Mark 7 for 9–10 minutes per 1 inch (2.5 cm) thickness of fish, plus 1–2 minutes to allow for the foil. If the fish was fresh in the first place, this is one of the most satisfying ways to serve it. The basic method can be dressed up with vegetables, as below, to add colour, flavour, and an even greater perception of freshness.

oil spray (page ix)
1 fillet of cod or haddock, or other similar fish
    weighing 4–5 oz (110–150 g)
salt and freshly ground pepper
1 small carrot, peeled and cut into very thin
    sticks
1 small courgette, thinly sliced
4–5 button mushrooms, halved or quartered
½ small red pepper, deseeded, peeled (page 49)
    and cut into 2 inch (5 cm) squares

½ small yellow pepper, peeled (page 49) and
    cut into 2 inch (5 cm) squares
6 cherry tomatoes, halved
2 tablespoons shredded fresh mint leaves
2 tablespoons chopped fresh parsley
1 tablespoon chopped spring onion or snipped
    chives
1½ tablespoons stock
1½ tablespoons dry white vermouth

1 Preheat the oven to 220°C, 425°F, Gas Mark 7. Put a baking sheet in the oven.

2 Tear off a sheet of heavy-duty foil large enough to enclose the fish and all the vegetables with room to spare. Fold in half, shiny side in and crease, then unfold so that it lies flat. Mist the foil with oil spray and position the fish, skin-side down, on one half of the foil. Season with salt and pepper, and arrange the vegetables – each in a neat, separate heap – around the fish. Place the cherry tomatoes, cut-side up, on the fish. Season the vegetables with salt and pepper. Sprinkle the herbs and spring onion all over. Dribble on the stock and vermouth.

3 Fold the foil up and over, and crimp the edges together to form a roomy but very well sealed 'tent' around the fish and vegetables. Place on the baking sheet and bake in the oven for 10–15 minutes. To serve, slash the foil open and slide the fish and vegetables on to a warm plate.

VARIATION *Smoky Fish and Vegetables in a Bag* Use one 4–5 oz (110–150 g) undyed fillet of smoked haddock. Instead of button mushrooms, use 2–3 small oyster mushrooms, quartered, and 2–3 fresh shiitake mushrooms, trimmed of their tough stems, and quartered. Before sealing the packet you could sprinkle the fish and vegetables with 1 tablespoon freshly grated Parmesan cheese. (Do not add any salt – the cheese and smoked fish contain enough.) Bake as above.

COD AND HERBS IN A BAG

SERVES 1

⊙

Another very simple combination: a fish fillet, a few herbs, and a sprinkling of orange juice and vermouth. Mix and match the fish and herbs to your taste.

oil spray (page ix)
1 cod fillet, weighing about 4 oz (110 g)
1 generous tablespoon each of chopped fresh
  parsley and shredded fresh mint

1 tablespoon each of orange juice and dry
  vermouth
salt and freshly ground pepper

1 Preheat the oven to 220°C, 425°F, Gas Mark 7. Put a baking sheet in the oven.

2 Tear off a sheet of heavy-duty foil large enough to enclose the fish. Fold in half, shiny-side in, and crease, then unfold so that it lies flat. Mist the foil with oil spray, and place the fish, skin-side down, on one half. Sprinkle with the remaining ingredients and season with salt and pepper.

3 Fold the foil up and over, and crimp the edges together to form a roomy but very well sealed 'tent' around the fish and vegetables. Place on the baking sheet and bake in the oven for 10–15 minutes. To serve, slash the foil open and slide the fish and vegetables on to a warm plate.

BARBECUED COD IN A BAG

SERVES 1

⊙

A mixture of mustard, tomato purée, vermouth and citrus juices makes an instant barbecue sauce to slather over smoked cod fillet. The sauce and the smokiness of the fish together make the finished fish redolent of a wood-smoked barbecue. Serve this with wild rice (page 116) and sautéed shiitake mushrooms. It will taste like autumn in the Canadian woods!

oil spray (page ix)
1 undyed smoked cod fillet, weighing about
  4 oz (110 g)
1 tablespoon each of Dijon mustard, tomato
  purée, dry vermouth and stock

juice of ½ lemon and ½ orange
freshly ground pepper

1 Preheat the oven to 220°C, 425°F, Gas Mark 7. Put a baking sheet in the oven.

2 Tear off a sheet of heavy-duty foil large enough to enclose the fillet. Fold in half, shiny-side in, and crease, then unfold and lay out flat. Mist the foil with oil spray.

3 Place the cod, skin-side down, on one half of the sheet of foil. Whisk together all the remaining ingredients, except the pepper. Pour this mixture over the fish, and grind on some pepper. Fold the foil up and over the fish, and crimp the edges together all around to make a roomy but very well sealed parcel. Put the parcel on the hot baking sheet and bake in the oven for 10–15 minutes.

4 To serve, cut open the parcel with scissors, and slide the contents on to a warm plate.

SALMON AND MUSHROOMS IN A BAG

SERVES 1

⊙

Here, salmon is given an oriental dimension with wild-tasting shiitake mushrooms and a sprinkling of teriyaki sauce and sherry. If you can't find shiitakes, use brown-caps.

oil spray (page ix)
1 salmon fillet, weighing about 8 oz (225 g)
⅛ inch (0.25 cm) slice fresh root ginger, peeled and crushed
1 small garlic clove, crushed

1 teaspoon teriyaki sauce
1 shiitake mushroom, stemmed and thinly sliced
1 tablespoon medium-dry sherry
freshly ground pepper

1 Preheat the oven to 220°C, 425°F, Gas Mark 7. Put a baking sheet in the oven.

2 Tear off a sheet of heavy-duty foil large enough to enclose the fish with room to spare. Fold in half, shiny-side in and crease, then unfold and lay out flat. Spray lightly with oil spray.

3 Put the salmon fillet, skin-side down, on one half of the foil, and massage the ginger, garlic and teriyaki into the top of the fillet. Scatter on the mushroom slices, and dribble on the sherry. Grind on some pepper. Fold the foil up and over the fish, and crimp the edges together all around to make a roomy but very well sealed pouch. Place on the hot baking sheet and bake in the oven for about 15 minutes. To serve, cut open the foil with scissors and slide the contents on to a warm plate.

'FRIED' FISH

Deep-frying is messy and smelly as well as unhealthy. The odour of abused grease lingers in one's hair and clothes (and in the curtains and upholstery) for ages. How nice to be able to dispense with the whole dangerous business once and for all! Crumbed fish fillets, baked in a hot oven or grilled, stand in very nicely for the old-fashioned submerged-in-oil method. Fish and chips, with the fish cooked this way, a heap of oven-fried Chips (page 51) and Green Pea Spread (page 74) standing in for the mushy peas, is a meal to cherish. The fish fillets are also good with one of the salsas (particularly Cucumber and Fennel Salsa, page 80, with Orange Mango Sauce (page 92) or Mango Sauce (page 88), with one of the tomato and pepper sauces (page 89), or simply with lemon or lime wedges.

OVEN-'FRIED' FISH

⊘

As always, the timing is approximate – it depends on the exact size of the fish, your oven, and the way you like your fish cooked. Ideally, the fish should be cooked right through, but still be pearly and moist – not dry and dusty.

oil spray (page ix)
flour
egg white, lightly beaten
plain breadcrumbs

salt and freshly ground pepper
cod fillets, or other firm white fish fillets of
    similar thickness

1 Preheat the oven to 220°C, 425°F, Gas Mark 7. Line a baking sheet with foil, shiny-side up and spray with oil spray.

2 Spread the flour out on a plate. Put the egg white into a wide, shallow bowl, and spread the breadcrumbs on a plate. Season the breadcrumbs with salt and pepper.

3 Dredge the fillets in flour on both sides, then dip in egg, and finally coat with crumbs, covering the fish well. Put the fillets on the lined baking sheet, and spray lightly with oil spray. Bake in the oven for about 10 minutes (no need to turn), then flash under the grill to brown.

Opposite: Meat Pie with Pumpkin and Swede Topping (page 165), served with Red and Red Salad (page 15) and Stir-fried Roman Broccoli (page 17)

GRILL-'FRIED' FISH

☙

Remember the aubergine and courgette 'fried fish' in the vegetable chapter (pages 5 and 29)? Needless to say, the technique works splendidly with real fish!

oil spray (page ix)
plain breadcrumbs
salt and freshly ground pepper

Fromage Frais 'Mayo' (page 97)
fillets of sole or plaice, or other fish fillets of
similar thickness

1 Preheat the grill to high. Line the grill pan with foil, shiny-side up. Put the grill rack in the pan and spray with the oil spray.

2 Spread the breadcrumbs out on a plate and season with salt and pepper. Spread the 'mayo', out on a plate.

3 Dredge the fish in the 'mayo', then coat in the crumbs. Both sides should be well coated. Place on the grill rack, skin-side up.

4 Position 4 inches (10 cm) from the heat, and grill for about 4 minutes on each side. Turn carefully with tongs and a fish slice. If, when turning, any bits of 'breading' come off, smear the fish with a little more 'mayo', sprinkle on more crumbs, and continue grilling. Serve at once.

Opposite: Pork and Apple Burgers (page 168), Baked Sweet Potato (page 54) and a dish of Sautéed Button Mushrooms (page 40)

OVEN-POACHED FISH

The next two recipes are for very simple oven-poached flat fish fillets. They may be served just as they are, accompanied simply by steamed new potatoes and a dark green leafy salad. If all the ingredients are top-notch, this meal – simple though it is – is a feast. It can also be dressed up in countless different ways. Serve the fish and its aromatic juices on a warm plate with a wide ribbon of sauce or salsa alongside. Cucumber and Fennel (page 80) salsa would go beautifully with the fillets, as would Mango Sauce (page 88) and Tomato Sauce (page 86).

SIMPLE OVEN-POACHED SOLE FILLETS

SERVES 2–4

☉

Oven-poaching is a lovely way to cook fresh fish fillets. Cook only until the fish is opaque, just beginning to flake, and still moist.

4 fl oz (100 ml) dry white vermouth
juice of ½ lemon

2–4 fillets of lemon sole or plaice
salt and freshly ground pepper

1 Preheat the oven to 220°C, 425°F, Gas Mark 7.

2 Combine the vermouth and lemon juice, and pour a little (just enough to coat the bottom) into a baking dish that will hold the fish in one uncrowded layer. Place the fillets, skin-side down, in the dish, season with salt and pepper, and pour the remaining liquid on to the fish. Bake, uncovered, in the oven for 7–10 minutes or until opaque and cooked through.

OVEN-POACHED SOLE FILLETS WITH HERBS

SERVES 2–4

☉

Fish stock is easily made from fish bones and trimmings and is also available in little tubs from many supermarkets. If you have none, use chicken or vegetable stock.

2–4 fillets of sole
salt and freshly ground pepper
4 fl oz (100 ml) dry vermouth
4 fl oz (120 ml) fish stock
juice of 1 small lemon

¼ teaspoon crumbled dried tarragon or 1
*   teaspoon chopped fresh tarragon*
4 fl oz (100 ml) sliced spring onions
4 fl oz (100 ml) chopped fresh parsley

1 Preheat the oven to 200°C, 400°F, Gas Mark 6.

2 Place the fish fillets, skin-side down, in a shallow baking dish that will hold them in one uncrowded layer. Sprinkle with salt and pepper.

3 In a small, non-reactive saucepan, combine the vermouth, stock, lemon juice and tarragon. Bring to the boil, and boil until reduced by half. Pour over the fish, and scatter on the spring onions and parsley.

4 Bake, uncovered, in the oven 7–10 minutes or until opaque and cooked through.

OVEN-POACHED COD WITH SPRING ONIONS AND MINT

SERVES 2–4

⊙

Fresh mint is particularly good with fish; I use it often. If fresh is unavailable, don't substitute dried – just depend on parsley, or try fresh basil, if you have it.

10 spring onions, trimmed and sliced
2 garlic cloves, crushed
4–6 tablespoons shredded fresh mint
4–6 tablespoons chopped fresh parsley
juice of ½ lemon

¼ pint (150 ml) fish stock
2–4 equal-sized pieces of cod fillet, or similar
  fish (such as haddock or hake)
salt and freshly ground pepper
lemon wedges, to serve

1 Preheat the oven to 230°C, 450°F, Gas Mark 8.

2 Combine the spring onions (save some of the sliced green part for garnish), garlic, mint and parsley, lemon juice and stock in a baking dish large enough to hold the cod in one uncrowded layer.

3 Place the cod fillets on the herb–garlic mixture and turn them to moisten. Season with salt and pepper.

4 Bake in the oven for 8–10 minutes or until opaque, just beginning to flake, and still moist. Sprinkle with the reserved fresh spring onion greens and serve at once with lemon wedges.

FISH IN PIQUANT TOMATO SAUCE

SERVES 2–4

⌣

Firm fish fillets can be baked in any of the tomato or pepper sauces (pages 85–89), but I particularly like it with piquant seasonings. The fish is baked on a bed of the sauce; a drizzle of lemon juice and balsamic vinegar helps to keep it moist.

about ½ pint (300 ml) Picadillo Tomato Sauce
(page 86), warmed
2–4 cod fillets, or other similar firm white fish
fillets

juice of ½ lemon
1 teaspoon balsamic vinegar
freshly ground pepper

1 Preheat the oven to 230°C, 450°F, Gas Mark 8.

2 Spoon the sauce into a baking dish large enough to hold the fish in one uncrowded layer. Place the fish on the sauce. Squeeze the lemon juice over the fish and sprinkle on the vinegar. Grind on some pepper.

3 Bake, uncovered, in the oven for 8–10 minutes or until opaque, just beginning to flake, and still moist. Put each fillet on a plate and spoon the sauce around it. Serve at once.

COD MARINATED IN LEMON AND GARLIC

SERVES 2–4

If time is short, pop the fish into the oven without the preliminary marinade, but – if you have the time – I think you will like what happens when the ingredients have a bit of time to themselves before they get oven-poached.

2–4 cod fillets, or other similar firm white fish
fillets
juice of 1 ½–2 lemons

2 tablespoons dry white vermouth
1–2 garlic cloves, crushed
freshly ground pepper

1 Put the fish in one uncrowded layer in a shallow baking dish. Squeeze the juice of 1 ½ lemons over and around the fish. Sprinkle in the vermouth, scatter in the garlic, and grind on some pepper. Turn the fish a few times to coat with the marinade. Cover the dish and refrigerate for a few hours or overnight. (Turn the fish in the marinade once or twice.)

2 Remove the dish from the refrigerator to warm up a bit while you preheat the oven to 230°C, 450°F, Gas Mark 8. If most of the marinade has been absorbed into the fish, squeeze on the juice of another ½ lemon.

3 Bake, uncovered, in the oven for about 10 minutes or until opaque, just beginning to flake, and still moist. Serve at once.

FISH FILLETS WITH FENNEL AND ORANGE

SERVES 2–4

⊙

Fish fillets can be seared quickly, in a heavy-bottomed frying pan, and then steamed in the residual heat in the pan.

2 bulbs fennel, trimmed
½ pint (300 ml) stock
1 large, juicy orange
2 fl oz (50 ml) orange juice

2 fillets of sole, plaice, or other similar flat fish
salt and freshly ground pepper
oil spray (page ix)

1 Cut the bulbs of fennel in half lengthways, then cut across into ¼ inch (0.5 cm) thick slices. Put into a frying pan with ¼ pint (150 ml) stock, and simmer briskly until the fennel is tender and the stock almost gone.

2 Peel the orange, removing every scrap of white pith, separate into segments and cut the segments into chunks. Add to the pan with the remaining stock and the orange juice. Bring to a simmer, stirring and scraping the bottom of the pan to dislodge any browned deposits. Tip the mixture into a bowl and cover loosely to keep warm. Wipe out and dry the frying pan.

3 Season the fish with salt and pepper on both sides. Spray the pan with oil spray and heat. Sear the fish on both sides for about 1 minute on each side, turning with tongs and a fish slice. Surround with the fennel and orange mixture, bring to a simmer and cover, then remove from the heat and leave to stand for about 5 minutes or until the fish is *just* cooked.

FISH SOUPS AND STEWS

A bowlful of soup or stew, laced with vegetables, herbs and chunks of fish, makes a wonderful supper. All you need to complete the feast is a big salad of dark, leafy greens dressed with one of the citrus dressings (pages 95–96) or the vinaigrette spray (page 95) and plenty of crusty bread for dunking. One big advantage of fish stews (aside from their splendid taste) is their ease of preparation. This and the recipes on pages 137–140 all take minimal time and effort.

FISH STEW WITH FENNEL

MAKES 3¾ PINTS (2.1 LITRES)
SERVES 4

Fennel and fish are a natural pairing. If you can't find fennel, use celery instead, and add ½ teaspoon fennel seeds in step 2.

1½ pints (900 ml) fish or chicken stock
2 large garlic cloves, chopped
1 onion, chopped
2 bulbs fennel, trimmed (save the feathery
* fronds) and chopped*
two 14 oz (400 g) cans tomatoes, drained and
* cut into strips*
¾ pint (450 ml) dry white wine

3 tablespoons tomato purée
1 bay leaf
1 teaspoon fresh or ¼ teaspoon dried oregano
salt and freshly ground pepper
2 lb (900 g) mixed fish fillets (cod, halibut, etc.),
* cut into 3 inch (7.5 cm) chunks*
2 tablespoons lemon juice
chopped fresh parsley

1 In a large, heavy-bottomed saucepan, combine half the stock, garlic, onion and fennel. Cover, bring to the boil, and boil for 5–7 minutes. Uncover, reduce the heat a little, and simmer until the vegetables are browning, and almost all the liquid is gone.

2 Stir in the tomatoes, remaining stock, wine, tomato purée, bay leaf and oregano, and season with salt and pepper. Bring back to the boil, then reduce the heat and simmer gently, partially covered for 30 minutes.

3 Increase the heat to a brisk simmer. Stir in the fish and cook for 3–5 minutes or until just done. Stir in the lemon juice, parsley and snipped reserved fennel fronds. Remove the bay leaf before serving.

HEARTY FISH AND VEGETABLE SOUP

MAKES ABOUT 4 PINTS (2.3 LITRES)
SERVES 4

⊙

As in the previous recipe, this main course soup again pairs fish with fennel, but adds mushrooms and potatoes as well. The previous soup was a red one (tomato-based); this one is based on stock and the rendered juices of the mushrooms.

3 medium onions, cut into wedges (eighths)
3 garlic cloves, crushed
2 celery stalks, destrung and cut into ¼ inch (0.5 cm) slices
1 small bulb of fennel, trimmed (save the feathery fronds), quartered, cored and sliced into ½ inch (1 cm) pieces
3½ pints (2 litres) stock (chicken, fish, vegetable or a combination)

4 fl oz (100 ml) dry white vermouth
8 oz (225 g) button mushrooms, quartered
12 oz (350 g) new potatoes, scrubbed and quartered
salt and freshly ground pepper
6 tablespoons chopped fresh parsley
1½ lb (700 g) cod fillets, or other white fish fillets, cut into 2 inch (5 cm) pieces

1 Combine the onions, garlic, celery, fennel, ½ pint (300 ml) stock and the vermouth in a large, heavy-bottomed saucepan. Cover, bring to the boil, and boil for 3–4 minutes. Uncover, reduce the heat a little, stir in the mushrooms, and simmer until the vegetables are 'frying' in their own juices. Cook, stirring, until everything is tender.

2 Add the potatoes and the remaining stock. Season with salt and pepper, and continue to cook, uncovered, until the potatoes are tender.

3 Stir in the parsley and fish. Simmer for 2–4 minutes or until the fish is just done. Serve at once.

FISH AND POTATO STEW WITH GARLIC SAUCE

MAKES ABOUT 3 PINTS (1.7 LITRES), SERVES 2

⌣

This deeply flavoured stew is designed for frozen fish fillets. They thaw and cook gently on a bed of olives, sundried tomatoes, enriched braised onions and potatoes. Serve with croûtons spread with a chilli-spiked garlic sauce for a meal that resonates with Provençal flavour.

*1 large onion, halved and sliced into thin half
   moons*
2 garlic cloves, crushed
2–3 sundried tomatoes, diced (use scissors)
*2–3 black olives in brine, drained and slivered
   off their stones*
pinch of crushed dried chillies
about 1½ pints (900) ml) boiling stock
*4 small potatoes, each weighing about 2 oz
   (50 g), peeled and cut into ¼ inch (0.5 cm)
   slices*

salt and freshly ground pepper
*2 large, ripe, flavourful tomatoes, peeled,
   deseeded and chopped (page 68)*
1–2 tablespoons shredded fresh basil
1 bay leaf
3 inch (7.5 cm) strip of orange zest
1 lb (450 g) frozen white fish fillets
chopped fresh parsley, to garnish
*toasted slices of bread and Garlic Sauce (see
   below), to serve*

1 Combine the onion, garlic, sundried tomatoes, olives, chillies and ½ pint (300 ml) stock in a heavy-bottomed flameproof casserole or wok. Cover, bring to the boil, and boil for 5 minutes. Uncover, and cook briskly until the onion is tender and the liquid almost gone.

2 Spread the onions evenly in the bottom of the pan. Arrange the sliced potatoes over the onions and season with salt and pepper. Spread the tomatoes over the potatoes. Add the basil, bay leaf and orange zest. Top with the frozen fish fillets and sprinkle on a little more salt and pepper. Pour in enough boiling stock just to cover the vegetables. Cover the pan.

3 Simmer for 20 minutes or until the potatoes are tender and the fish just cooked through. Sprinkle with chopped parsley. To serve, break up the fish with a spoon, and ladle some broth, vegetables and fish into soup plates. Spread a slice of toast with sauce, then drop the slice into the soup. The toast will disintegrate into the juices and the sauce will meld in ... delicious!

GARLIC SAUCE

MAKES ABOUT 6 FL OZ (175 ML)

6–8 garlic cloves
1–2 pinches crushed dried chillies
12–14 fl oz (350–400 ml) boiling vegetable stock

*2 thin slices white bakery bread, trimmed of
   crusts*
1 tablespoon tomato purée

1 Combine the garlic, chillies and 4 fl oz (100 ml) stock in a frying pan. Cover, bring to the boil, and boil for 7–10 minutes. Uncover and simmer until the garlic cloves are meltingly tender and the stock is greatly reduced and syrupy.

2 Scrape the garlic and all the pan juices into a blender. Tear the bread into pieces and add it along with the tomato purée and 1–2 spoonfuls of the hot stock. Blend to a paste. Slowly blend in the remaining liquid until the mixture is the texture of a loose mayonnaise.

SMOKY FISH CHOWDER

MAKES 4 PINTS (2.3 LITRES) SERVES 4–6

⊙

Fish chowders are many and varied. They always make me think of the line from Melville's Moby Dick: 'Chowder for breakfast and chowder for supper, till you begin to look for fishbones coming through your clothes.' This chowder combines firm white fish fillets with smoked haddock and sweetcorn.

1 large onion, coarsely chopped
24 fl oz (750 ml) fish stock
2 fl oz (50 ml) dry white wine
1 pint (600 ml) skimmed milk
3 medium all-purpose potatoes (such as Wilja),
   steamed until almost tender, peeled and
   coarsely diced
1 grilled red pepper (page 49), or use a drained
   bottled pepper, chopped

12 oz (350 g) can sweetcorn kernels, drained
12 oz (350 g) firm white fish fillets, skinned and
   cut into 1 inch (2.5 cm) cubes
12 oz (350 g) undyed smoked haddock, skinned,
   boned and cut into 1 inch (2.5 cm) cubes
6 oz (175 g) tiny cooked peeled prawns
freshly ground pepper
chopped fresh parsley

1 Combine the onion, 4 fl oz (100 ml) stock, and the wine in a large, heavy-bottomed saucepan. Cover, bring to the boil, and boil for 5 minutes. Uncover and simmer briskly until the onions are meltingly tender and beginning to brown.

2 Stir in the remaining stock and the milk, and gently bring to a simmer. Add the potatoes and simmer gently for 3–5 minutes. Stir in the red pepper and corn, and simmer for 5 minutes more. Cool slightly, then purée half the mixture in a blender. Return to the pan, and bring back to a simmer.

3 Stir in the fish cubes. Simmer gently for 2–3 minutes. Stir in the prawns and heat through. Season with pepper and serve at once, sprinkled with fresh parsley.

FESTIVE FISH AND SHELLFISH STEW

MAKES ABOUT 4 PINTS (2.3 LITRES) SERVES 4–6

This rustic casserole overflows with the bounty of the sea, and would make a beautiful focus for a celebration meal. To pull out all the stops, serve it with home-baked crusty bread – try the Potato Bread on page 196, baked with egg glaze and topped with fennel seeds.

2 large Spanish onions, chopped
22 fl oz (620 ml) chicken or fish stock, or a
  combination
1 yellow or red pepper, deseeded, peeled (page
  48) and chopped
2 garlic cloves, crushed
two 14 oz (400 g) cans chopped tomatoes
2 tablespoons tomato purée
12 fl oz (350 ml) dry white wine

salt and freshly ground pepper
2 lb (900 g) mixed firm white fish fillets (Cod,
  halibut, haddock, etc.), skinned and cut into
  1 inch (2.5 cm) cubes
1 lb (450 g) medium prawns, peeled and
  deveined
16–18 fresh mussels, thoroughly scrubbed
4 fl oz (100 ml) chopped fresh parsley

1 Combine the onions and 10 fl oz (300 ml) stock in a large, heavy-bottomed flameproof casserole that can be covered. Cover, bring to the boil, and boil for 5 minutes. Uncover, stir in the peppers and garlic, and simmer briskly until the stock is almost gone and the vegetables are tender.

2 Add the tomatoes, tomato purée, wine and 12 fl oz (350 ml) stock. Season with salt and pepper, and simmer, partially covered, for 25 minutes.

3 Uncover, and lay the fish on top of the tomato mixture. Cover tightly and simmer very gently for 3 minutes.

4 Uncover. Add the prawns, mussels and parsley, cover tightly and simmer gently for 3–5 minutes more, or until the mussels open and the prawns and fish are just cooked. Discard any mussels that do not open. Sprinkle with parsley and serve, straight from the casserole.

CHICKEN

Chicken is a relatively lean bird but there is a good deal of fat in and beneath the skin. If you are using chicken portions, skin them (or buy them skinned) before cooking. A whole roasted chicken needs the covering of skin to keep it moist, so roast with the skin on, but don't eat it. Pull off all the lumps of fat from the chicken and discard them. When you roast a chicken (skin and all), quite a lot of the fat will melt into the pan drippings. Either tilt the roasting tin and skim off the fat, or quick-chill the drippings in the freezer so that the fat rises to the top. It is then a cinch to skim the fat off, and discard.

LEMON-ROASTED CHICKEN

SERVES 4–6

Serve this golden, fragrant, sizzling roasted chicken, surrounded by Spicy Oven-Fried Potatoes (page 52) and a selection of gorgeous vegetables

1½ lemons
1 teaspoon freshly ground black pepper
2 teaspoons ground cumin
1 teaspoon paprika

2½–3 lb (1.1–1.4 kg) roasting chicken, trimmed of fat
stock
4–6 fl oz (100–175 ml) dry white wine

1 Squeeze the juice from the lemons and mix with the pepper and spices. (Reserve the squeezed lemon halves.) Make small incisions all over the chicken, except in the breast, and rub in the lemon mixture. Loosen the breast skin and rub the lemon mixture under the skin. Place the squeezed lemon halves in the chicken's cavity. Marinate overnight in the refrigerator.

2 Next day, bring the chicken to room temperature and preheat the oven to 230°C, 450°F, Gas Mark 8. Place a rack in a shallow flameproof roasting tin. Place the chicken, breast down, on the rack and roast in the oven for 15 minutes, then turn breast up and roast for about 45 minutes or until just done. Baste the chicken with the pan juices several times as it roasts. As the pan juices cook down, add a little stock. If the chicken is not cooked through after 45 minutes (the leg should move freely in its socket, the juices should run clear, and there should be no trace of red if you make an incision near the bone), turn it breast down again and roast for an additional 15 minutes or until done. When done, tip the juices from the cavity into the roasting tin.

3 Allow the chicken to rest on a plate, loosely covered with foil. Tilt the roasting tin, and prop it in a tilted position. Spoon out all the fat and discard. Put the roasting tin on the hob, and turn the heat to full. Stir and scrape up the drippings and browned bits. Pour in the wine, bring to the boil, and boil, stirring and scraping, until it has reduced by about one third, and formed a dark, thick, rich sauce. Serve with the carved chicken.

ROASTED SPICY CHICKEN

SERVES 4

If you wish, slip ½–1 teaspoon mild runny honey in with the lemon juice in step 1 to make a sweet and sour roasted chicken. If so, stir 4 fl oz (100 ml) passata and another ½ teaspoon honey into the roasting tin with the vermouth and stock at the end of step 4. Either way (with or without the honey), serve the chicken with Potato Pancakes (page 55).

1 lemon
2 garlic cloves, crushed
¼ teaspoon ground cinnamon
1–2 pinches cayenne pepper
1 teaspoon paprika
3–3¼ lb (1.4–1.5 kg) roasting chicken, trimmed
  of fat

4 thin lemon slices (pips removed)
1 large mild onion, halved and sliced into half
  moons
about 6 fl oz (175 ml) vermouth
about 6 fl oz (175 ml) stock
salt and freshly ground pepper

1 Squeeze the lemon and mix the lemon juice with the garlic and spices. (Reserve the squeezed lemon halves.) Make small incisions all over the chicken, except the breast. Loosen the skin over the breast. Rub the chicken all over (including under the breast skin) with the lemon mixture. Leave the garlic under the breast skin, and slip two lemon slices under the skin on each side. Put the squeezed lemon halves in the cavity. Marinate overnight in the refrigerator.

2 Next day, bring to room temperature and preheat the oven to 230°C, 450°F, Gas Mark 8.

3 Put the sliced onion and 2 fl oz (50 ml) each of vermouth and stock in a flameproof roasting tin. Put a rack in the tin. Season the chicken with salt and pepper, and place on the rack, breast down. Roast for 15 minutes, then turn the chicken breast up and roast for an additional 45 minutes. Baste with the pan juices several times during roasting. If the breast skin tears or shrinks, position the lemon slices over the breast to keep it moist. If the pan juices cook down too much, replenish with a splash of extra vermouth and stock. If the chicken is not cooked through after 45 minutes (see opposite), turn the chicken once more and roast, breast down, for 15 minutes or until done. When done, tip the juices from the cavity into the tin.

4 Put the chicken on a plate, cover loosely with foil, and leave to stand for 15 minutes for the juices to settle. Strain the pan juices into a bowl or jug, pressing down on the onions to extract all their goodness. Put the jug in the freezer for 10 minutes. Remove the jug, and skim off and discard the fat. Return the juices to the roasting tin and place on the hob. Bring to the boil, stirring and scraping up any deposits. Pour in 4 fl oz (100 ml) each of stock and vermouth, and boil until reduced by about a third. Pour into a gravy boat, and serve with the carved chicken.

VARIATION *Lemon and Rosemary Chicken* Follow the above recipe but omit the spices. Slip a sprig or two of rosemary under the skin of each breast, along with the garlic and lemon slices. Continue with the recipe.

ROASTED CHICKEN, CHINESE STYLE

SERVES 4

Five-spice powder is an exquisite Chinese blend of spices with sweet overtones. Here it imbues marinated roasted chicken with its subtle fragrance.

2½–3 lb (1.1–1.4 kg) roasting chicken, trimmed of fat

MARINADE

3 tablespoons thinly sliced spring onions

½ inch (1 cm) piece of fresh root ginger, peeled and crushed

1 garlic clove, crushed

2 fl oz (50 ml) teriyaki or soy sauce

2 fl oz (50 ml) dry sherry

¼ teaspoon Chinese five-spice powder

1 teaspoon sugar

STUFFING

1 lb (450 g) mushrooms, sliced

1 inch (2.5 cm) piece of fresh root ginger, peeled and crushed

8 spring onions, trimmed and cut into 1½ inch (4 cm) pieces

2 fl oz (50 ml) stock

2 fl oz (50 ml) dry sherry

dash of teriyaki or soy sauce

BASTING SAUCE

6 fl oz (175 ml) chicken stock

2 tablespoons teriyaki or soy sauce

4 fl oz (100 ml) dry sherry

½ tablespoon honey

¼ teaspoon Chinese five-spice powder

FINAL THICKENING

1 tablespoon cornflour

3 tablespoons water

1 Combine all the marinade ingredients. With the tip of a small sharp knife, make incisions all over the chicken, except in the breast. Loosen the breast skin. Rub the chicken thoroughly, inside and out, and under the breast skin, with the marinade. Leave the ginger and garlic under the breast skin. Marinate overnight in the refrigerator.

2 To make the stuffing, sauté the mushrooms, ginger and onions in the stock, sherry and teriyaki or soy sauce until tender. Cool and refrigerate until needed.

3 Next day, bring the chicken to room temperature and preheat the oven to 230°C, 450°F, Gas Mark 8. Combine the basting ingredients in a roasting tin. Put a rack in the tin. Stuff the chicken, then plug the opening with a ball of foil. Place the chicken, breast down, on the rack in the roasting tin. Add to the roasting tin any marinade that has drained off the chicken.

4 Roast the chicken for 15 minutes, then turn it on one side and roast for 15 minutes. Turn it on to its other side and roast for 15 minutes, then turn it breast up and roast for 15 minutes or until done. Baste frequently. Put the chicken on a plate, cover loosely with foil and leave to rest for 15 minutes.

5 Strain the juices into a jug, and place in the freezer for a few minutes. Skim off the fat and discard. Pour the skimmed juices into a saucepan. Whisk together the cornflour and water until well blended. Add to the saucepan and heat over moderate heat, stirring constantly, until simmering and thickened.

OVEN 'FRIED' TIKKA CHICKEN FILLETS

SERVES 4

These spicy breasts bake in no time at all. The secret here is to cook the chicken so that it is *just* done. There should be no trace of pink in the centre (the meat will be pearly white inside), and the texture should be creamy. If chicken breasts cook too long, they turn dry and stringy.

4 skinless chicken breast fillets, trimmed of fat and gristle
¼ pint (150 ml) very low-fat yoghurt
3 tablespoons tikka spices

oil spray (page ix)
plain breadcrumbs
lime wedges, raita and chutney, to serve

1 Remove the small flap of chicken on the underside of each fillet. With a thin skewer (a cake tester, for instance), pierce each piece of chicken, including the lower flaps, right through in several places.

2 Whisk together the yoghurt and tikka spices. Tip this mixture into a shallow glass or ceramic baking dish that is large enough to hold the chicken in a single layer. Dredge all of the chicken (including the under flaps) in the mixture, using a rubber spatula to coat the chicken well. Refrigerate for a few hours, or, even better, overnight. Leave to stand at room temperature for about 1 hour before cooking.

3 Preheat the grill to high. Line the grill pan with foil, shiny-side up. Put the grill rack in the pan and spray with oil spray.

4 Spread the breadcrumbs on a large plate. Dredge the chicken in the crumbs, pressing them in well on both sides. Put the breaded fillets and flaps on the grill rack.

5 Position the grill so the chicken is about 4 inches (10 cm) from the heat, and grill for 4–5 minutes on the first side, then turn and grill for 3–4 minutes on the second side or until just done. The chicken is done when it feels firm but springy when pressed; when the juices run clear when the chicken is pierced in the centre with a skewer, and when there is no trace of pink in the centre of each piece. Serve with lime wedges, raita and chutney.

PAN-BRAISED CHICKEN THIGHS

Skinless chicken thighs (they are easy to skin — just pull the skin off and trim away any bits of fat) are wonderful in a pan sauté with apples, or potatoes, or garlic, or whatever you choose. The traditional method is to sauté the chicken in butter or oil first until golden brown, then to simmer it in wine or cream, until tender. In order to achieve deep sauté flavour and rich sauce without the oil, butter or cream, I've reversed the process somewhat, first simmering the chicken and flavourings in stock and wine, then gently braising until the chicken is tender and browned in the reduced syrupy pan juices. It is a very quick way to cook chicken, and a remarkably savoury one.

CHICKEN WITH APPLES AND CIDER

MAKES 4 PIECES

⌣

What I especially love about this method of pan-braising chicken is the way the flavourings permeate the chicken right to the bone. The apples caramelize as they sauté. Serve with a nice heap of mashed potatoes.

4 chicken thighs, skinned and trimmed of fat
4 fl oz (100 ml) stock
4 fl oz (100 ml) medium dry cider
2 fl oz (50 ml) brandy
1 garlic clove, crushed
½ onion, chopped

1 tablespoon chopped fresh sage
1 tablespoon chopped fresh parsley
salt and freshly ground pepper
1 Granny Smith apple, peeled, cored and sliced
*   into ¼ inch (0.5 cm) thick wedges*

1 Arrange the chicken, skinned-side down, in a heavy-bottomed frying pan. Pour in the liquids, and scatter the garlic, onion, sage and parsley around the chicken. (The chicken should be in one uncrowded layer.) Season with salt and pepper, and bring to the boil.

2 Reduce the heat and simmer, uncovered, turning the chicken occasionally, for about 10 minutes, then add the apples and cook for about 10 minutes more. As it cooks, the liquid will cook down considerably. When the juices are thick and syrupy, the chicken will brown nicely (turn it frequently at this point). When the chicken is tender and cooked through (no pink at the bone) and the apple is soft, the dish is ready to serve. If, during the cooking, the liquid cooks away, add a little more, as needed. If, on the other hand, the chicken is tender and cooked through, and there is a considerable amount of liquid left, remove the chicken and apples to a plate, and boil the pan juices down, then return the chicken and apples to the sauce.

Pan-Braised Chicken with Red Vermouth

MAKES 4 PIECES

Red vermouth has a bitter-sweetness with herbal undertones, and bathes the chicken pieces in a rich, syrupy sauce. Serve with rice, sliced potato gratin or polenta.

4 chicken thighs, skinned and trimmed of fat
4 fl oz (100 ml) stock
4 fl oz (100 ml) red vermouth
2–3 garlic cloves, crushed
salt and freshly ground pepper

1 Arrange the chicken, skinned-side down, in a heavy-bottomed frying pan. Pour in the liquids, and scatter the garlic around the chicken. (The chicken should be in one uncrowded layer.) Season with salt and pepper, and bring to a simmer.

2 Cook, uncovered, turning the chicken occasionally, for about 20 minutes. As it cooks, the liquid will cook down considerably. When the juices are thick and syrupy, the chicken will brown nicely (turn it frequently at this point). When the chicken is meltingly tender, there is no pink at the bone, and the garlic is very tender in a thick syrupy sauce, the dish is ready to serve. If, during the cooking, the liquid cooks away, add a little more, as needed. If, on the other hand, the chicken is tender and cooked through, and there is a considerable amount of liquid left, remove the chicken to a plate, and boil the pan juices down, then return the chicken to the sauce.

Pan-Braised Chicken with Potatoes and Rosemary

MAKES 4 PIECES

If you use dried rosemary and thyme, sniff them first to make sure they haven't gone musty. Serve with Oven-Fried Potatoes with Mustard and Herbs (page 52).

4 chicken thighs, skinned and trimmed of fat
4 fl oz (100 ml) stock
4 fl oz (100 ml) dry white vermouth
1 garlic clove, crushed
2 all-purpose potatoes (such as Wilja), each weighing about 4 oz (110 g), peeled and diced into ½ inch (1 cm) pieces
1 small onion, very finely chopped
1½ teaspoons chopped fresh rosemary leaves, or ½ teaspoon dried rosemary
½ teaspoon fresh thyme leaves, or ¼ teaspoon dried thyme
salt and freshly ground pepper

1 Arrange the chicken, skinned-side down, in a heavy-bottomed frying pan. Pour in the liquids, and scatter the garlic, potatoes, onion and herbs around the chicken. (The chicken should be in one uncrowded layer.) Season with salt and pepper, and bring to a simmer.

2 Cook, uncovered, turning the chicken occasionally, for about 20 minutes. As it cooks, the liquid will cook down considerably. When the juices are thick and syrupy, the chicken will brown nicely (turn it frequently at this point). When the chicken is meltingly tender, there is no pink at the bone, and the potatoes are very tender in a thick syrupy sauce, the dish is ready to serve. If, during the cooking, the liquid cooks away, add a little more, as needed. If, on the other hand, the chicken and potatoes are tender and cooked through, and there is a considerable amount of liquid left, remove the chicken and potatoes to a plate, and boil the pan juices down, then return the chicken to the sauce.

PAN-BRAISED CHICKEN IN HONEY–MUSTARD SAUCE

MAKES 4 PIECES

⊙

Honey–mustard glazed chicken and the Simple Wheat Pilaf on page 121 are a wonderful combination. Garnish with generous bunches of peppery watercress, and serve with Cherry Tomato and Olive Salsa (page 81).

½ teaspoon teriyaki sauce
1 tablespoon mild runny honey
2 tablespoons Dijon mustard
juice of ½ lemon

8 fl oz (225 ml) stock
4 chicken thighs, skinned and trimmed of fat
1 small onion, very finely chopped
salt and freshly ground pepper

1 Whisk together the teriyaki, honey, mustard, lemon juice and stock.

2 Arrange the chicken, skinned-side down, in a heavy-bottomed frying pan. Pour in the honey–mustard mixture, and scatter the onion around the chicken. (The chicken should be in one uncrowded layer.) Season with salt and pepper, and bring to a simmer.

3 Cook, uncovered, turning the chicken occasionally, for about 20 minutes. As it cooks, the liquid will cook down considerably. When the juices are thick and syrupy, the chicken will brown nicely (turn it frequently at this point). When the chicken is meltingly tender, with no pink at the bone, in a thick syrupy sauce, the dish is ready to serve. If, during the cooking, the liquid cooks away, add a little more, as needed. If, on the other hand, the chicken is tender and cooked through, and there is a considerable amount of liquid left, remove the chicken to a plate, and boil the pan juices down, then return the chicken to the sauce.

STUFFED CHICKEN PARCELS

MAKES 6

Chicken thigh fillets are boned, skinned chicken thighs, available in many supermarkets. If not, it is easy to pull the skin off a chicken thigh, remove the bone, and trim away the bits of fat. Here, the fillets are wrapped around a lovely garlic, olive and chilli stuffing and simmered in a tomato and wine sauce. If you (and those you feed) don't like getting your fingers in the food, snip off the twine before serving the parcels. If not, do be sure to warn people that the twine is there.

6 chicken thigh fillets
salt and freshly ground pepper
4 spring onions, trimmed and sliced
1 garlic clove, crushed
2 olives in brine, drained and slivered off their stones
2 sundried tomatoes, diced (use scissors)
1 chilli, deseeded and chopped
about ¼ pint (150 ml) chicken stock

6 fl oz (175 ml) red wine
two 14 oz (400 g) cans chopped tomatoes
1 thin slice of smoked ham, finely chopped (use scissors)
1 tablespoon freshly grated Parmesan cheese
1 tablespoon plain breadcrumbs
3 tablespoons chopped fresh parsley
olive oil spray (page ix)
1 tablespoon tomato purée

1 Trim the chicken fillets of any signs of skin, fat and gristle. Put a piece of cling film on your work surface. Lay the chicken thigh fillets out on the film, skinned-side down, and cover with another piece of cling film. With a kitchen mallet, a rolling pin, or the side of a wide knife, gently pound the chicken to flatten and enlarge slightly. Peel off the top cling film. Sprinkle the fillets with some salt and pepper.

2 In a heavy-bottomed frying pan, combine the onions, garlic, olives, sundried tomatoes, chilli, ¼ pint (150 ml) stock and 4 fl oz (100 ml) red wine. Simmer briskly until the onions are tender and the liquid almost gone. Scoop half of this mixture into a bowl; leave the rest in the pan and add the canned tomatoes. Season with salt and pepper, and simmer for 5–10 minutes.

3 Meanwhile, stir the ham, Parmesan, breadcrumbs and 1 tablespoon parsley into the onion and garlic mixture in the bowl. Put a spoonful of this stuffing on each chicken thigh, roll up from one of the short ends, and tie crossways and lengthways with kitchen twine.

4 Spray a heavy-bottomed non-stick frying pan with olive oil spray, and heat. Add the chicken parcels, and cook, turning with tongs, until they are well browned on all sides. Stir 1 tablespoon parsley and the tomato purée into the tomato sauce, and place the chicken parcels, in a single layer, on the sauce.

5 Pour the remaining red wine into the frying pan in which you browned the chicken and boil, stirring and scraping up any browned deposits. When the wine has reduced by almost half, scrape it into the tomato sauce.

6 Cover the frying pan and simmer the chicken for about 25 minutes or until just done, stirring occasionally. If the sauce thickens too much and threatens to catch, stir in 1–2 tablespoons extra stock. Sprinkle with the remaining chopped parsley and serve with pasta or mashed potatoes.

GRILLED CHICKEN PARCELS FILLED WITH CREAMY GARLIC CHEESE

This is a sort of post-modern Chicken Kiev, with boneless, skinless chicken thighs replacing the breasts, and low-fat garlic and herb cheese replacing the butter. The secret is to be sure to seal the chicken parcels well (with the flour, egg and crumbs) so that the cheese does not ooze out too soon. When they are well sealed, the parcels swell up as they grill, and then, when you cut into them with a knife, the juices and the melted, creamy cheese spurt out. It's a lovely moment.

oil spray (page x)
chicken thigh fillets, trimmed of fat
Boursin Léger
flour

lightly beaten egg white
plain breadcrumbs seasoned with salt and
  pepper

I Preheat the grill. Line the grill pan with foil, shiny-side up. Put the rack in the pan and spray with oil spray.

2 Put a sheet of cling film on your work surface and lay the fillets, skinned-side down, on the film. Cover with another sheet of film. With a kitchen mallet, rolling pin or the flat side of a wide knife, gently pound the chicken to flatten and enlarge slightly. Remove the top sheet of cling film.

3 Spread about 1 teaspoon Boursin on each fillet. Fold over and press together so the flesh adheres. Dip each parcel in flour, then in egg white and then in breadcrumbs, coating well on all sides, including the edges. Place on the grill rack.

4 Position the grill pan so the chicken is about 5 inches (12.5 cm) from the heat, and grill for about 4 minutes on each side or until browned and cooked through. Serve at once.

OVEN-BAKED CHICKEN THIGHS

One of the easiest ways to cook bone-in, skinless chicken thighs (drumsticks are good this way, too) is spread out in a baking dish, smothered with a quick but interesting sauce, and baked. It's not one of those 10-minute dishes (it takes 45 minutes to cook), but the ingredients are thrown together in less than 5 minutes, and then baked unattended except for the occasional basting – cookery doesn't get much easier than this! And it fills the kitchen with such gorgeous aromas as it roasts! If you wish, throw the ingredients into the baking dish in the morning and put them in the fridge, then in the evening, just heave the dish into the oven.

CHICKEN IN CURRIED FRUIT SAUCE

MAKES 6 PIECES

Passata, curried fruit chutney and lime – that's all. They do wonderful things to a panful of chicken. In the summer, this instant sauce is great brushed on to chicken drumsticks and thighs as they barbecue. Serve with crusty bread to soak up the delicious juices.

4 fl oz (100 ml) passata
8½ oz (235 g) jar curried fruit chutney
juice and grated zest of ½ lime

several dashes Tabasco sauce (optional)
6 chicken thighs, skinned
freshly ground pepper

1 Preheat the oven to 180°C, 350°F, Gas Mark 4.

2 Combine the passata, chutney, lime juice, lime zest and Tabasco, if using.

3 Place the chicken, skinned-side up, in a baking dish so that the pieces do not touch each other. Grind over some pepper.

4 Pour the tomato and chutney mixture evenly over and around the chicken, and bake, uncovered, in the oven for 40–45 minutes or until just done, basting once or twice during baking.

CHINESE CHICKEN

MAKES 6 PIECES

I don't add garlic to this; believe it or not, it seems better without it. But do add a few cloves, by all means, if you miss the pungent bulb.

2 fl oz (50 ml) soy sauce
3 tablespoons mild runny honey
2 tablespoons lemon juice
2 tablespoons dry sherry

½ teaspoon mustard powder
½ inch (1 cm) piece of fresh root ginger, peeled
*   and crushed*
6 chicken thighs, skinned

1 Thoroughly combine all the ingredients, except the chicken.

2 Toss the chicken and the soy sauce and honey mixture together, and leave to marinate while you preheat the oven to 180°C, 350°F, Gas Mark 4.

3 When the oven is preheated, arrange the chicken pieces, skinned-side up, in a baking dish, so that they do not touch each other. Pour and scrape any remaining marinade over and around the chicken.

4 Bake, uncovered, in the oven for 40–45 minutes or until just done, basting once or twice during baking.

VARIATIONS Bake chicken thighs, as above, in any of the tomato sauces (pages 85–86). Best of all, blanket them with Mango Sauce (page 88), and bake as above. This particular sauce and chicken get on extremely well – the mango fragrance penetrates right to the bone.

'FRIED' CHICKEN

Like courgettes, aubergines and fish, chicken pieces can be 'fried' (this time in the oven rather than under the grill) if they are coated with crumbs. Serve with lemon, lime or orange wedges, or an interesting sauce.

OVEN 'FRIED' CHICKEN

⊙

A spicy coating sets off bland chicken breast very well, but leave out the spices if you crave a gentler piece of chicken. The chicken is roasted first then browned under the grill.

oil spray (page ix)
flour
lightly beaten egg white
breadcrumbs
salt and freshly ground pepper

1–2 pinches ground paprika, ground allspice,
   dried thyme, dried oregano and cayenne
   pepper (optional)
boneless chicken breast fillets, trimmed of fat
   and gristle

1 Preheat the oven to 220°C, 425°F, Gas Mark 7. Line a baking tray with foil, shiny-side up, and spray with oil spray.

2 Put the flour on a plate and the egg white in a wide, shallow dish. Spread the breadcrumbs on another plate and season with salt and pepper and the herbs and spices, if using. Pat the chicken dry with paper kitchen towels, and dredge in flour, the egg and then the breadcrumbs. Place on the foil-lined tray, and spray lightly with oil spray.

3 Bake in the oven for 10 minutes, then turn and bake for about 5 minutes more. Flash under the grill for 30–60 seconds on each side to brown. Serve at once.

OVEN 'FRIED' CHICKEN THIGHS

T he 'mayo' method of oven frying works beautifully for chicken thighs.

chicken thighs, skinned
Fromage Frais 'Mayo' (page 97)
dry breadcrumbs

salt and freshly ground pepper
oil spray (page ix)

1 Preheat the oven to 190°C, 375°F, Gas Mark 5. Dredge the thighs with 'mayo' (spread it thickly on the skinned side), then coat the skinned-side thickly with seasoned breadcrumbs.

2 Put on a rack on a foil-lined baking sheet and spray lightly with oil. Bake for 40–50 minutes.

CHICKEN SALADS

You could make chicken salad from here to eternity and never run out of ideas. Left-over roasted chicken, a quickly pan-sautéed chicken breast, or even an unsliced block of smoked chicken from the deli counter make tempting blank canvases. Embellish that canvas with fruit, herbs, vegetables, colourful sauces – the possibilities really are endless. A chicken salad makes a pleasing summer meal, or a beautiful addition to a buffet table.

SMOKED CHICKEN PESTO POTATO SALAD

MAKES 2¾ PINTS (1.6 LITRES)

The creamy pesto lovingly coats the chicken, the potatoes give a touch of carbo-comfort, and the peppers are a welcome blaze of colour. Arranged on a platter, with the garnishes, this salad is absolutely stunning.

1 lb (450 g) new potatoes, scrubbed
1 lb (450 g) boned and cubed smoked chicken
  (or turkey)
1 grilled red pepper (page 49), drained, or use
  canned or bottled peppers

6 fl oz (175 ml) Creamy Pesto (page 76), thinned
  with a little buttermilk
whole basil leaves and halved cherry tomatoes,
  to garnish

1 Do not peel the potatoes. Steam until cooked through but not mushy, then cool. When cool, cut into 1 inch (2.5 cm) chunks, or slice them.

2 Combine the potatoes, chicken and peppers. Add the pesto and fold together. Serve on a platter, garnished with whole basil leaves and cherry tomatoes.

CHICKEN MANGO SALAD

SERVES 4–6

This recipe, and Chicken–Berry Salad (below), are stars. They look splendidly colourful, and the chicken/fruit partnerships are very successful.

4 skinless chicken breast fillets
1 large onion, chopped
2 garlic cloves, crushed
1 inch (2.5 cm) piece of fresh root ginger, peeled and crushed
seeds of 5 cardamom pods
2 tablespoons teriyaki or soy sauce
2½ tablespoons dry sherry
2 tablespoons runny honey

3 fl oz (75 ml) white wine vinegar
salt and freshly ground pepper
1 small red pepper, peeled (page 48), deseeded and chopped
1 celery stalk, destrung, cut in half lengthways and thinly sliced
15 cherry tomatoes, halved
1 mango, peeled and cubed (page 69)
chopped fresh coriander or parsley, to garnish

1 Preheat the oven to 180°C, 350°F, Gas Mark 4.

2 Spread the chicken, skinned-side up, in one layer in a heavy, very shallow baking dish.

3 Combine the onion, garlic, ginger, cardamom seeds, teriyaki or soy sauce, sherry and honey in a saucepan. Bring to the boil and pour evenly over the chicken. Cover tightly with foil and bake in the oven for 20–30 minutes or until the chicken is *just* done (it will feel firm but springy).

4 Put the chicken, in one layer, on a platter. Cover loosely with foil. Pour and scrape the onions and juices into a saucepan. Boil the juices until they are syrupy and the onions are amber-coloured and tender.

5 Cut the chicken into ½ inch (1 cm) cubes. Sprinkle with the vinegar and toss together. Gently stir in the onion mixture. Season with salt and pepper, spread out in a shallow dish, cover and set aside.

6 Just before serving, stir in the pepper and celery. Arrange attractively on a serving plate, and surround with the cherry tomatoes and mango cubes. Sprinkle with the coriander and parsley, to garnish.

CHICKEN–BERRY SALAD

SERVES 4–6

⊙

I've been making variations of this salad for years, and I never get tired of it. Save it for that intoxicating time when the best berries are available in wild profusion. If you wish, dispense with the dressing entirely and just serve balsamic vinegar for sprinkling, or serve the salad with Mango Mayo (page 99).

oil spray (page ix)
4 skinless chicken breast fillets
salt and freshly ground pepper
1 lb (450 g) mixed fresh berries (use blueberries,
  blackberries, strawberries, tayberries,
  raspberries – whatever you can find)

8 oz (225 g) seedless grapes, halved
8 oz (225 g) very low-fat fromage frais
1 tablespoon balsamic vinegar
½ teaspoon mild runny honey
½ teaspoon Dijon mustard
fresh mint leaves, to garnish

1 Mist a frying pan with oil spray and heat. Season the chicken breast fillets with salt and pepper and cook, in one layer, for 3–4 minutes each side or until just cooked (they will feel firm and springy and the interior will be a delicate pearly white).

2 Slice each chicken breast crossways on the diagonal into wide slices. Overlap the chicken slices on a beautiful platter, and surround with the mixed berries and grapes.

3 Combine all the remaining ingredients, except the mint leaves, and season with salt and pepper. Pour a little dressing in a stripe down the centre of the chicken slices, and serve the remainder separately. Garnish the salad with mint leaves.

MEAT

If you love red meat, there is no need to cut it out in the name of a low-fat lifestyle. Although meat is a source of fat, much of it saturated, it is also a source of excellent protein, B vitamins, zinc and iron. In fact, the zinc and iron in meat are absorbed more efficiently into the body than the iron or zinc in any other foodstuff, or in food supplements. The trick is to accentuate the positive (all those valuable nutrients and that good taste) and eliminate as much of the negative (the fat) as possible. Here's how to do it:

1 If you are in the habit of eating meat once (or even twice) a day, cut back. Eat it 2–3 times a week, or even less.

2 Choose lean meat that has minimal fat marbling within the flesh, and always trim away any visible fat surrounding the meat.

3 When you cook with meat, use plenty of vegetables and grains to 'stretch' it and surround it. Stews and ragouts, for instance, can be prepared with more vegetables than meat, and then served with potatoes or rice, pasta or another grain. And mince can be 'stretched' and improved with all sorts of clever things in such a way that the amount of actual meat eaten is small, but the meaty taste is entirely satisfying.

4 There is never any need to brown meat in quantities of added fat or oil. At the most, a spritz of oil spray (page ix) in a non-stick pan or on the grill does the job nicely; in many cases, even that is unnecessary.

This section will take you through the techniques of low-fat meat cookery, including advice on low-fat cuts of meat. Meat is bred to be leaner these days, so finding lean cuts is not nearly as difficult as it used to be. There are many who believe that the only tasty meat is that which is well marbled with fat, but you will find that leaner meat, when cooked properly, can be wonderfully flavourful. The health benefits make the leaner cuts well worth using and you will be paying for far less waste too.

MINCE MATTERS

For many reasons, mince is the most satisfying of meats to work with. Mince is the basis of dishes that people really like to eat: sausages, meatballs, burgers, meat loaves, bolognese sauce, shepherd's pies – all those homely, comforting things that epitomize home cooking. These dishes are great fun to cook as well, because they can be endlessly varied. And mince can be subtly and discreetly 'stretched' so that a meaty-tasting dish is not quite so meat-filled as it seems. Supermarkets sell extra-lean mince, or a butcher will mince a cut of lean meat for you. And you can, of course, mince lean meat yourself by pulsing cubes of lean meat in a food processor.

The only problem of working with extra-lean mince is that without the fat, the finished product can be terribly disappointing. Meatballs, sausages and burgers can be dry and tough; bolognese sauce, shepherd's pie fillings, and so on, can be juiceless and 'bitty'. Fat adds smoothness, succulence and moistness; when the fat is gone, so are these properties. Fortunately, there are alternatives to the fat. Vegetable ingredients can add texture and moistness, 'stretch' the meat and make it taste rich and well rounded although the fat levels are very low indeed.

Aubergine Magic

Aubergine is a marvel. When you buy a batch of extra-lean mince, buy an aubergine or two as well, roast it or pan-braise it (see below), then use the pulp to enrich and improve the meat. The aubergine will allow you to stretch a small amount of meat much further than you would believe possible. It will also restore moistness and smoothness to the lean mince, and add lightness without adding any taste of its own. A half pound of mince, 'improved' with aubergine will yield 2½ pints (1.4 litres) bolognese sauce, or 4 generously plump burgers, or 15–20 meatballs. It will all taste rich and meaty, and the aubergine will not be intrusive at all; in fact, no one will know it is there.

ROASTED AUBERGINE

❅

A roasted aubergine is an odd sight, all shrivelled and collapsed, and the chopped pulp of the aubergine looks even odder. But once you have the chopped pulp safely mixed into the mince, it is practically invisible, and once the meatballs, sausages, sauces, etc., are cooked, it *is* invisible. Roasted aubergine pulp will keep in the fridge for several days and in the freezer for months, so it pays to roast, peel and chop several at once.

whole aubergines, each weighing 8–12 oz
  (225–350 g)

1 Preheat the oven to 200°C, 400°F, Gas Mark 6.

2 Pierce the aubergines in several places with a fork or thin skewer. Bake directly on the oven shelf for 30–40 minutes or until soft and collapsed. Cool.

3 Cut away the stems, and strip off and discard the skins, which should come away easily. Chop the aubergine flesh to a pulp, or process to a rough purée in a blender or food processor.

VARIATION *Microwave Roasted Aubergine* Pierce an 8 oz (225 g) aubergine in several places with a fork or thin skewer. Place it in an 8 inch (20 cm) square, 1–2 inches (2.5–5 cm) deep glass baking dish. Cover tightly with microwave cling film, and microwave on high (full power) for 6 minutes. Remove (do not uncover) and stand for 5 minutes. Pierce the cling film to allow steam to escape (avert your face and stand back). Very carefully remove the cling film. When the aubergine is cool enough to handle, strip off the skin with a dull knife. Chop the pulp finely.

PAN-BRAISED AUBERGINE

⌄ ❄

If you have no roasted aubergine on hand, and you don't want to wait the 40 minutes of roasting before you can continue with a particular recipe, pan-braised aubergine can be quickly prepared instead. The two methods are interchangeable. Roasted aubergine is incredibly convenient when you have some, preroasted and chopped, tucked away in the fridge or freezer, but if none is on hand, pan-braised aubergine can be prepared in about 15 minutes. Pan-braised aubergine is simmered with wine, garlic and onions, along with sundried tomatoes and black olive slivers (although these two are optional). The advantage of this method is the wonderful way that the aubergine becomes infused with the delicious flavours of the braising ingredients. Any herbs or seasonings you like can be added to the basic mixture. Once the braised aubergine has been puréed, it can be refrigerated for several days, or frozen for several months, so it makes sense to prepare a big batch to keep for future dishes.

2 aubergines, peeled and chopped
2 onions, chopped
2 garlic cloves, crushed
2–3 black olives in brine, drained and slivered
  off their stones (optional)

2 sundried tomatoes, chopped with scissors
  (optional)
pinch of crushed dried chillies
4 fl oz (100 ml) red wine
½ pint (300 ml) stock

1 Combine all the ingredients in a frying pan, cover, and simmer briskly for 5–7 minutes. Uncover and simmer until very tender and the liquid absorbed. Cool slightly.

2 Put the aubergine mixture into a food processor or blender, and process to a rough purée.

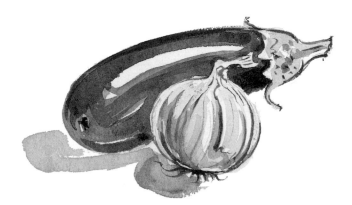

BOLOGNESE SAUCE WITH ROASTED AUBERGINE

MAKES 2½ PINTS (1.4 LITRES)

❅

Spag bol – no home-cooking repertoire would be complete without it. This version, which is enriched with roasted aubergine pulp, is delicious and very meaty, although it contains no more than 8 oz (225 g) very lean meat.

1 medium onion, chopped
2 large garlic cloves, crushed
1 small carrot, peeled and finely diced
1 small red pepper, peeled (page 48), deseeded and chopped
1 small yellow pepper, peeled (page 48), deseeded and chopped
8 fl oz (225 ml) stock
5–6 sundried tomatoes, chopped (use scissors)
pinch of crushed dried chillies
8 oz (225 g) extra-lean minced beef, pork, or a combination

four 14 oz (400 g) cans chopped tomatoes
chopped pulp of two 8 oz (225 g) roasted aubergines (page 157)
4 tablespoons tomato purée
1 tablespoon chopped fresh oregano, or ¼ teaspoon dried oregano
1 tablespoon chopped fresh basil, or ¼ teaspoon dried basil
salt and freshly ground pepper

1 Put the onion, garlic, carrot and peppers in a non-stick, heavy bottomed frying pan with the stock, sundried tomatoes and chillies. Cover, and simmer over medium heat until the carrots are tender, then uncover and simmer until the liquid has almost gone.

2 Add the meat to the pan and continue to cook, stirring to break up any lumps, until the meat is completely cooked through and the onions are limp.

3 Add the canned tomatoes, aubergine, tomato purée and dried herbs, if using, and season with salt and pepper. Partially cover the frying pan and simmer for 20 minutes.

4 Adjust the seasoning. Add the fresh herbs, if using, and simmer, partially covered, for about 15 minutes more, or until the sauce is thick and the vegetables tender.

CHILLI WITH VEGETABLES

MAKES ABOUT 3 PINTS (1.7 LITRES)

�
❄

hilli con carne is more 'Texican' than Mexican. There are as many versions as there are cooks preparing it, and each cook is sure that his or hers is the only true chilli. Chilli can be prepared with mince, as it is here, or with cubes of beef. When serving chilli, don't just tip it in a bowl and heave it on to the table. A chilli meal should be something of an event: put the chilli into a beautiful pottery casserole and arrange all the garnishes in pretty bowls, on the table, surrounding it. Ladle the chilli into shallow soup plates rather than flat plates. Rice is good with chilli but I prefer the Simple Wheat Pilaf on page 121. Everyone should take some bulghur, then some chilli, and then add the garnishes to their hearts' content. It is colourful, fun and delicious. This mostly vegetable chilli can be prepared *without* the meat to make a colourful vegetarian main dish; indeed you will hardly miss it. Or leave out the mince and choose one of the meatball recipes in this chapter. Grill them, and add them to the chilli during the last 7–10 minutes of simmering.

1 aubergine, weighing about 12 oz (350 g), chopped into 1 inch (2.5 cm) pieces
1 red or yellow pepper, deseeded, cut into its natural sections, peeled (page 48) and diced
2 carrots, peeled and diced
2 large onions, diced
2 garlic cloves, crushed
4 sundried tomatoes, chopped (use scissors)
1 chilli, deseeded and chopped (optional)
½ pint (300 ml) red wine
½ pint (300 ml) stock
1 tablespoon dried oregano, crumbled
1 teaspoon ground cumin
1 teaspoon ground coriander
1 teaspoon paprika

1–2 pinches crushed dried chillies
½–1 teaspoon mild chilli powder (optional)
1 tablespoon brown sugar
8 oz (225 g) extra-lean minced pork
salt and freshly ground pepper
two 14 oz (400 g) cans chopped tomatoes

GARNISHES
lime wedges
very low-fat fromage frais
freshly grated Parmesan cheese
chopped fresh herbs (parsley, coriander, mint)
thinly sliced spring onions or chopped red onion
Pepper Salsa (page 80)
Green Pea Spread (page 24)

1 Combine the aubergine, pepper, carrots, onions, garlic, sundried tomatoes, chilli (if using), wine, stock, oregano, spices and sugar in a heavy-bottomed frying pan or flameproof casserole. Cover and simmer briskly for 10 minutes. Uncover and simmer until the vegetables are tender and the liquid about gone.

2 Add the meat and season with salt and pepper. Stir and cook, breaking up the lumps of meat, until the pork loses its redness.

3 Stir in the tomatoes and simmer, partially covered, for 15–20 minutes, stirring occasionally, until thick and savoury. Taste and adjust the seasonings.

4 Serve with the Simple Wheat Pilaf on page 121, and an array of the garnishes.

KEEMA CURRY

MAKES ABOUT 2 PINTS (1.1 LITRES)

❄

Keema is like an Indian bolognese. Curry powder may be substituted for the mix of spices, and peas may be used in place of some of the potatoes. Serve keema with rice and raita.

2 medium onions, cut into eighths
1 pint (600 ml) stock
1 inch (2.5 cm) piece of fresh root ginger, peeled and crushed
2 garlic cloves, crushed
1 green chilli, deseeded and finely chopped
1 teaspoon ground coriander
½ teaspoon ground cinnamon
tiny pinch of ground cloves
½ teaspoon ground allspice
6 whole green cardamom pods, lightly crushed
cayenne pepper, to taste
1 bay leaf
1 lb (450 g) extra-lean minced beef or lamb
2 medium boiling potatoes, cut into 1 inch (2.5 cm) dice
3 tablespoons tomato purée
chopped pulp from one roasted aubergine (page 157)
14 oz (400 g) can chopped tomatoes
salt and freshly ground pepper
1 teaspoon garam masala

1 Separate the layers of the onion segments, and put them in a heavy-bottomed frying pan with ½ pint (300 ml) stock, the ginger, garlic, chilli, spices and bay leaf. Cover and bring to the boil, then reduce the heat and simmer briskly for 5–7 minutes. Uncover and simmer, stirring frequently, until the onions are tender and the spices are 'frying' in their own juices. Don't rush this step; it is essential that the spices should not have a raw, harsh taste. Taste, add a little more stock and cook very gently for a few more minutes, if necessary.

2 Add the meat, stir and cook, breaking up the lumps, until cooked through.

3 Add the potatoes and stir until they are well combined with the spicy meat. Stir in the tomato purée, the remaining ½ pint (300 ml) stock, the aubergine purée and the tomatoes. Season with salt and pepper, and bring to the boil. Reduce the heat and simmer briskly for about 30 minutes, partially covered, until the mixture is thick and savoury. Cover and simmer for a few minutes more, if necessary, until the potatoes are done. Stir in the garam masala.

SHEPHERD'S PIE

Nothing spells home cooking the way shepherd's pie or cottage pie does. And like so many dishes made from mince, the fun of shepherd's pie is in fiddling around with it, once you have made it the classic way a few million times. I'm giving you the classic (but low-fat) version, and then two extraordinarily savoury variations. I'm sure that you will think up quite a few variations of your own.

Potato-topped shepherd's pies can be prepared in one gratin or baking dish or several individual casserole dishes. They can be prepared in advance, then refrigerated or frozen before the final baking. To cook from the refrigerator, add about 10 minutes to the cooking time. To cook from the freezer, allow 40–60 minutes in total.

TOPPINGS FOR SHEPHERD'S PIES

1 Mashed potato is the classic topping, and will happily blanket any shepherd's pie. To make mashed potato from 'scratch', prepare the mash from 3 lb (1.4 kg) baking potatoes, baked, boiled or steamed and then mashed with an old-fashioned masher or put through a ricer. Stir in 1–2 tablespoons fromage frais, season with salt and pepper, and add 2–3 tablespoons freshly grated Parmesan or medium-fat Cheddar cheese, if liked.

2 Packet potatoes (unseasoned potato flakes like Mr Mash or Waitrose own brand) are excellent as a topping for shepherd's pies of all descriptions. Prepare them with very well seasoned stock instead of water, and when they are done, stir in 1–2 tablespoons fromage frais and 2–3 tablespoons freshly grated Parmesan cheese.

3 If you can find those tubes of unbaked baguette dough in the chill cabinet of your supermarket (they are called Kool French Experience) then they can be used as a wonderful topping. Spread the piping hot shepherd's pie filling in a baking dish. Open the tube, unroll the dough, and separate the pieces. Lay the dough pieces flat, and evenly spaced, on the meat, brush lightly with 2–3 tablespoons skimmed milk, and bake in the oven at 200°C, 400°F, Gas Mark 6 for 12 minutes or until the bread topping has risen and browned.

Opposite: Tomato and Mango Salad (page 69), Pâté with Chicken (page 176) served with Redcurrant and Vermouth Sauce (page 92) and toasted Chive and Mustard Seed Bread (page 202)

SHEPHERD'S PIE

SERVES 4–6

※

This is the basic shepherd's pie – it makes a very satisfying and filling supper. The pan-braised aubergine infusion (page 158) may be used in place of the roasted aubergine pulp.

1 lb (450 g) extra-lean minced lamb
3 onions, finely chopped
1–3 garlic cloves, crushed
¾ pint (450 ml) stock
dash of teriyaki or soy sauce
½ pint (300 ml) dry red wine
chopped pulp from three 8–12 oz (225–350 g)
  peeled, roasted aubergines (page 157)

1 tablespoon Worcestershire sauce
2 tablespoons tomato purée
salt, freshly ground pepper and cayenne pepper
several pinches of freshly grated nutmeg
mashed potato topping (see opposite)
3–4 tablespoons skimmed milk

1 Cook the lamb in a large non-stick frying pan, breaking up the lumps as it cooks. When the lamb is cooked through, drain it well in a colander over a bowl. Blot the frying pan.

2 Combine the onions, garlic, ½ pint (300 ml) stock, teriyaki or soy sauce and ¼ pint (150 ml) wine in the frying pan. Cover and simmer briskly, stirring occasionally, until the onions are tender and the liquid almost gone. Add the drained lamb and the aubergine pulp.

3 Stir in the Worcestershire sauce and tomato purée, and season with salt, pepper, cayenne pepper and nutmeg. Stir in the remaining stock and wine, and simmer, uncovered, for 20–30 minutes, stirring occasionally, until thick and savoury. Taste and adjust the seasonings.

4 Spread the meat mixture in a gratin dish. Season the potatoes with a little nutmeg, and spread them over the meat. At this point the pie may be cooled, covered tightly with cling film and refrigerated for up to 2 days, or it can be frozen. If refrigerated, bring to room temperature before proceeding. If frozen, cook from frozen.

5 Dribble the top of the pie with a little skimmed milk. If the components of the pie are freshly made and piping hot, grill for 4–6 minutes until browned. If not, cook, uncovered, in the oven at 180°C, 350°F, Gas Mark 4 for 30–40 minutes (40–60 minutes if frozen) or until browned and bubbly. Serve at once.

Opposite: Braised Brisket (page 185) served with its sauce and Braised Red Cabbage and Apples (page 21) and Potato Pancakes (page 55)

MEXICAN SHEPHERD'S PIE

SERVES 4–6

❄

This is a lively, zesty, South-of-the-Border flavoured shepherd's pie topped with mashed potatoes.

1 aubergine, weighing about 10 oz (275 g), peeled and diced
½ teaspoon chilli powder
¼ teaspoon ground cinnamon
½ teaspoon ground cumin
½ teaspoon crushed dried chillies (or less, to taste)
1 teaspoon crumbled dried oregano
3–4 sundried tomatoes, chopped (use scissors)
1 large onion, finely chopped
2 carrots, peeled and finely chopped
1 red pepper, peeled (page 48), deseeded and chopped
1 garlic clove, crushed

1 pint (600 ml) stock
½ pint (300 ml) red wine
1 lb (450 g) extra-lean minced pork
4 fl oz (100 ml) passata
14 oz (400 g) can chopped tomatoes
salt and freshly ground pepper
TOPPING
3 lb (1.4 kg) baking potatoes
1–2 tablespoons fromage frais
salt and freshly ground pepper
a few pinches ground cumin
pinch of cayenne pepper
2 tablespoons skimmed milk
3 tablespoons freshly grated Parmesan cheese

1 Combine the aubergine, spices, oregano, sundried tomatoes, onion, carrots, pepper and garlic, ½ pint (300 ml) stock and the red wine in a heavy-bottomed saucepan. Simmer briskly until the vegetables are tender and the liquid absorbed. Add the pork. Cook, stirring to break up the lumps, until the pork loses its raw look.

2 Stir in the passata and chopped tomatoes, and season with salt and pepper. Simmer, uncovered, for 30 minutes, or until the mixture is thick and savoury. While the mixture cooks, prepare the potato topping (page 57), omitting the cheese, and seasoning with a few pinches of ground cumin and a pinch of cayenne pepper.

3 Spoon the pork mixture evenly into a gratin dish. Spread the freshly made potato topping over the meat. Sprinkle with the milk and cheese.

4 If the components of the pie are freshly made and piping hot, grill for 4–6 minutes or until browned. If not, cook, uncovered, in a preheated oven at 180°C, 350°F, Gas Mark 4 for 30–40 minutes (40–60 minutes if frozen) or until browned and bubbly. Serve at once.

MEAT PIE WITH PUMPKIN AND SWEDE TOPPING

SERVES 4–6

❄

This is a gorgeous variation of shepherd's pie with a smooth, tawny purée of baked swede and pumpkin standing in for the mashed potato. The whole dish can be prepared a day or so ahead of time. Prepare it up to the end of step 4 and store it in the refrigerator. To serve, sprinkle with cheese and milk, and bake in a preheated oven at 190°C, 375°F, Gas Mark 5 until browned and bubbling.

12 oz (350 g) swede, peeled
12 oz (350 g) pumpkin, peeled and cleaned of seeds and fibre (page 66)
2 tablespoons very low-fat fromage frais
4 tablespoons freshly grated Parmesan cheese
salt and freshly ground pepper
1 large onion, chopped
1 carrot, peeled and finely chopped
2 garlic cloves, crushed
13 fl oz (375 ml) stock

1 teaspoon each of paprika, mild chilli powder, ground cumin and dried oregano
12 oz (350 g) extra-lean beef or pork mince
pulp of two 8–12 oz (225–350 g) roasted, peeled aubergines (page 157)
two 14 oz (400 g) cans chopped tomatoes
¼ pint (150 ml) passata
1 tablespoon tomato purée
1–2 tablespoons skimmed milk

1 Cut the swede and pumpkin into pieces and steam for 15–20 minutes or until very tender. Alternatively, wrap in foil and roast in a preheated oven at 200°C, 400°F, Gas Mark 6 for about 1 hour. (If you choose to oven-roast – it gives a beautiful, deep caramelized flavour – roast the aubergine at the same time.) Cool the pumpkin and swede pieces, then put into a food processor with the fromage frais and 2 tablespoons grated Parmesan. Season with salt and pepper, and process until smooth.

2 While the vegetables are cooking, make the meat mixture. Combine the onion, carrot, garlic, ½ pint (300 ml) stock, the spices and oregano in a heavy-bottomed frying pan. Cover, bring to the boil, and boil for 5–7 minutes, then uncover and simmer briskly, stirring occasionally, until the carrots are very tender and the liquid almost gone.

3 Add the meat and cook, stirring to break up the lumps of meat, until it is cooked through. Chop the aubergine pulp or purée it in a blender or food processor. Stir it into the meat mixture with the canned tomatoes, passata, tomato purée and remaining stock. Season with salt and pepper and simmer, partially covered, for 25 minutes or until thick and savoury.

4 Put the meat mixture into a 10–12 inch (25–30 cm) round or square baking dish. Top with the pumpkin–swede purée. Sprinkle with the remaining (2 tablespoons) grated cheese and drizzle on the skimmed milk. Flash under the grill until the cheese is melted and the top is flecked with brown.

MOUSSAKA

SERVES 6

❄

Traditional moussaka usually oozes rivulets of oil. Eating a non-oily rendition of the Greek classic is a revelation – all that lovely creamy and meaty taste and texture, unpolluted by greasiness – what a pleasure! Moussaka is, essentially, another version of shepherd's pie. The seductively creamy topping makes it a particularly delicious one.

2 garlic cloves, crushed
2 large onions, finely chopped
½ teaspoon each of freshly grated nutmeg and
  ground cinnamon
½ pint (300 ml) stock
2 fl oz (50 ml) dry red wine
1 lb (450 g) extra-lean minced lamb
½ pint (300 ml) passata

14 oz (400 g) can chopped tomatoes
chopped pulp from two 8–12 oz (225–350 g)
  roasted, peeled aubergines (page 157)
salt and freshly ground pepper
3 aubergines, peeled in strips, sliced and grilled
  (page 4)
1 quantity Feta Cheese Sauce (page 94)
4 tablespoons freshly grated Parmesan cheese

1 Preheat the oven to 200°C, 400°F, Gas Mark 6.

2 Combine the garlic, onion, nutmeg, cinnamon, stock and wine in a heavy-bottomed frying pan. Cover, bring to the boil, and boil for 5 minutes, then uncover and simmer briskly until the onions are almost tender. Add the lamb and cook, stirring to break up the lumps, until the lamb is cooked through. Stir in the passata, tomatoes and roasted aubergine pulp. Season with salt and pepper, and simmer for about 15 minutes or until thickened and savoury.

3 Line a gratin dish or shallow baking dish with an overlapping layer of half the grilled aubergine slices. Spread the lamb mixture over the slices, and top with an overlapping layer of the remaining aubergine slices.

4 Spread the cheese sauce smoothly over the aubergine slices. (It will look quite attractive if the aubergine peeks through the sauce here and there.) Sprinkle evenly with the grated Parmesan. Bake, uncovered, in the oven for about 30 minutes or until browned and bubbly.

HAMBURGERS

Dry, flat, fast-food flaps of greasy meat in a flabby bun are not the only hamburgers in the world. Consider plump, juicy burgers, laced with wonderful seasonings, that leak delicious juices as you bite into them. The addition of aubergine, courgette, or apple guarantees juicy burgers, even though the mince is very lean. These burgers, plump and thick though they are, contain only a small amount of meat. They may be grilled or pan-braised.

PORK AND COURGETTE BURGERS WITH BRAISED CABBAGE

MAKES 4

✻

Apurée of courgettes, wine and seasonings add flavour and succulence to lean mince. After searing, the burgers are braised in red vermouth on a bed of cabbage. Serve with mashed potatoes.

4 oz (110 g) courgettes, sliced
1½ tablespoons red wine
1–2 pinches crushed dried chillies
2 tablespoons chopped fresh parsley
2 tablespoons chopped fresh basil
juice of ½ small lemon
1 garlic clove
8–10 tablespoons plain dry breadcrumbs
8 oz (225 g) extra-lean minced pork

salt and freshly ground pepper
1 egg white, lightly beaten
6 tablespoons plain flour
oil spray (page ix)
6–8 oz (175–225 g) white cabbage, cored and
    shredded
pinch of cayenne pepper
about 1 pint (600 ml) stock
about ½ pint (300 ml) red vermouth

1 Combine the courgettes, red wine, chillies, parsley, basil, lemon juice and garlic in a food processor or blender. Process to a rough purée. Transfer to a bowl and add 3 tablespoons breadcrumbs and the pork. Season with salt and pepper, and mix very well. Fry a tiny piece in a non-stick frying pan, taste and adjust the seasonings, if necessary.

2 Tip the egg white into a shallow soup plate or bowl. Spread the flour on a plate. Sprinkle several tablespoons of breadcrumbs on to another plate, and season lightly with salt and pepper. Form the pork mixture into four oval burgers. Dredge each in flour, then egg, and finally in breadcrumbs, pressing the crumbs on firmly. Place the burgers on a large plate.

3 Spray a heavy, non-stick frying pan with oil spray, and heat. When very hot, put in the burgers, and cook over moderately high heat for about 3 minutes or until crusty on the underside. Loosen and turn carefully and cook on the second side for 3 minutes or until crusty and brown. Remove to a plate. Stir the cabbage into the pan, add salt and a pinch of cayenne, and pour in some of the stock and vermouth. Return the burgers to the pan, and cook, partially covered, over medium heat for about 10 minutes, carefully turning the burgers occasionally. Add more stock and vermouth as the liquids threaten to boil away. Remove the cover completely and cook for 1–2 minutes more or until the cabbage is tender, and the pan juices are scant, thick and syrupy.

PORK AND APPLE BURGERS

MAKES 4

�֍

These elegant burgers are seared in a frying pan until browned and crusty, and then braised on a bed of onions.

4 oz (110 g) Granny Smith apples, peeled, cored
and roughly diced
1½ tablespoons medium dry cider
pinch of crushed dried chillies
2 tablespoons chopped fresh parsley
2 tablespoons shredded fresh mint
juice of ½ small lemon
2 garlic cloves
salt and freshly ground pepper

8–10 tablespoons plain dry breadcrumbs
8 oz (225 g) lean minced pork
1 egg white, lightly beaten
6 tablespoons plain flour
oil spray (page ix)
about 1 pint (600 ml) stock
about ½ pint (300 ml) medium dry cider
1–2 onions, thinly sliced
Pan-Fried Onions and Apples (page 47), to serve

1 Combine the apples, cider, chillies, parsley, mint, lemon juice and garlic in a food processor or blender. Process to a rough purée. Transfer the apple mixture to a bowl, season with salt and pepper, and add 3 tablespoons breadcrumbs and the pork. Mix very well. Fry a tiny piece in a non-stick frying pan, taste and adjust the seasonings if necessary.

2 Tip the egg white into a shallow soup plate. Spread the flour on a plate. Sprinkle several tablespoons of breadcrumbs on to another plate, and season lightly with salt and pepper. Form the pork mixture into four oval patties and dredge each on all sides with flour, then egg, and finally with the crumbs, pressing them in so that they adhere. Put the burgers on to a plate.

3 Mist a heavy frying pan with oil spray and heat. Put in the burgers and cook on a moderately high heat for 3 minutes or until crusty on the underside. Loosen and then turn carefully and cook for 2–3 minutes or until the second side is crusty and brown. Return the burgers to the plate. Pour ½ pint (300 ml) stock, ¼ pint (150 ml) cider and the onions into the pan. Cover, bring to the boil, and boil for 5–7 minutes, then uncover and return the burgers to the pan. Cook, partially covered, over medium heat, for about 10 minutes, occasionally turning the burgers. Add a little more stock and cider if the liquid threatens to cook away.

4 When done, the burgers will be beautifully glazed, the pan juices thick and syrupy, and the onions caramelized. Remove to a platter and cover loosely with foil to keep warm.

5 Pour about another 1 fl oz (25 ml) stock and cider into the pan, and simmer, scraping up all the browned bits, for a moment or so. Put the Pan-Fried Onions and Apples on to a serving platter and top with the burgers. Pour the onions and pan sauce over and serve at once.

BRAISED LAMB BURGERS

MAKES 4

❄

The pan-braised aubergine infusion enriches these deeply flavoured lamb burgers which are braised in red wine on a bed of shredded savoy cabbage.

about 1 pint (600 ml) stock
1 aubergine, weighing about 8 oz (225 g), peeled and diced
4 garlic cloves, crushed
4 sundried tomatoes, chopped (use scissors)
4 black olives in brine, drained and slivered off their stones
1 red onion, chopped
pinch of crushed dried chillies
about 1 pint (600 ml) dry red wine

salt and freshly ground pepper
4 tablespoons chopped fresh parsley
8–10 tablespoons plain dry breadcrumbs
4 tablespoons freshly grated Parmesan cheese
8 oz (225 g) extra-lean minced lamb
1 egg white, lightly beaten
6 tablespoons plain flour
oil spray (page ix)
4–5 oz (110–150 g) cored savoy cabbage, shredded

1 Combine half the stock with the aubergine, half the garlic, the sundried tomatoes, olives, onion, chillies and ½ pint (300 ml) wine in a frying pan. Cover and simmer briskly for 5–7 minutes, then uncover and simmer for 10 minutes, stirring occasionally, until the vegetables are very tender and the liquid absorbed. Season with salt and pepper, cool slightly, then purée in a food processor or blender.

2 Combine the parsley, breadcrumbs and the Parmesan and season lightly. Add 2 tablespoons of this mixture to the lamb and mix well. Mix in the aubergine purée. Fry a tiny piece in a non-stick frying pan, taste and adjust the seasonings. Form into four oval burgers.

3 Spread the remaining breadcrumb mixture on a plate, tip the egg white into a shallow bowl or soup plate, and spread the flour out on another plate.

4 Spray a non-stick frying pan with oil spray and heat. Dredge the lamb burgers on both sides in the flour, then the egg, and finally the crumbs, pressing the crumbs in so that they adhere. Cook the lamb burgers in the hot pan for 2–3 minutes on each side or until they are golden and crusty on both sides, then remove to a plate.

5 Put the cabbage and remaining garlic in the pan and pour in 4 fl oz (110 ml) wine and 4 fl oz (110 ml) stock. Bring to the boil, stirring with a wooden spoon to dislodge any browned bits in the pan. Reduce the heat and arrange the burgers on the cabbage. Simmer, partially covered, for about 10 minutes or until the burgers are done. Turn the burgers occasionally, and add a little more stock and wine as the liquid threatens to cook away. At the end, the juices should be thick and syrupy, the burgers a gorgeous winey purple, and the cabbage very tender.

SAUSAGES AND MEATBALLS

I am a great fan of sausages and meatballs, both in the cooking and the eating, but, obviously, in their low-fat incarnations. Under ordinary circumstances, very low-fat sausages and meatballs are dry as dust and hardly worth eating, but, as with the burgers and bolognese, roasted aubergine pulp or puréed pan-braised aubergine works miracles. I have a vast repertoire of low-fat sausage and meatball recipes; you might call me a maestro of meatballs, a sausage sage, a mince maniac. In fact, I firmly believe that there is a sausage or meatball for every occasion, whether a solitary snack, an informal family meal, an elegant dinner party, or a buffet for hordes of friends. The following collection encompasses a selection from that repertoire.

Most of the recipes can be used to make meatballs *or* sausages, although some are better one way or the other. If so, it is indicated in the title of the recipe. One pound (450 g) of mince will yield approximately 30 little meatballs or sausage patties.

TO MAKE MEATBALLS

1 Preheat the grill to its highest setting. Line the grill pan with foil, shiny side up. Put the rack in the pan, and spray lightly with oil spray (page ix).

2 Combine the recipe ingredients very well. Depending on the moisture content of the aubergine and the meat, the pulp of either one or two 8 oz (225 g) aubergines will be needed for each 1 lb (450 g) meat. The idea is to have as much of the aubergine as possible, while still allowing the mixture to hold together. Fry a tiny piece of the mixture in a non-stick frying pan, taste and adjust the seasonings.

3 Form the mixture into walnut-sized balls. (I think this size is best – the meatball is delicate, and several on a plate with sauce, garnishes and vegetable accompaniments look enchanting.) Space the meatballs on the oil-sprayed grill rack so that they are not touching each other, and grill with the rack in the upper position (close to the heat) for 3–4 minutes on each side. The idea is to cook them through, so that they are *just* done, and not dried out. They should be quite juicy. You will soon get the hang of cooking them for the right amount of time on your particular grill.

4 Line a platter or shallow baking dish with paper kitchen towels, and put the meatballs on them in one layer to blot up any rendered fat. (They most likely will not all fit, so put one layer of meatballs in the dish, cover with more paper towels, top with another layer of meatballs and so on.)

5 The cooked meatballs may be served at once, or refrigerated for later. To reheat, put some stock in a large frying pan or flameproof casserole to a depth of ½ inch (1 cm). Add the meatballs in one layer, cover, bring to a bare simmer, and simmer *very gently* for about 10 minutes or until heated through. If you plan to serve the meatballs with a sauce, simmer them gently in the sauce to reheat them. The meatballs may also be frozen, as they are, or in a tomato sauce.

TO MAKE SAUSAGES

In low-fat sausages, aubergine replaces the fat, and, instead of stuffing the mixture into animal intestine casings (not the easiest thing to do without the proper equipment), the mixture is formed into little patties or ovals. It is traditional in England to include rusk or breadcrumbs in the sausage mix so, in the following recipes that *do not* include breadcrumbs, 2–3 tablespoons plain dry breadcrumbs can be added if you prefer it that way. To make sausages, follow the directions for meatballs but form the mixture into plump patties, sausage shapes or ovals instead of little balls. Grill them as described for meatballs.

PORK–SAGE MEATBALLS OR SAUSAGES

⊙ ❄

Fresh sage is so much better than dried – it really pays to try to find it (many supermarkets sell it, or you might consider growing your own). If you can't find fresh, use ½ teaspoon dried rubbed sage, crumbled between your fingers. For a blameless breakfast 'fry-up', have these sausages with a poached egg, no-fat Sautéed Mushrooms (page 40) and a pile of oven-fried Chips (page 51).

1 lb (450 g) extra-lean minced pork
chopped pulp from one or two 8–12 oz (225–350g) roasted aubergines (page 157)
2 tablespoons plain dry breadcrumbs
1 tablespoon chopped fresh sage

½ teaspoon fresh thyme leaves, or a pinch of dried thyme
¼ teaspoon ground allspice
salt and freshly ground pepper
pinch of freshly grated nutmeg

Mix all the ingredients together, season with salt and pepper, form into sausages or meatballs, and grill as described on page 170.

PAPRIKA MEATBALLS

⊙ ❄

These would be perfect in the Sweet and Sour Cabbage Soup (page 110) or served with the Mushroom Paprikash (page 42).

1 lb (450 g) extra-lean minced beef
chopped pulp from one or two 8–12 oz (225–350 g) roasted aubergines (page 157)

juice of ½ lemon
1 tablespoon paprika
salt and freshly ground pepper

Mix all the ingredients together, season with salt and pepper, form into meatballs, and grill as described on page 170.

ITALIAN SAUSAGES OR MEATBALLS

⊙ ❄

My favourite sausage – I never tire of making it, eating it, and serving it to friends. Serve with pasta and a tomato sauce (pages 85–86); in crusty bread with a heap of Stir-Fried Peppers (page 50); sliced or crumbled on to pizza; or stuffed into a Calzone (page 200).

1 lb (450 g) extra-lean minced pork
chopped pulp from one or two 8–12 oz (225–
* 350 g) roasted aubergines (page 157)*
1 teaspoon fennel or anise seeds
¼ teaspoon crushed dried chillies

1–3 garlic cloves, crushed
4 tablespoons chopped fresh parsley
3 tablespoons dry red wine
salt and freshly ground pepper

Mix all the ingredients together, season with salt and pepper, form into sausages or meatballs, and grill as described on page 170.

GARLIC SAUSAGES OR MEATBALLS

⊙ ❄

The garlic is pronounced, but mild and mellow. These are lovely with one of the tomato sauces (pages 85–86), or – for an over-the-top version of sausages and mash – with the potato gratin on page 60.

1 lb (450 g) extra-lean minced pork
chopped pulp from one or two 8–12 oz (225–
* 350 g) roasted aubergines (page 157)*
6–8 garlic cloves, pan-braised (page 35) and
* thoroughly mashed*

1 bunch chives, snipped
2–3 tablespoons chopped fresh parsley
2–3 fl oz (60–75 ml) dry red wine
4–6 tablespoons freshly grated Parmesan cheese
salt and freshly ground pepper

Mix all the ingredients together, season with salt and pepper, form into sausages, or meatballs, and grill as described on page 170.

INDIAN SAUSAGE PATTIES

⊙ ❄

A low-fat version of shami kebab, these are delicious served with Mint and Coriander Raita (page 101), shredded cucumber, diced red onion and chutney.

1 lb (450 g) extra-lean minced lamb
8 spring onions, finely chopped
4 garlic cloves, crushed
1 inch (2.5 cm) piece of fresh root ginger, peeled
 and crushed
1 teaspoon ground cumin
½ teaspoon ground cardamom

¼ teaspoon cayenne pepper (or to taste)
6 tablespoons shredded fresh mint leaves
6 tablespoons chopped fresh coriander
chopped pulp from one or two 8–12 oz
 (225–350 g) roasted aubergines (page 157)
salt and freshly ground pepper

Mix all the ingredients together, form into sausages, and grill as described on page 170.

MORROCAN-STYLE MEATBALLS OR SAUSAGES

☙ ❄

These are perfect with the Simple Wheat Pilaf (page 121), or the Vegetable Stew (page 72).

1 lb (450 g) extra-lean minced lamb
chopped pulp from one or two 8–12 oz
 (225–350 g) roasted aubergines (page 157)
3 garlic cloves, crushed
4 tablespoons chopped fresh mint or parsley,
 or a mixture

1 tablespoon tomato purée
2 teaspoons ground cumin
1 teaspoon ground coriander
½ teaspoon cayenne pepper (or to taste)
salt and freshly ground pepper

Mix all the ingredients together, form into meatballs or sausages, and grill as described on page 170.

MEXICAN MEATBALLS OR SAUSAGES

☙ ❄

A bean stew or chilli would make a wonderful meal with these sausages nestling in their depths. Or serve in tortillas with Green Pea Spread (page 74) and a salsa.

1 lb (450 g) extra-lean minced pork
chopped pulp from one or two 8–12 oz
 (225–350 g) roasted aubergines (page 157)
2 spring onions, trimmed and chopped
4 tablespoons plain dry breadcrumbs
1 tablespoon chopped fresh mint or coriander

½ teaspoon each of ground cumin and
 coriander
1–2 pinches cayenne pepper
juice and grated zest of ½ lime
1 tablespoon tomato purée
salt and freshly ground pepper

Mix the ingredients together, form into meatballs or sausages and grill as described on page 170.

CABBAGE-WRAPPED SAUSAGES

MAKES 12

❄

When a sausage or meatball mixture is pan-braised in a savoy cabbage wrapper, the results are wonderfully savoury. Half of any of the meatball or sausage mixtures will work nicely given this treatment. Here, a pork and aubergine mixture fills the cabbage leaves.

1 savoy cabbage
5 oz (150 g) aubergine, peeled and diced
1 red onion, chopped
2 garlic cloves, crushed
4 sundried tomatoes, chopped (use scissors)
3 black olives in brine, drained and slivered off
  their stones

1 pint (600 ml) stock
1 pint (600 ml) dry red wine
8 oz (225 g) extra-lean minced pork
2 tablespoons soft plain breadcrumbs
salt and freshly ground pepper
3–4 tablespoons freshly grated Parmesan cheese
  (optional)

1 Bring some water to the boil in the bottom of a steamer. Remove any tough outer leaves from the cabbage, then carefully peel off 12 inner leaves. Set aside the heart of the cabbage. With a vegetable peeler or a sharp paring knife, pare down the tough central vein on each of the 12 leaves. Steam for 5–7 minutes or until the leaves are flexible. Drain well.

2 Meanwhile, combine the aubergine, onion, garlic, sundried tomatoes, olives, ½ pint (300 ml) stock and ½ pint (300 ml) red wine in a frying pan. Cover, and simmer briskly for 5–7 minutes.

3 Cut the cabbage heart into quarters, remove the core, and chop 3 oz (75 g). Uncover the aubergine, stir in the chopped cabbage, and simmer briskly until the vegetables are tender and the liquid absorbed. Cool slightly.

4 Put the cabbage-aubergine mixture into a food processor or blender and process until roughly chopped. Stir it into the pork, along with the breadcrumbs, and season with salt and pepper. Fry a tiny piece in a non-stick frying pan, taste and adjust the seasonings if necessary.

5 Film the frying pan in which the aubergine mixture cooked with a little stock. Spread out the cabbage leaves on the work surface. Put a generous spoonful of the pork mixture on each leaf, tuck in the ends, fold over the sides, and roll to form neat parcels. Place, seam-side down, in the frying pan. Pour in the remaining stock and wine, and bring to a simmer.

6 Clap on the cover, and simmer gently for 30–40 minutes or until the cabbage is very tender and the sausage cooked through. The pan juices will be greatly reduced and syrupy. If the juices cook down too much, before the parcels are done, add a little bit more wine and stock. (If you are not sure if the stuffing is cooked, carefully unwrap one parcel to check.) If you are using the cheese, sprinkle it evenly over the rolls, re-cover and stand for 3–5 minutes until it melts.

STUFFED MUSHROOMS

MAKES 12

❄

Any of the meatball or sausage mixtures can be formed into balls, grilled, and then set into grilled mushroom caps. The caps can be filled first with a puddle of tomato or pepper sauce, or a dollop of Boursin Léger, or left in its natural state, depending on your mood. And the meatball-filled mushrooms can be served as they are, or set on a vegetable purée or a tomato sauce (pages 85–86). Half a pound (225 g) of mince fills 12 medium mushrooms.

12 medium mushrooms (brown-caps or white)
1 aubergine, weighing about 8 oz (225 g), peeled and diced
2 garlic cloves, crushed
½ small onion, chopped
4 sundried tomatoes, chopped (use scissors)
4 black olives in brine, drained and slivered off their stones
4 fl oz (110 ml) dry red wine

4 fl oz (110 ml) stock
2–3 dashes teriyaki or soy sauce
salt and freshly ground pepper
oil spray (page ix)
8 oz (225 g) extra-lean minced pork
3 tablespoons freshly grated Parmesan cheese (optional)
4 tablespoons Boursin Léger or 4 tablespoons Basic Tomato Sauce, page 85 (optional)

1 Clean the mushrooms and remove the stems. Chop the stems.

2 Combine the mushroom stems, aubergine, garlic, onion, sundried tomatoes, olives, wine, stock and teriyaki in a frying pan. Cover and simmer briskly for 5–7 minutes, then uncover and simmer until the vegetables are very tender and the liquid absorbed. Season lightly with salt and pepper, cool slightly, then purée in a food processor or blender.

3 Preheat the grill. Line the grill pan with foil, shiny side up, and spray with oil spray. Arrange the mushrooms, open side down, in the tray and spray lightly. Grill for 1–2 minutes, then turn and grill for 1–2 minutes or until juices begin to collect in the mushroom caps, but they are still firm. Set aside and keep warm.

4 Put the grill rack in the grill pan and spray lightly with oil spray. Combine the pork with the aubergine mixture, and, if you like, the Parmesan and mix well. Fry a tiny piece in a non-stick frying pan, taste and adjust the seasonings. Form into 12 balls. Space them evenly on the grill rack, and grill for 4–5 minutes, then turn and grill for 3–4 minutes on the second side.

5 Meanwhile, put a teaspoon of Boursin Léger or tomato sauce (if using either of them), in each mushroom cap. When the meatballs are done, flash the mushrooms under the grill for a few seconds just to soften the Boursin or heat the tomato sauce. Place one meatball in each mushroom cap, and serve at once.

PATE

I started fiddling with low-fat versions of pâtés when a reader sent me a copy of her favourite pâté recipe along with a request to de-fat it. Actually, it wasn't that hard to do, and when I had a version that I was pleased with, my assistant and I cooked the original and the low-fat version side-by-side. The low-fat version won the taste test, hands down, so don't feel that a low-fat pâté is a compromised version of a richer reality. For an equally delicious and low-fat liver pâté, see page 74.

PATE WITH CHICKEN

MAKES ABOUT 12 SLICES

A most elegant pâté with a layer of brandy-marinated chicken breasts sandwiched between herbed minced pork and beef, this would look splendid on a buffet table, or as part of a very special picnic spread. (Arrange to keep it chilled up to serving time.) Serve chilled, in thin slices with Redcurrant and Vermouth Sauce (page 92).

1 skinless chicken breast fillet, trimmed and cut
*   into ½ inch (1 cm) wide strips*
4 fl oz (110 ml) brandy or cognac
½ teaspoon freshly grated nutmeg
salt and freshly ground pepper
2 garlic cloves, crushed
1 onion, finely chopped
¼ pint (150 ml) stock
12 oz (350 g) each of extra-lean minced pork
*   and beef*

chopped pulp from two 8–12 oz (225–350 g)
*   roasted aubergines (page 157)*
3 egg whites, lightly beaten
4 fl oz (110 ml) red wine
¼ teaspoon dried thyme
1 teaspoon dried tarragon
salt and freshly ground pepper
2 tablespoons chopped fresh parsley
a few bay leaves and fresh thyme sprigs

1 Toss the chicken strips with half the brandy, half the nutmeg and a little salt and pepper.

2 Sauté the garlic and onion in the stock until they are tender and the liquid almost gone. Cool slightly.

3 Preheat the oven to 180°C, 350°F, Gas Mark 4. Put the kettle on to boil.

4 Combine the onion mixture with all the remaining ingredients, including the remaining brandy and nutmeg, but not the chicken, bay leaves and thyme. Use your hands to mix thoroughly. Fry a tiny piece in a non-stick frying pan, taste and adjust the seasonings if necessary.

5 Spread half the mixture into a glass or non-stick 2 pint (1.1 litre) loaf tin and press it down. Lay the chicken strips evenly on top in one layer, then cover with the remaining meat mixture. Press down and top with bay leaves and thyme. Cover with foil so that it is well sealed but the foil does not touch the top of the pâté.

6 Put the loaf tin in a shallow baking dish, put in the oven, and pour boiling water into the baking dish to come halfway up the sides of the loaf tin.

7 Bake in the oven for 45 minutes, then uncover and bake for 45–60 minutes more or until the juices run clear. Remove from the oven, and put the loaf tin on a wire rack to cool for a few minutes. Carefully pour the accumulated juices into a jug or bowl through a sieve and refrigerate (see the box below for what to do with them). Scrape off any coagulated matter from the pâté and discard. Cover the pâté with cling film and place a weight on top (a cling-film-wrapped brick or canned goods). Refrigerate the pâté (with the weights in place) overnight. Serve in thin slices with Redcurrant and Vermouth Sauce (page 92).

SAVE THE JUICES

The rendered juices from Pâté with Chicken are delicious and useful, and should never be discarded. As the juices cool, the fat rises to the top. Scrape it off and discard. When the juices are thoroughly chilled, they jell. This savoury jelly is wonderful served alongside the pâté. Otherwise, freeze the de-fatted juices, and use them at a later time for roasting chunks of root vegetables or potatoes (page 58). The spicy, meaty juices permeate the tender, starchy roots – believe me, it is a culinary experience to cherish.

BEEF STEWS

Braising steak (beef chuck) is lean, yet it braises to melting tenderness. To prepare it, cut it into cubes, trimming away any fat as you do so, then braise it in stock and/or wine with vegetables and herbs, to make all manner of sustaining and aromatic beef stews. These stews improve in flavour if they are made a day ahead of time, cooled, refrigerated and then gently reheated the next day. After chilling, any rendered fat will rise to the surface and harden, and so can easily be skimmed away. But today's beef chuck seems to be so lean that the fat in the fibres of the meat is far from excessive. If you want to cook and serve the stew on the day, do not hesitate to do so.

BEEF, MUSHROOM AND CARAMELIZED ONION STEW

MAKES 2 PINTS (1.1 LITRES) SERVES 4
❄

The onions are gently sautéed in stock with a bit of sugar (along with the olives, garlic and sundried tomatoes that flavour the stew), so that they caramelize as they reach melting, amber tenderness. Serve the stew with mashed potatoes, rice or couscous, or use as a dark, rich winy filling for a meat pie in a bread case (page 199).

2 large onions, chopped
2 garlic cloves, crushed
3 sundried tomatoes, chopped (use scissors)
19 fl oz (550 ml) stock
1 tablespoon caster sugar
7 fl oz (200 ml) dry red wine

1½ lb (700 g) well-trimmed beef chuck (braising steak), cut into cubes
1 tablespoon tomato purée
1 lb (450 g) mushrooms, cut into quarters or eighths, depending on size
1–2 dashes teriyaki sauce

1 Preheat the oven to 180°C, 350°F, Gas Mark 4.

2 Combine the onions, garlic, sundried tomatoes, 10 fl oz (300 ml) stock and the sugar in a shallow flameproof casserole. Cover, bring to the boil, and boil for 5–7 minutes, then uncover and simmer briskly until the onions are tender and turning amber, and the liquid has greatly reduced and turned syrupy. Stir in 5 fl oz (150 ml) red wine and simmer until it has cooked down. Add the meat and cook, stirring, until it has lost its raw look. Stir in the tomato purée and 5 fl oz (150 ml) of the remaining stock. Cover tightly and cook in the oven for 1 hour.

3 Meanwhile, simmer the mushrooms in the remaining wine and stock, and the teriyaki sauce until tender. After the beef has simmered for 1 hour, stir in the mushrooms and simmer for 30–60 minutes more or until the beef is fork-tender. Reduce the oven temperature as needed to keep the stew at a gentle simmer.

BEEF GOULASH

MAKES 2 PINTS (1.1 LITRES) SERVES 4
❄

Not quite a real goulash (a real one would be soupier), this stew of tender beef bathed in a rosy sauce of several kinds of peppers (red and yellow capsicums and ground paprika) gives a taste of Hungary without the traditional lard.

3 large onions, coarsely chopped
1½ tablespoons Hungarian paprika
3–4 sundried tomatoes, chopped (use scissors)
4 large peppers (a mixture of yellow and red, peeled (page 48), deseeded and coarsely chopped

3 garlic cloves, crushed
¾ pint (450 ml) stock
1½ lb (700 g) well- trimmed beef chuck (braising steak), cut into 1 inch (2.5 cm) cubes
1½ tablespoons tomato purée
salt and freshly ground pepper

1 Preheat the oven to 180°C, 350°F, Gas Mark 4.

2 Combine the onions, paprika, sundried tomatoes, peppers, garlic and ½ pint (300 ml) stock in a flameproof casserole. Cover and bring to the boil, then reduce the heat and simmer briskly for 7–10 minutes. Uncover, reduce the heat, and continue simmering until the liquid is almost gone and the vegetables are very tender, stirring occasionally.

3 Add the beef, stir and cook over a low heat until it loses its redness. Stir in the tomato purée and the remaining stock, and season with salt and pepper. Bring to the boil, cover, and cook in the oven for 1½–2 hours or until the meat is very tender and the sauce is thick and savoury. Reduce the oven temperature as needed to keep the stew at a gentle simmer. Serve the goulash in shallow soup plates, with mashed or roasted potatoes.

VARIATION *Beef Chilli* Turn the goulash into a chilli by omitting the paprika and substituting this seasoning mix: 1 tablespoon dried oregano (crumbled); 1 teaspoon each of ground cumin, ground coriander and paprika; pinch or two of crushed dried chillies; ½ teaspoon mild chilli powder; 1 tablespoon brown sugar and 1 chopped chilli (if liked). Serve with garnishes as described for Chilli with Vegetables (page 160).

Opposite, clockwise from top right: Rice Fritters (page 117), Fillet Steak on a Bed of Onions with Red Pepper Sauce (page 187), Mushrooms Paprikash (page 42)

Opposite, clockwise from top: Orange Watercress Salad (page 39), Wild Rice Pilaf with Dried Cherries (page 118), Roasted Spiced Pork Tenderloin (page 191), Sweetcorn and Mushroom Saute (page 28)

BEEF STEW WITH ROSEMARY

MAKES 2 PINTS (1.1 LITRES); SERVES 4

✻

The garlic and rosemary give this beef stew an exquisite fragrance. If you wish, add one large all-purpose potato, peeled and cubed, during the last 20–30 minutes of braising.

3–4 sundried tomatoes, chopped
3 black olives, in brine, drained and slivered off
*   their stones*
3 onions, finely chopped
¾ pint (450 ml) stock
½ pint (300 ml) red wine
1½ lb (700 g) well-trimmed beef chuck (braising
*   steak), cut into 1 inch (2.5 cm) cubes*

4 garlic cloves, peeled
1½ tablespoons fresh rosemary leaves
1 tablespoon tomato purée
salt and freshly ground pepper
2–3 tablespoons chopped fresh parsley

1 Preheat the oven to 180°C, 350°F, Gas Mark 4.

2 Combine the sundried tomatoes, olives, onions, ½ pint (300 ml) stock and ¼ pint (150 ml) wine in a flameproof casserole and bring to the boil. Cover and simmer briskly for 10 minutes, then uncover, reduce the heat and simmer until the onions are tender and the liquid almost gone.

3 Add the beef, garlic and rosemary, stir, and cook until the beef has lost its redness. Stir in the tomato purée, season with salt and pepper, and stir in the remaining stock and wine. Cover tightly and cook in the oven for 1½–2 hours or until the meat is fork-tender. Reduce the oven temperature as needed to keep the stew at a gentle simmer. Sprinkle with parsley and serve.

SKIRT STEAK

Red meat lovers who wish to maintain a low-fat lifestyle should look into skirt steak, one of the best-kept secrets in the country. I say 'secret', because most supermarkets do not stock skirt, and some younger butchers seem never to have heard of it. Most butchers, however, *will* have it, but not in great quantity, so you might want to get into the habit of asking your local butcher to put some aside for you each week.

There are two cuts of skirt (both are delicious and useful): goose skirt (sometimes called flank skirt) and rump skirt (not rump *steak*; rump *steak* and rump *skirt* are two different things). Goose (flank) skirt is a neat, rather flat, paddle-shaped steak. A whole goose skirt weighs 12 oz–1 lb (350–450 g). Rump skirt is thicker, longer and not as neatly shaped. Both are very lean and superbly flavourful. The goose (flank) skirt, and the rump skirt are from the flank of the animal, next to the brisket and sirloin. Rump skirt is the tail end of the sirloin; goose skirt is just behind the sirloin. They both just need to be trimmed of any bits of surrounding fat. The butcher can do most of the trimming for you, or it is easily done at home with a small, sharp knife.

To confuse you even more, there is a strip of meat that comes from the diaphragm that is sometimes called skirt too. Cheap and tough, it is occasionally sold during the barbecue season. It has to be specially tenderized, and is not the same skirt as goose (flank) skirt and rump skirt.

Is it worth all this palaver? Yes, indeed. Both goose skirt and rump skirt are the leanest, most flavourful and most economical cuts of beef you could ever hope to find. Because of its neat shape and convenient size, goose (flank) skirt is exceptionally useful. One goose skirt will feed at *least* four people. It can be grilled, pan-fried or stir-fried.

BASIC GOOSE (FLANK) SKIRT TECHNIQUES

Here are some general guidelines, followed by specific recipes.

Grilling

1 Preheat the grill to its highest setting. Line the grill pan with foil, shiny side up. Place the grill rack in the grill pan.

2 Season the goose skirt on both sides with salt and freshly ground pepper. Place on the grill rack and position 3 inches (7.5 cm) from the heat. Grill for 5–7 minutes (depending on thickness, and your preference) on each side. (It tastes best and most tender when it is *not* well done. Poke it with your finger. When it feels firm but springy, it is medium rare. If it feels mushy, it is very rare. If it feels very firm, it is well done.) Let rest for 5 minutes for the juices to redistribute. With a sharp carving knife, slice the steak thinly, on the diagonal, across the grain. Leftover slices of meat make the ultimate steak sandwich. Saturate a slice of bread with any meat juices. Spread on some roasted garlic purée (page 42), should you have any on hand. Lay on the meat, spread another slice of bread with mustard and put it on top. Press down.

Pan-frying

1 Heat a heavy-bottomed non-stick frying pan until hot. Season a goose skirt steak with salt and pepper. Sear it on both sides in the hot pan (use tongs to turn it). Once seared, reduce the heat a little and cook for 5–7 minutes on each side. It is medium rare when it feels firm but springy. Remove to a platter, cover loosely with foil, and let rest for 5 minutes.

2 A quick sauce can be prepared in the same pan while the meat is resting: sauté mushrooms or onions in the pan with some stock or wine, scraping up any browned bits from the bottom of the pan with a wooden spoon. Pour in more stock and wine, or some chopped tomatoes or passata. Return the meat and cook for a few minutes. To serve, slice the steak thinly on the diagonal, across the grain.

NOTE

You can pan-*grill* your goose skirt, if you have a non-stick ridged frying pan. Simply heat the ridged pan on the hob, then cook your steak in the pan, turning it with tongs. Goose skirt grilled in a ridged pan has an enticing, smoky, barbecued taste. You'll need a good extractor fan over your cooker, or the kitchen may get a bit smoke-filled.

Braising

Skirt steak is fibrous, so a braised goose skirt is a bit stringy, but not so stringy that it is unpleasant to eat. Braised goose skirt makes an easy, economical and tasty everyday family meal.

1 Sear the goose skirt on both sides in a heavy-bottomed non-stick frying pan, then put it into a baking dish.

2 Sauté some vegetables (whatever you like – onions and garlic, chopped carrots and celery, sliced mushrooms) in the pan with some stock, or stock and wine, scraping up the browned bits with your wooden spoon. Scrape this mixture over the meat, add some wine or stock, and braise, tightly covered, in the oven for 1½–1¾ hours at 180°C, 350°F, gas 4 or until meltingly tender. Slice on the diagonal, across the grain, and serve with the vegetables and pan juices.

Stir-frying

1 Cut the goose skirt down the centre, lengthways, into two equal-sized pieces. With a very sharp carving knife, carve each piece of steak on the diagonal, crosswise (across the grain), into slices as thin as you can manage.

2 Whisk together 2 tablespoons soy or teriyaki sauce, 1 tablespoon dry sherry and 1 tablespoon cornflour. Toss this mixture with the beef slices.

3 Heat a non-stick wok or frying pan. Pour in 2 fl oz (50 ml) stock. When it boils furiously, add the meat. Stir and cook with two wooden spoons, using the spoons to pull apart the meat strips as they cook. When the strips have lost their red, raw look, scoop them on to a plate.

4 Add 4 fl oz (110 ml) stock to the wok with some finely chopped fresh ginger and garlic. Add whatever vegetable you like: cauliflower, sliced peeled broccoli stalks, mangetout, sliced mushrooms. Cook and stir until tender and surrounded by a thick but scant sauce. Return the beef and its juices. Cook and stir for another minute or so. Serve with rice.

CHINESE BEEF WITH MUSHROOMS

MAKES 1½ PINTS (900 ML); SERVES 3–4

❋

Goose-skirt is the perfect cut for Chinese beef and vegetable stir-fries. The sesame oil spray (page ix) is for flavour, as is the preliminary marinating time.

1 oz (25 g) dried shiitake mushrooms
1 pint (600 ml) hot water
1 lb (450 g) goose (flank) skirt steak, very well trimmed
2 tablespoons teriyaki sauce
4 tablespoons dry sherry
1 tablespoon cornflour

sesame oil spray (page ix)
about 4 fl oz (110 ml) stock
4 oz (110 g) button mushrooms, quartered
1 bunch (about 10) thin spring onions, trimmed and cut into 1½ inch (4 cm) pieces
salt (optional)
chopped fresh parsley and coriander, to garnish

1 Place the dried mushrooms in a bowl. Pour on the hot water and leave to soak for 30–60 minutes. Lift the mushrooms out of the liquid, and strain the liquid through a sieve lined with a double layer of coffee filters or muslin, reserving the liquid. Rinse the mushrooms under cold running water, and squeeze dry. Trim off and discard the stems. Cut each mushroom in half.

2 With a very sharp carving knife, cut the skirt steak lengthways in two. Slice each piece crossways, on the diagonal, against the grain, into slices that are as thin as you can manage. Put the slices in a large bowl.

3 Whisk together the teriyaki, 2 tablespoons sherry and the cornflour until the cornflour has dissolved. Pour over the beef and toss together with two wooden spoons until the strips are well coated. Cover and set aside at room temperature for 1 hour.

4 Heat a large non-stick wok or frying pan, and spray with sesame oil spray. Pour in 2 fl oz (50 ml) stock. When it boils furiously, tip in the meat. Cook for 2 minutes, constantly turning the meat with two wooden spoons. Pull the strips of meat apart as they cook. When they have lost their red raw look, scoop on to a platter, cover loosely with foil, and set aside.

5 Immediately pour another 2 fl oz (50 ml) stock, 2 fl oz (50 ml) of the mushroom soaking liquid and the remaining sherry into the wok. Tip in the Chinese mushrooms and the button mushrooms, stir and cook over high heat until the mushrooms are surrounded by a scant, thick sauce. Stir in the spring onions and cook for another 30–40 seconds.

6 Return the beef to the wok, along with any meat juices that have accumulated. Season with a little salt, if necessary. Stir together to mingle and heat through for about 1 minute, then heap on to a platter and sprinkle with herbs. Serve at once with rice.

GRILLED MARINATED SKIRT

Marinate skirt steak in a mixture of garlic, ginger, onions and soy sauce for at least 24 hours before grilling, for one of the most delicious pieces of meat you have ever put into your mouth. The meat can marinate for up to three days before grilling; the longer the marinating period, the deeper and more spectacular the flavour. After three days of marinating, the meat will stand up and boogie when you open the fridge door! (A pork tenderloin is delicious marinated in this mixture and then roasted – see page 191 for roasting instructions.)

12 oz –1 lb (350–450 g) goose (flank) skirt steak,
    or 1 lb (450 g) rump skirt
1 inch (2.5 cm) piece fresh root ginger, peeled
    and crushed
½ bulb of garlic, cloves separated, peeled and
    crushed (or fewer cloves, to taste)

1 bunch of spring onions, trimmed and sliced
    (green and white parts)
4 oz (110 g) sugar
8 fl oz (225 ml) water
4 fl oz (110 ml) soy sauce

1 Put the goose skirt in a shallow glass baking dish.

2 Add the ginger, garlic and spring onions to the meat. Combine the sugar, water and soy sauce, and pour over the meat. Add a little more water, if necessary, to barely cover the meat. Cover and leave in the refrigerator to marinate for at least 24 hours, turning the meat with tongs occasionally.

3 Drain the meat, reserving the marinade, and cook in a ridged grill pan on the hob, under the grill, or on a charcoal barbecue, for 6–10 minutes on each side so that it remains pink inside. As it cooks, brush it occasionally with the marinade. To serve, slice thinly against the grain.

BEEF BRISKET

If you talk to your local butcher about skirt steak, talk to him about brisket as well. Brisket is another lean, deeply flavoured cut. There is no better piece of meat for long, slow braising, and it makes a splendid roasted joint for Sunday lunch, or for a celebration meal. Although the meat is lean (not too fatty *within* the meat fibres), it has a thick *covering* of fat, and this must be completely trimmed away. The butcher can do it for you (if you can convince him that you really want all of the fat removed) but you will probably need to do a bit more fat trimming yourself when you get the meat home.

The leaner part of the brisket is called the point end (because it ends in a point), and the fattier back end is called the flank end. Briskets are often sold rolled, with most of the covering fat still on, and sometimes with the bone in, as well. So ask for the point end brisket, flat (unrolled), boned, and trimmed of fat. It will cost more than the bone-in, fat-on meat, but you will have no waste. The end product will be a long, lean, flattish piece of meat.

Cook the boneless unrolled (flat) trimmed brisket by browning it on each side, then slow-braising it in the oven with vegetables, wine and stock until it is melt-in-the-mouth tender. The meat produces copious juices which, puréed with the braising vegetables, make a rich, luscious natural gravy. It is very convenient to braise the meat the day before you plan to serve it, so that the meal, on the next day, is effortless. Also, the meat is easier to slice after it has been well chilled. Four to five pounds (1.8–2.3 kg) of trimmed point end brisket will serve six to eight people. To serve more, buy a larger piece of point end, but follow the recipe as written – there is no need to increase the other ingredients.

BRAISED BRISKET

SERVES 6–8

❊

The perfect Sunday lunch, served with an array of vegetables, and Potato Pancakes (page 55) or a puréed root vegetable gratin (page 64). It can be made the day before (or even several days or weeks before; it freezes well). The gravy is rich and deeply flavoured, and the meat so buttery tender that you could eat it with a spoon.

5 lb (2.3 kg) boned, unrolled, point end of
   brisket, trimmed of all fat
8 fl oz (225 ml) stock
2 large onions, halved and sliced into thin half
   moons
4 fl oz (110 ml) red wine
2 fl oz (50 ml) brandy

4 sundried tomatoes, chopped (use scissors)
2 fl oz (50 ml) tomato purée
salt and freshly ground pepper
4 large garlic cloves
2 large carrots, peeled and sliced
1 celery stalk with leaves, de-strung and sliced

1 Preheat the oven to 180°C, 350°F, Gas Mark 4.

2 In a large non-stick frying pan, sear the brisket on both sides, then put it on a platter and cover loosely with foil to keep warm. (It may be too large for your pan, in which case simply brown the piece in sections, letting the excess overlap the edge of the pan, then repositioning it.)

3 Pour any fat drippings out of the frying pan and blot the pan with paper towels, but do not wipe off the browned bits. Pour 4 fl oz (110 ml) stock into the frying pan. Add the onions, cover and boil for 4–5 minutes, then uncover, turn down the heat and cook gently until the onion is browned and almost tender. Pour in the wine and brandy, and stir in the sundried tomatoes. Boil, scraping the pan with a wooden spoon to release all the browned bits, until the liquid has almost cooked away. Stir in the tomato purée, and season with a little salt and pepper. Scrape the mixture into a 9 × 13 × 2 inch (23 × 33 × 5 cm) baking tin. Pour the remaining stock over the onion.

4 Season the meat on both sides with salt and pepper. Place the meat on the onion, and pour in any meat juices that have accumulated on the platter. Tuck the garlic, carrot and celery slices around the meat. Cover tightly with heavy-duty foil, shiny side down, so that the dish is well sealed but the foil does not touch the meat.

5 Cook in the oven for 1 hour, then reduce the oven temperature to 120°C, 250°F, Gas Mark ½ and bake for an additional 2–2½ hours, or until the meat is very tender. Adjust the oven temperature as necessary so the contents of the pan simmer very gently.

6 When tender, remove the meat to a platter, cover to prevent it drying out, and leave to cool. Discard the celery. Pour the pan juices and remaining vegetables into a jug, add any juices that have accumulated under the meat, cool and refrigerate. When the meat has cooled, wrap well in cling film and refrigerate. It can remain in the fridge for a day or two.

7 Skim any fat from the juices in the jug. Purée the vegetables and de-fatted juices in a blender, then rub the purée through a sieve.

8 With a sharp carving knife, slice the meat thinly against the grain (starting at the 'point' end), and arrange in a baking dish. Pour and spread some of the puréed sauce over the slices. Cover and refrigerate until serving time (or freeze). To serve, reheat, covered, in the oven at 170°C, 325°F, Gas Mark 3 for 35–40 minutes. Reheat the remaining puréed sauce in a saucepan and serve in a gravy boat.

STEAK

A lean pork or beef steak makes an elegant, quick meal. Try a buttery tender fillet steak with a bravura sauce (below) or a boneless pork loin steak, split, filled and grilled.

FILLET STEAK ON A BED OF ONIONS WITH RED PEPPER SAUCE

SERVES 4

Fillet steak makes a luxurious low-fat meal. The sauce and onion marmalade can be prepared several days ahead of time; the meat itself cooks in less than 5 minutes.

4 fillet steaks, each about ½ inch (1 cm) thick
salt and freshly ground pepper
oil spray (page ix)
1 bunch spring onions, thinly sliced

4 tablespoons chopped fresh parsley
4 fl oz (110 ml) dry red wine
1 recipe Red Pepper Sauce (page 87)
1 recipe Onion Marmalade (page 46), warmed

1 Trim the steaks of all fat, trim them into neat rounds, and slice horizontally in two.

2 Spread a sheet of greaseproof paper on your work surface. Sprinkle with freshly ground pepper. Place the steaks on the paper. Grind pepper on the steaks and press into the meat.

3 Mist a non-stick frying pan with oil spray and heat. Place the meat in the pan so that the pieces are not touching. (Cook in batches, if necessary.) Cook over high heat for 1–2 minutes on each side. The steaks will be brown on the outside and juicy and pink within. Season with salt, transfer to a platter, cover loosely with foil and keep warm.

4 Tip the spring onions and parsley into the frying pan and pour in the wine. Boil, stirring and scraping the browned bits, until almost all the liquid is gone. Reduce the heat, stir in the Red Pepper Sauce and juices that have collected under the meat. Stir and cook for a few minutes.

5 Spread the Onion Marmalade out on a warm platter. Overlap the steaks on top. Pour a ribbon of sauce down the length of the meat. Serve with the rest of the sauce in a gravy boat.

VARIATION *Fillet Steak with Red Wine and Mustard Sauce* Prepare the steak up to the end of step 3. Put 1 bunch of trimmed, thinly sliced spring onions into the frying pan with ½ teaspoon crumbled dried thyme and ½ pint (300 ml) dry red wine. Simmer for 5 minutes or until reduced by one quarter. Whisk in 4 tablespoons Dijon mustard, and simmer for 5 minutes, stirring frequently. Return the meat to the pan and simmer gently for 1–2 minutes.

PORK STEAKS STUFFED WITH ONIONS AND APPLES

MAKES 4

Boneless pork steaks cut off the loin are remarkably lean; they just need to be trimmed of a thin surrounding rim of fat. Because they are so lean, they cook in no time at all – long cooking will only make them tough. 'Butterfly' them so that each one opens like a hinged book, then fill with a savoury mixture, coat them with crumbs and grill. If you have time, refrigerate them first for about 30 minutes to help the coating adhere, but if time is a problem, just slam them under the grill and hope for the best. Be careful as you turn them, and there should be no problem. As they grill, they puff up slightly, and the crumbs form a golden crunchy crust. A beautiful sight, and – if you are careful not to overcook them – a juicy delight to eat.

oil spray (page ix)
4 boneless pork loin steaks, ½–¾ inch (1–2 cm) thick, trimmed of all fat
salt and freshly ground pepper
6 tablespoons plain flour

2 egg whites, lightly beaten
6–8 tablespoons plain breadcrumbs
3–4 tablespoons freshly grated Parmesan cheese
Pan-Fried Onions and Apples (page 47)
watercress, to garnish

1 Preheat the grill to its highest setting. Line the grill pan with foil, shiny side up. Place the rack in the pan. Mist with oil spray.

2 To 'butterfly' the pork steaks, place them flat on the work surface. Put your palm firmly on a steak. With a very sharp knife, carefully slice the steak almost through horizontally so that it opens like a book. Sprinkle the inside with salt and pepper. Repeat with the remaining steaks.

3 Put the flour on a plate. Put the egg white into a shallow bowl. Combine the breadcrumbs and Parmesan on another plate and season with pepper.

4 Open each steak and fill with a spoonful of the onion and apple mixture. Close up the steak and press the edges together. Dredge each filled steak in the flour, coating each side and the edges well, then dip both sides and the edges into the egg white, then dredge well with the crumb mixture, making sure that the sides and edges are well coated. Have a plate ready so that as each steak is ready, it can go on the plate. (If you have time, refrigerate the steaks for 30–60 minutes, but this is not necessary if time is short.)

5 Place the steaks on the grill rack, and position the pan so the meat is 5 inches (12.5 cm) from the heat. Grill for 2–3 minutes on each side, until browned and crusty. Serve at once, garnished with watercress. Serve with the remaining pan-braised onions and apples, and mashed potatoes.

PORK STEAKS STUFFED WITH MUSHROOMS

MAKES 4

A sliver of mozzarella or a dollop of Boursin Léger may be slipped inside the steaks as well as the mushrooms, so you have the pleasure of the melted cheese oozing out when you cut into the crusty pork.

oil spray (page ix)
4 boneless pork loin steaks, ½–¾ inch (1–2 cm)
   thick, trimmed of all fat and 'butterflied'
   (page 188)
2 teaspoons Dijon mustard

6 tablespoons plain flour
6–8 tablespoons plain breadcrumbs
3–4 tablespoons freshly grated Parmesan cheese
2 egg whites
¾ pint (450 ml) Red Wine Mushrooms (below)

1 Preheat the grill to its highest setting. Line the grill pan with foil, shiny side up. Place the rack in the pan, and mist with oil spray.

2 Sprinkle the inside of each steak with salt and pepper, and spread on ¼ teaspoon mustard.

3 Spread the flour on a plate. Combine the breadcrumbs and Parmesan on another plate, and season with freshly ground pepper. Put the egg whites in a shallow bowl with 1 teaspoon Dijon mustard, and beat lightly together with a fork.

4 Open each steak and fill with a tablespoon of the mushrooms. Close up the steaks and press the edges together. Dredge each filled steak in the flour, coating each side and the edges well, then dip both sides and the edges into the egg white, then dredge well in the crumb mixture, making sure that the sides and edges are well coated. Place each coated steak on a plate as soon as it is ready. (If you have time, refrigerate the steaks for 30–60 minutes.)

5 Place the steaks on the grill rack and position the pan so the meat is about 5 inches (12.5 cm) from the heat. Grill for 3 minutes on each side or until browned and crusty. Serve at once, with the remaining mushrooms.

RED WINE MUSHROOMS

MAKES ¾ PINT (450 ML)

2 garlic cloves, crushed
5 sundried tomatoes, chopped (use scissors)
4 black olives in brine, drained and slivered off
   their stones
pinch of crushed dried chillies

dash of teriyaki or soy sauce
6 fl oz (175 ml) stock
4 fl oz (110 ml) dry red wine
1 lb (450 g) button mushrooms, sliced

Combine the garlic, sundried tomatoes, olives, chillies, teriyaki, 4 fl oz (110 ml) stock and all the wine in a saucepan. Simmer briskly until the liquid has reduced to about 2 tablespoons. Add the mushrooms and remaining stock, and simmer, stirring occasionally, until the mushrooms are tender, and the liquid almost gone.

PORK STEAKS STUFFED WITH CHEESE

MAKES 4

Be sure that the egg and crumbs coat the pork all around the edges, so that the cheese does not ooze out before time. A fresh sage leaf is a nice addition, but the simplicity of the cheese alone has a lot to recommend it.

oil spray (page ix)
4 boneless pork loin steaks, ½–¾ inch (1–2 cm)
*   thick, trimmed of all fat and 'butterflied'*
*   (page 188)*
salt and freshly ground pepper
6 tablespoons plain flour
6–8 tablespoons plain breadcrumbs

3–4 tablespoons freshly grated Parmesan cheese
2 egg whites, lightly beaten
four ¼ inch (0.5 cm) thick slices mozzarella
*   cheese, each weighing about ¼–½ oz*
*   (7–15 g)*
4 fresh sage leaves (optional)

1 Preheat the grill to its highest setting. Line the grill pan with foil, shiny side up. Place the grill rack in the grill pan and mist with oil spray. Sprinkle the inside of each pork steak with salt and pepper.

2 Spread the flour on a plate. Combine the breadcrumbs and Parmesan on another plate, and season with freshly ground pepper. Put the egg whites in a shallow bowl.

3 Trim the mozzarella slices so they fit into the butterflied steaks. Open each steak and put a slice of cheese and a sage leaf, if using, inside. Close up the steaks and press the edges together.

4 Dredge each filled steak in the flour, coating the sides and the edges well. Dip both sides and the edges into the egg white, then dredge well in the crumb mixture. Place each coated steak on a plate as soon as it is ready. (If you have time, refrigerate the steaks for 30–60 minutes, but this is not necessary if time is short.)

5 Place the steaks on the grill rack and position the pan so the meat is about 5 inches (12.5 cm) from the heat. Grill for 3 minutes on each side or until browned and crusty. Serve at once.

PORK ROAST

Pork tenderloin makes a juicy, *quick*, very low-fat roast. The meat roasts perfectly in just 30 minutes or less in a very hot oven. One tenderloin will feed three or four people (depending on what you serve with it). Because of their size, it is easy to cook two or three tenderloins at once, should you want to feed more people. Just position them on the rack so that they are well spaced (not touching each other). A marinade or basting sauce will give the delicate pork plenty of pizzazz – the meat can marinate for at least 24 hours if you wish. Roast the meat until it is just cooked through, but still juicy. The pork is delicious both hot and cold. Serve the sliced roast with rice, couscous or bulghur, and an array of interesting vegetables.

ROASTED SPICED PORK TENDERLOIN

This marinade (it's actually more of a spice rub) is zippy; the longer the meat marinates, the zippier will be the finished roast. And consider trying the powerful marinade on page 184 with the tenderloin, and leave to marinate for 2–3 days before roasting. It will knock your socks off.

3 garlic cloves, crushed
½ inch (1 cm) piece fresh root ginger, peeled and crushed
4 spring onions, trimmed and chopped
generous pinch each of ground cumin and cayenne pepper

pinch of ground coriander
½ tablespoon teriyaki or soy sauce
juice of ½ lemon
1 teaspoon mild runny honey
salt and freshly ground pepper
1 pork tenderloin, trimmed of all fat

1 Roughly purée all the ingredients, except the pork, in a blender. Season with salt and pepper. Rub the mixture all over the pork. Put the pork and the mixture in a plastic bag and seal. Marinate for at least 4 hours (or overnight), turning the bag occasionally.

2 Preheat the oven to 240°C, 475°C, Gas Mark 9.

3 Remove the pork from the bag and place it on a rack in a shallow roasting tin. Put any of the marinade you can squeeze out of the bag into the tin, along with water to a depth of ½ inch (1 cm). Roast in the oven for 25–35 minutes, turning once halfway through, until done (the internal temperature will be 155–160°F). Leave to rest for 5–10 minutes, then slice thinly on the diagonal.

CHINESE ROASTED PORK

Chinese roast pork is delicious served with a selection of vegetables and rice. Or try serving the slices on top of a bowl of very thin spaghetti in fat-free chicken broth. Season the broth with crushed garlic and ginger, a dash or two of teriyaki and a teaspoon of fermented black beans or Chinese chilli sauce (look in the supermarket, near the hoisin and soy sauces).

3 tablespoons hoisin sauce
3 tablespoons tomato ketchup

1 tablespoon soy sauce
1 pork tenderloin, trimmed of all fat

1 Mix together the hoisin sauce, ketchup and soy sauce. Rub thoroughly over the pork, and leave to marinate in a glass baking dish for at least 4 hours (or overnight), turning the meat in the marinade occasionally.

2 Preheat the oven to 240°C, 475°F, Gas Mark 9. Line a roasting tin with foil, shiny side up. Pour water into the tin to a depth of ½ inch (1 cm). Put a rack in the tin, and place the meat on the rack. (Use the one from your grill pan.) Roast for 25–35 minutes, basting and turning once halfway through.

3 Allow to rest for 5–10 minutes, then slice, slightly on the diagonal, across the grain, and serve.

ROASTED HONEY-MUSTARD TENDERLOIN

❈

The honey and mustard combination is brilliant with pork. Use a mild honey, such as clover, or the flavour will be too strong.

¾ tablespoon mild runny honey
juice of ¼ lemon
1 garlic clove, crushed
¼ teaspoon teriyaki or soy sauce

pinch of cayenne pepper
1 tablespoon Dijon mustard
freshly ground pepper
1 pork tenderloin, trimmed of all fat

1 Preheat the oven to 240°C, 475°F, Gas Mark 9.

2 Whisk together all the ingredients, except the pork. Coat the tenderloin with the mixture.

3 Line a roasting tin with foil, shiny side up. Pour water into the tin to a depth of ½ inch (1 cm). Put a rack in the tin and place the meat on the rack. Roast in the oven for 25–35 minutes, basting and turning once halfway through.

4 Allow to rest for 5–10 minutes, then slice, slightly on the diagonal, across the grain, and serve.

BREAD

There is nothing quite so satisfying as wrestling a hunk of yeast dough into submission. The entire process is enormous fun in a very primitive way. Yes, it takes time, and yes, store-bought breads (even low-fat ones) are readily available. But once you get your fingers into the dough and feel how responsive it is, and how it comes to life in your hands; once you begin the whole sensual activity: the kneading, the punching, the rising, and finally that incomparable moment when a golden, fragrant, crusty loaf emerges from *your* oven, you will realise that it is not just a practical matter of putting a good low-fat loaf on the table – it is *therapy*.

Bread-making is a very forgiving kitchen activity; there is a lot more leeway involved than in making cakes and pastries. Once a few simple basics are understood, and once the yeast is working, it is almost impossible to ruin a loaf of bread.

EQUIPMENT

You don't need anything fancy: a large crockery bowl for mixing the dough, a wooden spoon, a set of scales and some measuring spoons, and a non-stick baking sheet. You can cut the kneading down drastically if you have a food processor. Simply put the dry ingredients (flour, yeast, salt) into the processor, turn on and pour the warm water in through the feed tube. Process for a few minutes or until a ball of dough is formed. Sometimes it gets caught under the blade and the machine stops before the dough is properly formed. Simply pull up the blade, clear the flour mixture out of the way, then start the machine again. When the dough has formed, stop the machine, gather the dough into a ball, turn out on to a lightly floured surface and knead for a few minutes or until it feels ready (page 194).

INGREDIENTS

FLOUR Bread flour (strong white flour), on its own or combined with wholemeal flour, will produce the best loaf. Flour contains a protein called gluten. It forms the web that allows the yeast action to rise the flour. Strong flour is high in gluten and will produce a superior loaf. Although wholemeal flour can contain as much gluten as white flour, the bran and germ in the whole grain are sharp, and tend to cut the developing strands of gluten, producing a loaf of less volume than a comparable white loaf. If you want a brown loaf, a mixture of wholemeal flour and strong white flour will give you a finished loaf with the colour and texture of the former, but the height and lightness of the latter.

YEAST Yeast is a living organism. As it grows (it is activated by warm water) it releases carbon dioxide gas. As the dough is kneaded, its gluten is developed into a web-like structure. The carbon dioxide gas gets trapped in the gluten framework and causes it to expand. This, in turn, causes the dough to rise. The most convenient yeast to use is easy-blend (fast-action) dried yeast, available in little sachets from all supermarkets. This yeast does not have to be dissolved in water first; simply add it to the flour, mix in some warm water, and start kneading.

A GOOD LOAF

MAKES TWO 12 OZ (350 G) LOAVES
V ❋

Agood loaf needs little more than flour, yeast and salt. The amount of flour called for in this (and any) bread recipe is approximate. The amount of liquid the flour will absorb depends on the flour, the weather, the humidity in the kitchen, the baker's hands and other variables. You will be able to feel whether enough flour has been added. If you add too much, you can always add a bit more liquid.

about 1¼ lb (550 g) strong white flour
1 sachet easy-blend yeast
½ tablespoon salt
about ½ pint (300 ml) warm water

maize meal, such as polenta (optional)
skimmed milk or a lightly beaten egg or egg
white, to glaze (optional)

I Put 1 lb (450 g) flour, the yeast and salt in a large bowl and mix with your fingers. Pour in ½ pint (300 ml) warm water while stirring with a wooden spoon. When it forms a cohesive mass, begin kneading in the bowl, sprinkling in a little flour as needed, to make a malleable dough.

2 Sprinkle some flour on the work surface and turn the dough on to it. Knead rhythmically, sprinkling on a little more flour as needed, until you have a smooth, lively, not-too-sticky dough. You will know when you've added enough by the state of the dough – it will be elastic and extremely responsive. To test if it is ready for its first rising, press it with your finger. It should spring straight back. Form into a ball and let it rest while you wash and dry the bowl. Put the kettle on to boil if your oven is electric. Knead the dough for another turn or two.

3 Lightly flour the bowl and put the dough in. Lightly flour the top of the dough and cover the bowl with cling film. Put the bowl into the oven. If it is a gas oven, the pilot light will provide a nice warm environment for the dough to rise; leave the oven door slightly ajar. If it is an electric oven, put a baking dish on the oven floor and pour boiling water into it. In this case, leave the oven door closed. Leave the dough for about 1 hour or until doubled in bulk. When you think it is ready, very gently push a finger into the risen dough to make a hole. Leave it for 5–10 minutes. If the hole remains, the dough is ready. Empty the water from the baking dish.

4 Flour your fist, and punch the dough down in the bowl. Turn it out on to a lightly floured surface and knead a few turns. Preheat the oven to 200°C, 400°F, Gas Mark 6. Sprinkle a non-stick baking sheet with maize meal (it gives the finished loaf a crunchy bottom) or flour. Cut the dough into two equal pieces, knead, and nudge, pat and cajole each piece into a bloomer shape. Alternatively, roll out each piece into a flat oval, then roll it up into a baguette shape. Place the loaves on the prepared baking sheet, and gently, with a sharp knife, slash across the tops of the loaves in three equally spaced places. Cover lightly with a tea-towel and leave in a warm draught-free place for 20–30 minutes or until doubled in bulk.

5 Uncover the loaves. Brush with milk, egg or egg white if you want a glaze. Don't let it drip down to the bottom of the loaf or it will stick to the baking sheet as it bakes. (For really crusty loaves, omit the glaze and use a water spray – a clean, plant-mister or even a water-pistol filled with water. Spray the bread two or three times during the first 10 minutes of baking.) Pour more boiling water into the baking dish on the bottom of the oven. Bake the loaves for 40–50 minutes. When almost done, slide them off the baking sheet on to the oven shelf. If browning too much on top, turn them upside-down for the last few minutes. They are done when golden brown, and hollow sounding when knuckle-thumped on the bottom. Cool on a wire rack.

VARIATIONS *Wholemeal Bread* Replace up to half of the white flour with wholemeal flour.
Garlic Bread Roast (or pan-braise) one or two bulbs of garlic, and rub it through a sieve as directed on page 35. Prepare the bread dough and give it its first rising, then punch it down, cut it in half and roll each piece into a flat oval with a rolling pin. Spread each oval with half of the garlic purée, and fold the dough over the purée. Knead each one thoroughly until the garlic is totally absorbed into the dough, then continue with the basic recipe.
Mushroom Bread Soak 2 oz (50 g) dried *porcini* mushrooms (ceps) in 1 pint (600 ml) warm water for 30 minutes (page 40). Lift the mushrooms out of the water, rinse them and chop them finely. Strain the soaking water through a sieve lined with dampened muslin or a double layer of paper coffee filters. Add the chopped mushrooms to the basic flour and yeast mixture. Replace the water with an equal amount of the mushroom soaking water. Proceed with the recipe.
Pita Bread After the first rising of the dough, punch it down and pull off lumps, weighing about 4 oz (110 g) each. Shape each into a round ball, and, with a rolling pin on a lightly floured surface, roll each into a flat round or oval, ⅛–¼ inch (0.25–0.5 cm) thick. Gently place them, well spaced, on a lightly floured baking sheet and bake in the oven at 200°C, 400°F, Gas Mark 6 for 30–40 minutes or until they billow into hollow-centred balloons. Cool on a wire rack.
Focaccia (flat bread much like a pizza base). Pull off lumps of dough after the first rising, and roll into balls, as described for pita bread. With a rolling pin on a lightly floured surface, roll each piece into a flat ⅛–¼ inch (0.25–0.5 cm) thick round or oval. Knuckle dent them in several places, so that they will not balloon into pita. Bake in the oven at 200°C, 400°F, Gas Mark 6 on a lightly floured baking sheet for about 30 minutes or until done. Cool on a wire rack.
Bread Rolls Roll the dough (after the first rising and punching down) into balls, place on a baking sheet that has been sprinkled with flour or maize meal, and leave to rise until almost doubled in size. Brush with beaten egg or egg white and bake for 30–40 minutes at 200°C, 400°F, Gas Mark 6.
Bread Sticks This works well with the Potato Bread dough (page 196). Pull off a small piece (after its first rising and punching down), and roll, on a floured surface, into ⅛ inch (0.25 cm) thick rectangle. Cut the rectangle into strips ½ inch (1 cm) wide. Lay on a non-stick baking sheet that has been lightly sprinkled with flour or maize meal. Bake at 200°C, 400°F, Gas Mark 6 for 7–12 minutes until crisp and lightly browned. Turn over for the last few minutes. Cool on a wire rack. Turn into Cheese Straws by kneading in a bit of Parmesan before rolling out.

POTATO BREAD

V ❄

My favourite breads are made from potato dough. Spuds give bread the dense moistness, and earthy flavour of the ethnic breads I love. The potato adds to the keeping quality of the finished loaf as well. If you have no potato flakes, bake or boil 8 oz (225 g) baking potatoes, then peel and push through a ricer or a mouli. Add to the flour in step 1. Decrease the amount of water to about ½ pint (300 ml).

about 1¼ lb (550 g) strong white flour
4½ oz (120 g) sachet potato flakes (Mr Mash
   or Waitrose brand)
one sachet easy-blend yeast
½ tablespoon salt
about ¾ pint (450 ml) water

skimmed milk or lightly beaten egg or egg
   white, to glaze (optional)
seeds, such as fennel, anise, caraway or cumin
   (optional)
coarse sea salt crystals (optional)

1 Combine 1 lb (450 g) flour, the potato flakes, yeast and salt in a large bowl and mix with your fingers. Pour in the water while mixing with a wooden spoon. When it forms a cohesive mass, begin kneading in the bowl, sprinkling in a little more flour as necessary to make a malleable dough.

2 Gather up the dough and place it on a very lightly floured work surface. Knead rhythmically for about 10 minutes or until the dough is smooth and lively. Add a sprinkling of additional flour, only if the dough is hard to handle, but remember that this dough should be a little sticky. Too much flour will make the finished loaf too heavy. If necessary, add a little more water. You know the dough has been kneaded sufficiently when it is very lively, and when you poke it with a finger, the indentation springs back straight away. Put the kettle on to boil if your oven is electric. Form the dough into a smooth ball, and place it in a very lightly floured large bowl. Very lightly dust the top with flour. Cover with cling film.

3 Put the bowl into the oven. If it is a gas oven, the pilot light will provide a nice warm environment for the dough to rise; leave the oven door slightly ajar. If it is an electric oven, put a baking dish on the oven floor and pour boiling water into it. In this case, leave the oven door closed. Leave the dough for about 1 hour or until doubled in bulk. (Note the size of the ball of dough when you leave it, so that you know when it has doubled.) When you think it is ready, very gently push a finger into the risen dough to make a hole. Leave it for 5–10 minutes. If the hole remains, the dough is ready for the next step.

4 Punch the dough down in the bowl, and knead it a few turns to expel the gas. Let it rest, while you lightly sprinkle a non-stick baking sheet with flour. Remove the pan of water from the oven.

5 Form the dough (by this time it is so lively it is practically talking back to you!) into a plump round loaf or into two bloomer shapes. Lightly slash twice across the top with a sharp knife. Put it on the floured baking sheet, cover loosely with cling film or a clean tea towel, and leave in a warm quiet corner for 30–45 minutes or until doubled in bulk. In the meantime, put the kettle on again and preheat the oven to 200°C, 400°F, Gas Mark 6.

6 Put another baking dish of boiling water on the oven floor. Uncover the loaves and brush with milk, egg or egg white, if you want a glaze, and sprinkle with seeds and/or coarse sea salt. Alternatively, for really crusty loaves, spray the bread three times during the first 10 minutes of baking with water from a clean plant-mister or water-pistol. Bake the bread in the oven for 55–65 minutes for a single loaf; 45–55 minutes for two loaves. For the last few minutes of baking, turn the loaf upside-down directly on the oven shelf. The bread is done when it is golden brown, and a knuckle-thump on the bottom produces a hollow sound. Although it is very difficult to wait, the flavour of this bread (and its variation) is best when it has cooled.

VARIATION *Rye Bread* Follow the directions for Potato Bread, but substitute 8 oz (225 g) pure rye flour for half of the strong white flour. Add 1–2 tablespoons caraway seeds in step 1. Continue as directed in the Potato Bread recipe, but the baking time will be a little longer.

TO STORE BREAD

Do not wrap in cling film or plastic bags; wrapping in plastic makes the crust flabby. Leave in a cool part of the kitchen with a piece of cling film against the cut end, or store in a paper bag.

QUICKER YEAST BREAD

V ❄

This is a milk-enriched (for extra nutrition), slightly sweetened yeast dough that has only one rising (30 minutes), and then is baked in a loaf tin for an additional 30 minutes. If you have a food processor, quite a bit of time can be knocked off the kneading as well. Great for family cooking.

½ pint (300 ml) warm water
1 generous tablespoon mild runny honey
8 oz (225 g) wholemeal flour
8 oz (225 g) strong white flour
4 tablespoons skimmed milk powder

1 sachet easy-blend yeast
½ teaspoon salt
skimmed milk for brushing
seeds (caraway, fennel, anise, poppy or sesame)
  for topping

1 Combine the water and the honey, mixing well.

2 Put the flours, milk powder, yeast and salt in a food processor. Turn on the processor and pour the honey and water mixture in through the feed tube. Process for a few minutes or until a ball of dough is formed. If some of the mixture gets stuck under the blade and the machine stops before the dough has properly formed, pull up the blade, clear the flour mixture out of the way, then start the machine again.

3 If you have an electric oven, bring a kettle of water to the boil. Put a shallow roasting tin in the bottom of the oven, and pour in the boiling water. Do not turn the oven on. Turn the dough out on to a lightly floured board and knead it briefly, kneading in a bit more flour if necessary. Form into a ball, and put it into a large lightly floured bowl. Lightly flour the top and cover the bowl with cling film. Put into the steamy oven, and leave to rise for 30 minutes. (If you have a gas oven, you will not need the boiling water – the pilot light will create a warm enough environment. In this case, leave the dough in the oven, with the door slightly ajar.)

4 Remove the dough from the oven and, if necessary, remove the water-filled roasting tin. Preheat the oven to 200°C, 400°F Gas Mark 6. Knead the dough firmly a few turns to knock it down. Pat and shape the dough into a loaf shape and put it into a 2 lb (900 g) non-stick loaf tin. (Or form it into a bloomer shape, cut three evenly spaced shallow slashes across the top, and put it on a flour-sprinkled baking sheet.)

5 Brush the top of the loaf with skimmed milk (don't let it trickle down, or the loaf may stick), and sprinkle on the seeds of your choice. Bake the loaf in the oven for 25–35 minutes. It is done when it is billowed, beautifully browned and glossy, it smells wonderful, and when you knock on the bottom of the loaf with your knuckles, it sounds hollow. (To remove the loaf from the tin, loosen around the sides with a palette knife and gently shake it out.) If it is not yet done, continue baking upside-down directly on the oven shelf. Cool on a wire rack. This bread is delicious warm or thoroughly cooled. It keeps well.

PIZZA

MAKES 1–2 PIZZAS

Everyone loves pizza, but it is far from junk food. In fact, it is one of the healthiest meals around. Leave off the olive oil, use mozzarella cheese, and avoid fatty sausage toppings, and pizza could win first prize in a high nutrition contest.

basic bread dough (page 194)   *toppings (see below)*
polenta (maize meal) or flour

1 Prepare the dough and give it its first rise. Punch it down, and divide it in two if you want to make two pizzas. Knead each piece briefly and form into compact rounds.

2 Preheat the oven to 200°C, 400°F, Gas Mark 6. On a lightly floured surface, roll each piece of dough out into a circle, rolling from the centre out to the edges, turning the dough as you roll. It doesn't need to be a perfect circle, so there's no need to fuss with it too much. If the dough is so lively that it refuses to roll out the way you want it to, then pick it up and turn and stretch it into shape with your hands. (If you're dexterous, you could even try flinging and turning it the way seasoned pizza chefs do!) Put one round on to a lightly floured (or maize-mealed) baking sheet. Spread the sauce (see below) on to the dough, leaving a 1 inch (2.5 cm) border all around, and sprinkle on any additional ingredients. (If you are baking two, leave the second half of dough to rest, lightly covered, while the first bakes. Punch it down when you are ready for it; (it can stay in the fridge overnight, if you wish.)

3 When the oven is thoroughly hot, put the pizza in and bake for 15–25 minutes or until the filling is bubbly, and the edges of the dough are puffed and golden. Slide the pizza on to a board and cut into wedges.

TOPPINGS FOR PIZZA Tomato sauce and shredded mozzarella cheese are the basics, or choose one of the sauces on pages 85–86) and add whatever you like: grilled courgettes, peppers and/or aubergine; crumbled meatballs or sausages (pages 170–173); cooked, well drained fresh spinach; sautéed mushrooms; raw, ripe tomato slices or cubes; braised fennel; whatever makes your mouth water.

MEAT AND VEGETABLE PIES

A batch of bread dough can be filled with one of the beef stews, bolognese sauces or vegetable stews, and baked until golden. Serve them in wedges, piping hot, with a green salad on the side, for a very special informal supper. Or make small individual pies for a packed lunch. Beef, Mushroom and Caramelized Onion Stew (page 178) with its dark rich sauce and melting cubes of beef, is just right to fill a meat pie.

basic bread dough, prepared to the end of step 2 (page 194)

1 Preheat the oven to 200°C, 400°F, Gas Mark 6.

2 On a lightly floured surface, roll half the dough out into a circle, rolling from the centre out to the edges, turning the dough as you roll. It doesn't need to be a perfect circle. If it refuses to roll the way you want it, pull and stretch it into shape with your hands. Put on a lightly floured baking sheet. Spread on the filling, leaving a ½ inch (1 cm) border all around.

3 Roll out the other half of the dough, a little smaller than the first half, and lay it over the top of the pizza. Fold over the bottom edge all around and pinch to seal. Bake in the oven for 20–25 minutes or until a knuckle-thump produces a hollow sound.

CALZONE

A calzone is a folded pizza. Instead of spreading the filling on the dough, and then baking open-faced, the dough is folded over the filling. All the suggested fillings for pizza work well in calzone. Grilled vegetables or peppers are particularly good.

basic bread dough, prepared to the end of step 2 (page 194)

1 Cut the bread dough into quarters or eighths and form each piece into a smooth ball. Put one ball of dough on a lightly floured surface, and roll it out to a circle. If it refuses to roll, pull and stretch it out by hand. Repeat with the remaining balls of dough.

2 Put some filling (see suggestions, above) across the centre of each circle. Fold over and pinch the edges to seal. Put the calzone on a lightly floured, non-stick baking sheet.

3 Cover loosely, and leave in a warm place for 20 minutes to rise. Bake in a preheated oven at 200°C, 400°F, Gas Mark 6 for about 15 minutes (for small ones) or about 25 minutes (for larger ones). They are done when they sound hollow when knuckle-thumped on their bottoms.

SODA BREADS

When time is a real problem, but you want to whip up a loaf of homemade bread, try a soda bread. Soda breads are raised by the chemical action of baking soda (contained in self-raising flour), they require a bare minimum of kneading (easily done in the mixing bowl) and bake relatively quickly. The texture is cake-like, and the flavour is quite different from that of a yeast-raised loaf, but it is a crusty, satisfying loaf of bread none-the-less. Since soda bread is mixed and kneaded in the bowl, the cleaning up is minimal. Fromage frais thinned with skimmed milk is the liquid and self-raising sponge flour, white (or a mixture of brown and white), is the flour to use. Sponge flour has a *low* gluten content, just right for these non-yeast breads. Each of the following recipes makes two loaves, or about 18 scone-like rolls. They don't keep well but a day-old soda bread makes wonderful toast.

BASIC SODA BREAD

MAKES 2 LOAVES
V ❋

This is a plain, honest loaf that goes very well with stews and casseroles.

8 oz (225 g) white self-raising sponge flour
8 oz (225 g) brown self-raising sponge flour
1 teaspoon salt

8 fl oz (225 ml) very low-fat fromage frais,
thinned with 7 fl oz (200 ml) skimmed milk
extra milk, as needed

1 Preheat the oven to 200°C, 400°F, Gas Mark 6.

2 Combine the flours and salt in a large bowl. Lightly mix with your hand. Make a well in the middle of the flour. Pour the thinned fromage frais into the well.

3 With a wooden spoon, stir the flour into the liquid. When the mixture forms a cohesive mass, squeeze it with your hands to help smooth it out, then knead it, in the bowl. If the dough is too crumbly, add a bit more milk; if too wet, add a bit more flour, but the dough should remain soft, smooth and malleable.

4 Cut the dough into equal halves and knead briefly. Form each piece into two plump round loaves and place them, well spaced, on a lightly floured, non-stick baking sheet. With a sharp knife, cut a shallow cross on the top of each one. Alternatively, form each piece of dough into a bloomer shape, and, with a sharp knife, cut three slashes, evenly spaced, across the top. Bake in the oven for about 35 minutes. If the loaves are browning too fast, turn them upside-down for the last few minutes of cooking. When done, they will sound hollow if tapped on the bottom, and they will be beautifully browned. Cool on a wire rack.

CHIVE AND MUSTARD SEED BREAD

MAKES 2 LOAVES
V ❄

Aquick and splendid bread to serve as a dinner accompaniment or with spreads. Try it with Duxelles (page 41) or one of the tuna spreads (page 97).

8 oz (225 g) white self-raising sponge flour
8 oz (225 g) brown self-raising sponge flour
1 teaspoon salt
2–2½ tablespoons yellow mustard seeds
6 tablespoons snipped fresh chives

2 tablespoons Dijon mustard
8 fl oz (225 ml) very low-fat fromage frais
thinned with 7 fl oz (200 ml) skimmed milk
extra skimmed milk, as needed

1 Preheat the oven to 200°C, 400°F, Gas Mark 6.

2 Put the flours into a large bowl. Sprinkle the salt, mustard seed and chives over it, and mix lightly with your hand. Make a well in the middle of the flour. Whisk together the mustard and the thinned fromage frais, and pour into the well.

3 Follow steps 3 and 4 of the method for Basic Soda Bread (page 201).

CORN BREAD

MAKES 2 LOAVES
V ❄

One of my favourite breads for a buffet, corn bread is perfect with highly seasoned soups and stews. This bread mops up gravies and sauces very nicely indeed.

10 oz (275 g) white self-raising sponge flour
5 oz (150 g) maize meal or polenta
2 pinches of salt
6 tablespoons freshly grated Parmesan cheese
freshly ground pepper

10½ oz (285 g) can creamed sweetcorn
very low-fat fromage frais thinned with
skimmed milk
extra skimmed milk, as needed

1 Preheat the oven to 200°C, 400°F, Gas Mark 6.

2 Put the flour and maize meal into a large bowl. Sprinkle the salt and cheese over it, and season generously with pepper. Mix lightly with your hand, and make a well in the middle of the flour. Pour the creamed corn into a measuring jug and make up to ¾ pint (450 ml) with fromage frais thinned with skimmed milk. Pour the mixture into the well.

3 Follow steps 3 and 4 of the method for Basic Soda Bread (page 201), but sprinkle the non-stick baking sheet with maize meal or polenta instead of flour.

CHEESE BREAD

MAKES 2 LOAVES
V ❄

The addition of Parmesan cheese elevates humble soda bread to ambrosia. This is a marvellous loaf to serve with bean or vegetable stews. If there is any left for the next day, it makes the best cheese toast you can imagine.

1 lb (450 g) white self-raising sponge flour
2 pinches of salt
6 tablespoons freshly grated Parmesan cheese
freshly ground pepper

8 fl oz (225 ml) very low-fat fromage frais
*   thinned with 7 fl oz (200 ml) skimmed milk*
extra skimmed milk, as needed

1 Preheat the oven to 200°C, 400°F, Gas Mark 6.

2 Put the flour into a large bowl. Sprinkle the salt and cheese over it, and season generously with pepper. Mix lightly with your hand, and make a well in the middle of the flour. Pour the thinned fromage frais into the well.

3 Follow steps 3 and 4 of the method for Basic Soda Bread (page 201).

SCONES

Scones are particularly good made with Cheese Bread (above), Raisin Bread or Cranberry and Maple Bread (pages 204–205). Form the dough into small balls, about 18 per batch of dough. Place them, well spaced, on a floured non-stick baking sheet and bake at 200°C, 400°F, Gas Mark 6 for 20–30 minutes or until they have risen, browned, and sound hollow when tapped on the bottom. Cool on a wire rack for a few minutes. (They are delicious when they are still a bit warm and when they have cooled as well.) Split and spread with Apricot Spread (page 73). If you wish, you could bake one loaf, and 9–10 scones from one batch of dough.

RAISIN BREAD

MAKES 2 LOAVES
V ❄

Speckled with raisins, flecked with citrus zest (be sure to scrub the lemons and oranges first, unless they are not waxed), this is a lovely breakfast, brunch or tea bread.

2 fl oz (50 ml) orange juice
2 fl oz (50 ml) water
4 oz (110 g) raisins or sultanas
grated zest of ½ lemon
grated zest of ½ orange
8 oz (225 g) white self-raising sponge flour

8 oz (225 g) brown self-raising sponge flour
pinch of salt
8 fl oz (225 ml) very low-fat fromage frais
thinned with 7 fl oz (200 ml) skimmed milk
2 tablespoons mild runny honey
extra skimmed milk, as needed

I Preheat the oven to 200°C, 400°F, Gas Mark 6.

2 Combine the juice, water, raisins and citrus zests in a small frying pan. Simmer until the raisins are plump and have absorbed the liquid, then remove from the heat and cool.

3 Combine the flours and salt in a large bowl. Sprinkle the raisin mixture over the flour. Mix well, and make a well in the middle of the flour. Pour the thinned fromage frais into the well.

4 With a wooden spoon, stir the flour into the liquid. Add the honey and continue stirring until the mixture forms a cohesive mass. Squeeze it with your hands to help smooth it, and knead it in the bowl. If the dough is too crumbly, add a little more milk; if it is too wet, add a little more flour, but the dough should remain soft, smooth and malleable. Cut the dough into two equal pieces, and knead briefly.

5 Form the dough into two plump, round loaves and place, well spaced, on a lightly floured non-stick baking sheet. With a sharp knife, cut a shallow cross in the top of each loaf. Alternatively, form the dough pieces into two bloomer shapes and, with a sharp knife, cut three evenly spaced slashes across the top of each. Bake in the oven for about 35 minutes. When done, the bread will sound hollow if tapped on the bottom, and it will be beautifully browned. If the loaves seem to be browning too fast, bake upside-down for the last 5–10 minutes. Cool on a wire rack.

VARIATION *Fruit Loaf* Use a mixture of dried cherries, dried blueberries and dried cranberries in place of the raisins, and orange or lemon marmalade in place of the honey. This version is good with half brown, half white flour, or all white.

CRANBERRY AND MAPLE BREAD

MAKES 2 LOAVES
V ❄

If your supermarket stocks 'Craisins' (sweetened dried cranberries) and maple syrup, you will be able to bake this North-American-influenced version of soda bread.

4 fl oz (110 ml) orange juice
4 oz (110 g) sweetened dried cranberries
  ('Craisins')
8 oz (225 g) white self-raising sponge flour
8 oz (225 g) brown self-raising sponge flour

pinch of salt
8 fl oz (225 ml) very low-fat fromage frais
  thinned with 7 fl oz (200 ml) skimmed milk
3 tablespoons maple syrup
extra skimmed milk, as needed

1 Preheat the oven to 200°C, 400°F, Gas Mark 6.

2 Combine the orange juice and cranberries in a small frying pan, and simmer until the cranberries are plump and have absorbed the liquid. Remove from the heat and cool.

3 Combine the flours and salt in a large bowl. Sprinkle the cranberry mixture over the flour. Mix well, and make a well in the middle. Pour the thinned fromage frais into the well.

4 With a wooden spoon, stir the flour into the liquid. Add the maple syrup and continue stirring. When the mixture forms a cohesive mass, squeeze it with your hands to smooth it, then knead it in the bowl. If the dough is too crumbly, add a bit more milk; if too wet, add a bit more flour, but the dough should remain soft, smooth and malleable. Cut the dough into two equal pieces and knead briefly.

5 Form the dough pieces into two plump, round loaves and place, well spaced, on a lightly floured, non-stick baking sheet. With a sharp knife, cut a shallow cross in the top of each loaf. Alternatively, form the dough pieces into two bloomer shapes and, with a sharp knife, cut three evenly spaced slashes across the top of each. Bake for about 35 minutes. If the loaves seem to be browning too fast, bake upside-down for the last 5–10 minutes. When done, the bread will sound hollow if tapped on the bottom, and it will be beautifully browned. Cool on a wire rack.

VARIATION *Sweet Crescent* Divide the dough into two. Roll each out with a rolling pin on a lightly floured surface. Spread each with a tablespoon or so of marmalade and roll up like a Swiss roll. Curve into a crescent shape. Arrange on a lightly floured baking sheet, and bake at 200°C, 400°F, Gas Mark 6 for 30–40 minutes or until browned and hollow-sounding when tapped on the bottom. Cool on a wire rack, then serve in slices. You could bake sweet crescents from the Raisin Bread dough (opposite) too.

SAVOURY BREAD PUDDINGS

I t pays to sequester old bread the way a squirrel hoards nuts for the winter, so that you can revel frequently in the glories of bread pudding. Savoury versions provide economical suppers that, although prepared from humble ingredients, overflow with luxurious comfort. These low-fat bread puddings contain two whole eggs and three egg whites, so that each diner gets just a fraction of an egg yolk, which should be no problem unless you have been told to restrict fat and whole-egg consumption totally.

Bread puddings are prepared by saturating dried bread in a low-fat custard, along with various savoury ingredients, then baking in a hot water bath until the mixture billows into cloud-like tenderness. Bread puddings rise almost like soufflés, then settle down somewhat as they cool.

It helps to know how to store the bread so that it gets properly dried and stale (not mouldy). The secret is never to wrap it in cling film or a plastic bag. These encourage flabbiness, excess moisture, and moulding. Store the bread in a paper bag, a bread box, or on the work surface draped with a clean tea-towel.

MUSHROOM BREAD PUDDING

SERVES 4–6

V

M ix the bread cubes with mushrooms that have been sautéed in the mushroom 'trinity', along with mustard and a touch of tarragon, and the resulting bread pudding will taste like essence of mushroom. If you add reconstituted dried mushrooms, and use some of the soaking liquid in place of the stock, the essence will be even stronger (page 41).

1 lb (450 g) button mushrooms, quartered
4 fl oz (110 ml) medium sherry
2 fl oz (50 ml) stock
1–2 dashes teriyaki or soy sauce
1 teaspoon dried tarragon, crumbled
1 tablespoon Dijon mustard
freshly ground pepper

6 oz (175 g) several-days-old, crustless bread,
  cut into cubes
2 eggs
3 egg whites
16 fl oz (475 ml) skimmed milk mixed with 3
  tablespoons skimmed milk powder

1 Preheat the oven to 190°C, 375°F, Gas Mark 5.

2 Combine the mushrooms, sherry, stock, teriyaki sauce and tarragon in a heavy-bottomed frying pan. Bring to the boil and cook, stirring occasionally, until the mushrooms have exuded a great deal of liquid. Stir in the mustard and season with pepper. Simmer until the mushrooms are tender, and the liquid greatly reduced. Cool slightly, then mix with the bread cubes in a bowl until well combined.

3 Lightly beat the eggs and egg whites together. Beat in the milk, then pour over the bread. Mix gently with two spoons until the bread is thoroughly saturated with the liquid. Leave to stand for a few minutes. Put the kettle on to boil.

4 Pour the mixture into a round, oval or square shallow glass or ceramic baking dish. Put the dish into a larger baking dish or roasting tin, and place in the oven. Fill the larger dish with boiling water to come halfway up the sides of the smaller dish. Bake for 40–50 minutes or until puffed and set, and a knife inserted near the centre emerges clean.

PORK, APPLE AND SAGE BREAD PUDDING

SERVES 4–6

One of the best savoury bread puddings of all, this would not only make a welcome supper dish, but is an excellent accompaniment to the Christmas turkey. (As a main dish, it will serve 4–6, but as one component of an enormous Christmas dinner, it will serve 8–10.) It's good hot or at room temperature. The pudding is even good cold, straight out of the fridge (should you have any left over – but you probably won't).

8 oz (225 g) extra-lean minced pork
1 large onion, chopped
1 small Bramley apple, peeled, cored and diced
1 aubergine, roasted, peeled and chopped (page 157)
4–6 fl oz (110–175 ml) cider
1 tablespoon chopped fresh sage

salt and freshly ground pepper
6 oz (175 g) several-days-old, crustless bread, cut into cubes
2 eggs
3 egg whites
16 fl oz (475 ml) skimmed milk mixed with 3 tablespoons skimmed milk powder

1 Preheat the oven to 190°C, 375°F, Gas Mark 5. Meanwhile, in a heavy-bottomed frying pan, sauté the pork and onions, breaking up the lumps as you stir. When the pork is browned and the onions softened, drain and blot dry then return to the pan.

2 Add the apple, aubergine, cider and sage. Season with salt and pepper, and simmer until the liquid evaporates. Cool slightly, then toss with the bread in a bowl until well combined.

3 Lightly beat the eggs and egg whites together. Beat in the milk, then pour over the bread. Mix gently with two spoons until the bread is thoroughly saturated with the liquid. Leave to stand for a few minutes. Put the kettle on to boil.

4 Pour the mixture into a round, oval or square shallow glass or ceramic baking dish. Put the dish into a larger baking dish and place in the oven. Fill the larger dish with boiling water to come halfway up the sides of the smaller dish. Bake for 40–50 minutes or until the pudding is puffed and set, and a knife gently inserted near the centre emerges clean.

VEGETABLE AND CHEESE BREAD PUDDING

SERVES 4–6
V

Why not bread pudding with a Mediterranean soul? It's only old bread and some vegetable bits and pieces, but it tastes so good!

2 courgettes, each weighing about 8 oz (225 g), cut into ½ inch (1 cm) cubes

2 peppers (1 red, 1 yellow), peeled (page 48), deseeded and cut into ½ inch (1 cm) cubes

8 spring onions, trimmed and sliced

1–2 garlic cloves, crushed

3–4 sundried tomatoes, chopped (use scissors)

pinch of crushed dried chillies

2–3 black olives in brine, drained and slivered off their stones

½ pint (300 ml) stock

3 tablespoons chopped mixed fresh herbs (parsley, oregano, basil)

6 oz (175 g) several-days-old, crustless bread, cut into cubes

salt and freshly ground pepper

2 eggs

3 egg whites

16 fl oz (475 ml) skimmed milk mixed with 3 oz (75 g) skimmed milk powder

3–4 tablespoons freshly grated Parmesan cheese

1 Combine the vegetables, garlic, sundried tomatoes, chillies, olives and stock in a frying pan. Simmer briskly, stirring, until the vegetables are tender and the liquid greatly reduced. Stir in the herbs. Remove from the heat and leave to cool.

2 Combine the vegetables with the bread in a large bowl. Season with salt and pepper, and toss with two spoons to thoroughly combine. Lightly beat the eggs and egg whites together, then beat in the milk. Add to the bread mixture along with the cheese, and mix with two spoons to thoroughly saturate the bread with the liquid. Leave to stand while you preheat the oven to 180°C, 350°F, Gas Mark 4. Put the kettle on to boil.

3 Put the bread and vegetable mixture into a baking dish. Set this dish in a larger baking dish and place in the oven. Fill the larger dish with boiling water to come halfway up the sides of the smaller dish. Bake for 40–50 minutes or until puffed and set (a knife inserted near the centre will emerge clean). Serve warm or at room temperature.

DESSERTS AND CAKES

Life without pudding? Don't be silly. Not only are low-fat, high-nutrition puddings easy to make, but they are more delicious than you would have dreamed possible. With fruit (fresh, dried, frozen and canned), non-fat dairy products, egg whites (and the occasional whole egg), low-fat unsweetened cocoa powder, high cocoa solid whole chocolate and a supply of liqueurs and flavourings, the potential for low-fat pudding development is limitless.

Some words of advice before you begin.

SWEETENERS

Sugar is a seasoning that helps to sweeten food and make it palatable. There is no reason not to use it judiciously here and there. No one sugar is better than another as far as health matters are concerned. As far as low-fat cookery is concerned, a form of sugar that deepens flavour and adds a perception of richness along with its dose of sweetness, is the most useful. Here are the sweeteners I depend upon for just these reasons:

Fruit Marmalades (and jams, preserves and conserves):

I use these invaluable ingredients to provide the sweetness in ice creams, bread puddings, crumbles, and any number of old-fashioned desserts. Two tablespoons or so are all that is needed, and the complex flavour that they deliver along with their sweetness is incomparable. I also find *pure maple syrup*, and *mild honey* extremely valuable.

Liqueurs and Wines

A shelf of liqueurs (they are used a few fluid ounces at a time) adds terrific pizzazz to low-fat desserts. The most useful are: Cointreau (orange); Crème de Pêche (peach); Amaretto di Saronne (almond); Kirsch (cherry), and dark rum. A bottle each of sweet red vermouth and medium sweet sherry will come in handy, too.

Flavour Extracts

These are basic to excellent desserts as well. Real vanilla extract is worth seeking out – it is much smoother and gentler than the harsh essences readily available in supermarkets. Pure vanilla extract is a revelation if you have never tried it before. Vanilla extract, in addition to lemon and almond extracts, are available through mail order (page 242).

Amaretti and Grape Nuts

Grape Nuts cereal (what a silly name!) and Amaretti biscuits (almond-flavoured meringues) make great no-fat crumbs for crumbles, cheesecake crusts and toppings. Grape Nuts are available in most supermarkets on the breakfast cereal shelf. Look for the Amaretti biscuits that contain egg whites and are flavoured with apricot kernels (no added fat, and no high-fat nuts).

Longlife Milk

Boxed longlife skimmed milk is excellent for cooking. The milk has been subjected to high heat, giving it a cooked taste. As a result, it is not particularly appropriate for drinking. But in recipes where it will be cooked anyway, it works perfectly. I use it mixed with skimmed milk powder for extra richness and nutrition.

Chocolate

With low-fat unsweetened cocoa powder and an excellent quality high-cocoa-solids dark chocolate (at least 70% cocoa solids, see page 242 for a mail order supply), all the compelling, erotic splendour of chocolate can be yours – without the usual accompaniment of fat and guilt.

FOOD PROCESSOR ICE CREAMS

Once you have a food processor you'll wonder why it took you so long to acquire one. They are useful for many things, but it is these ice creams that you will find yourself making again and again. They are prepared from a few ingredients in less than 5 minutes, contain no fat, overflow with good nutrition, and taste so damned good!

INSTANT ICE CREAM

MAKES 1 PINT (600 ML)
V

These ice creams do not freeze well (they freeze harder than a brick, and, if then left out to soften, taste icy rather than creamy). So make what you need, when you need it. A recipe this fast is instant gratification, so it is no inconvenience. Virtually any frozen fruit can be used: ready-frozen raspberries or blueberries, or fruit you have frozen yourself: peeled sliced banana, cubed mango, peeled, cubed apple, any berries (unless you have a problem with the tiny pips) – whatever you like. Freeze the fruit flat, on non-stick trays. When frozen, gather into plastic bags and store in the freezer. When you want to use the fruit, if it has frozen into a solid mass, knock it sharply on the work surface to separate the pieces. I'm giving you a standard recipe that will make 1 pint (600 ml) ice cream, but you could easily make double, or half the amount.

1 lb (450 g) cubes of frozen fruit, or whole
berries (strawberries should be quartered)
1–3 tablespoons very low-fat fromage frais
1–2 tablespoons marmalade, preserves or jam

½–1 tablespoon liqueur (optional) – Cointreau,
Amaretto di Saronne, Crème de Pêche –
whatever goes with the fruit
1 teaspoon vanilla extract

1 Put the *still frozen* fruit pieces into the container of a food processor, along with 1 tablespoon fromage frais, 1 tablespoon marmalade, the optional liqueur and the vanilla extract. Turn the machine on. It will rattle and clatter all over the place, but these machines are designed to crush ice if necessary, so there should be no problem. Add another ½ tablespoon fromage frais and process. (With some machines you will have to stop and scrape down the sides.)

2 Stop and taste for sweetness. Add more marmalade or preserves if necessary. Start the machine again. When it forms a super-creamy, smooth, (no ice crystals) ice cream consistency, it is done. Add a bit more fromage frais, if necessary, to reach that state, but it should be like ice cream, not like a frozen fruit fool. Serve *at once*. Everyone will think you are a genius.

INSTANT SORBETS

Sorbets are made in the same way as the ice cream opposite, but use fruit juice (orange in most cases, but apple juice works well too) in place of the fromage frais. Each type of fruit is different, so always taste as you go – some are very sweet and need a bare minimum of the sweetener (marmalade or preserves), some are tart and need more. A good ripe mango is sticky and sweet and voluptuous all by itself and may need nothing at all, not even fruit juice. Ditto for ripe bananas. So experiment, taste, adjust, and have fun.

MORE ICE CREAM AND SORBET IDEAS

Here are some good fruit and preserve combinations to get you started, though I'm sure you will think up plenty more. Remember, to each combination, add fromage frais (or fruit juice) and vanilla extract, then follow the master recipe.

Peach Ice Cream

frozen peach cubes
peach preserves
Amaretto di Saronne
   (optional)
1 teaspoon Crème de Pêche
   (optional)

Pear Ice Cream or Sorbet

frozen pear cubes
orange marmalade
Cointreau (optional)

Blueberry Ice Cream or Sorbet

frozen blueberries
wild blueberry conserve
Cointreau (optional)

Melon Sorbet

This one needs no sweetener
   (if the melon is ripe)
frozen melon balls or cubes
orange juice
Cointreau (optional)

Banana Ice Cream or Sorbet

(use very ripe bananas – you
   will not need to add
   sweetener)
frozen banana slices
rum (optional)

Raspberry Ice Cream or Sorbet

frozen raspberries
cherry conserve
Cointreau (optional)

Pineapple Sorbet

frozen pineapple chunks
pineapple preserves
orange juice
rum (optional)

Opposite page 210: Chocolate Angel Sheet Cake (page 216) filled with Orange Ricotta Cream (page 218) and fresh strawberries and topped with Chocolate Icing (page 217), slices of Banana Cake (page 220), Cranberry Maple Scones (page 203) served with Apricot Spread (page 73)

Opposite, clockwise from top: Summer Pudding Parfait (page 233), Caramelized Bananas and Pears with Mango Cream (page 233), Cherry Ricotta Tiramisu (page 225)

OLD-FASHIONED PUDDINGS

Nursery puddings bring much pleasure to life. They are usually quite substantial, and so contribute quite a bit of good nutrition. Unfortunately, they contribute plenty of sugar and fat as well – not much of a problem in the nursery, but disastrous for adults trying to pursue a low-fat lifestyle. You will be delighted at how well two beloved nursery puds (rice pudding and bread pudding) take to low-fat methods. No one believes it until they try these recipes for themselves, so I implore you to give them a go.

RICE PUDDING

MAKES ABOUT 2 PINTS (1.1 LITRES)

v

This is a *no-fat* rice pudding that overflows with nutrition: calcium, protein, vitamins A and D (from the milk powder), yet it tastes so wicked! It is true nursery food – smooth, creamy, rich, sweet (but not cloying), with just that touch of liqueur to remind us that we *are* adults, after all. As the pudding cooks slowly in the oven, the sugar and the milk sugars caramelize. This is what gives the pudding its incredible depth of flavour. The only drawback to this miracle is that you must stir every 20–30 minutes. Believe me, it's worth it. Serve warm or cold.

6 tablespoons raisins or sultanas
6 tablespoons Amaretto di Saronne
2 pints (1.1 litres) skimmed milk (at room temperature)

6 rounded tablespoons skimmed milk powder
1 oz (25 g) caster sugar
1 vanilla pod
4 oz (110 g) pudding rice

1 Combine the raisins and Amaretto in a small bowl and leave to soak while you preheat the oven to 150°C, 300°F, Gas Mark 2.

2 Thoroughly stir together the milk, milk powder and sugar. Split the vanilla pod lengthways and scrape out the contents with the tip of a knife. Stir this into the milk and stir to mix thoroughly. (Save the scraped pod to make vanilla sugar: bury the pod in a canister of sugar. The pod will give its fragrance to the sugar.) Stir in the rice, and the raisins with their liqueur.

3 Pour this mixture into a 9 inch (23 cm) square, 2 inches (5 cm) deep baking dish. Place the baking dish in a larger baking dish or roasting tin, and pour boiling water into the larger baking dish, so it comes two-thirds of the way up the sides. Bake in the oven for 2–2¼ hours, stirring after each 20–30 minutes. It is done when the rice is tender and bathed in a thick, creamy sauce. It should not be *too* soupy, but, on the other hand, the liquid should not be completely absorbed.

LEMON BREAD PUDDING

Even without butter and cream, bread puddings are as voluptuous and custardy as one could hope for. The custard in these puddings contains two whole eggs and three egg whites, so each diner gets only a fraction of the yolk. The eggs are combined with skimmed milk and whisked with skimmed milk powder. The skimmed milk powder adds splendid nutrition – calcium, vitamins A and D – but, even more important, it adds richness to the finished pudding. The puddings are sweetened with preserves or marmalade – this adds still more richness and a much nicer flavour than ordinary sugar. To ensure a maximum custardy texture, be sure to gently but *thoroughly* mix the bread cubes with the liquid, so the cubes are completely saturated. These puddings billow up like soufflés, then deflate a bit. Eat them warm, or at room temperature.

SERVES 6

V

6 oz (175 g) several-days-old, crustless white
    bread, cut into 1 inch (2.5 cm) cubes
4 tablespoons lemon marmalade
1 teaspoon lemon extract (page 242)

2 whole eggs
3 egg whites
16 fl oz (475 ml) skimmed milk mixed with 3
    tablespoons skimmed milk powder

1 Preheat the oven to 150°C, 300°F, Gas Mark 2.

2 In a bowl, toss the bread cubes with the marmalade and lemon extract until well combined.

3 Lightly beat the eggs and egg whites. Beat in the milk, and pour over the bread. Mix gently with two spoons until the bread is thoroughly saturated with the liquid. Leave to stand for a few minutes. Put the kettle on to boil.

4 Pour the mixture into a round, oval or square shallow glass or ceramic baking dish. Put the dish into a larger baking dish or roasting tin and place in the oven. Fill the larger dish with boiling water to come halfway up the sides of the smaller dish. Bake for 40 minutes.

5 Raise the oven temperature to 180°C, 350°F, Gas Mark 4 and bake for a further 40–45 minutes or until puffed, set and golden. Place the dish on a wire rack and leave to cool to room temperature.

PEACH BREAD PUDDING

SERVES 6
V

Canned fruit in fruit juice helps to make a great bread pudding. Crème de Pêche and Amaretto di Saronne (almond liqueur) complement the peaches beautifully. (Most of the alcohol in the liqueurs evaporates during baking, but the flavour remains.) The recipe can also be prepared with canned pears and orange marmalade, or canned, crushed pineapple and rum.

14 oz (400 g) can sliced peaches in fruit juice
6 oz (175 g) several-days-old, crustless white
* bread, cut into 1 inch (2.5 cm) cubes*
4 tablespoons peach preserve
4 tablespoons Crème de Pêche (peach liqueur)
* or Cointreau*

1 tablespoon Amaretto di Saronne
2 whole eggs
3 egg whites
16 fl oz (475 ml) skimmed milk mixed with 3
* tablespoons skimmed milk powder*

1 Preheat the oven to 150°C, 300°F, Gas Mark 2.

2 Drain the peaches, reserving the juice. Coarsely chop the peaches.

3 In a bowl, toss together the bread, peaches, peach juice, preserve and liqueurs.

4 Lightly beat the eggs and egg whites together. Beat in the milk, and pour over the bread. Mix gently with two spoons until the bread is thoroughly saturated with the liquid. Leave to stand for a few minutes. Put the kettle on to boil.

5 Pour the mixture into a round, oval or square, shallow, glass or ceramic baking dish. Put the dish into a larger baking dish or roasting tin, and place in the oven. Fill the larger dish with boiling water to come halfway up the sides of the smaller dish. Bake for 45 minutes.

6 Raise the oven temperature to 180°C, 350°F, Gas Mark 4 and bake for a further 40 minutes or until puffed, set and golden. Place the dish on a wire rack and leave to cool to room temperature.

IT'S NO YOLK

To prepare a virtually *fat-free* bread pudding (for those who cannot eat whole eggs), replace the three egg whites and two whole eggs in each recipe with five egg whites. A no-yolk bread pudding will be very pale, so you might want to use wholemeal bread, and sprinkle the top of the pudding, before baking, with a tablespoon of brown sugar.

Swiss Rolls and Layer Cakes

The basic sheet cake used for both Swiss rolls and layer cakes is made from a fat-free angel cake mixture. Angel cakes are prepared from egg whites, flour and sugar, so there really is no fat at all, not even an egg yolk. Baked flat on a silicone-paper-lined baking sheet, the finished cake can be spread with a filling and rolled, or cut into three pieces, then filled and stacked. These cakes will fool everybody; although they are fat-free, they taste nothing like diet food – there is not the slightest hint of austerity about them.

ANGEL SHEET CAKE

MAKES 1 SWISS ROLL OR 1 LAYER CAKE
V

Use this cake to make a Swiss roll or a layer cake (see page 216) or use as a base for one of the tiramisu recipes on pages 223–225. A chocolate version follows.

2 oz (50 g) self-raising flour
3½ oz (100 g) caster sugar
5 egg whites (at room temperature)

pinch of cream of tartar
1 teaspoon vanilla extract

1 Preheat the oven to 180°C, 350°F, Gas Mark 4.

2 Sift the flour and 1½ oz (40 g) sugar together into a bowl. Set aside.

3 Beat the egg whites until foamy. Add the cream of tartar and beat until they hold soft peaks. Continue beating, adding the remaining sugar, 2 tablespoons at a time, until the sugar is dissolved, and the whites are stiff and glossy. Fold in the vanilla.

4 A little at a time, sprinkle the sifted flour/sugar mixture over the batter and fold in gently but thoroughly.

5 Spread the mixture on to a Swiss roll tin lined with non-stick (silicone) baking paper.

6 Bake in the oven for 15–18 minutes or until firm but springy to the touch, and a cake tester comes out of the cake clean.

7 Place the tin on a wire rack and leave to cool. Spread a tea-towel on the work surface, and turn the cooled cake out on to it. Peel off the lining paper. It will appear rather flat, but, when rolled or stacked, will meld beautifully with the filling.

CHOCOLATE ANGEL SHEET CAKE

V

1½ oz (40 g) plain flour
3 tablespoons unsweetened cocoa powder
3½ oz (100 g) caster sugar

5 egg whites (at room temperature)
pinch of cream of tartar
1 teaspoon vanilla extract

1 Preheat the oven to 180°C, 350°F, Gas Mark 4.

2 Sift the flour, cocoa and 1½ oz (40 g) sugar together into a bowl. Set aside. Follow stages **3** to **7** of the previous recipe.

TO MAKE A SWISS ROLL

With a palette knife, spread the sheet cake with a filling (see below). Starting at a long edge, begin to roll up the cake. Use the tea-towel to help it roll. If it cracks, don't worry – it will still look good. Brush it with a glaze, or ice it (see below) and refrigerate, covered, until needed.

TO MAKE A LAYER CAKE

Cut the sheet cake into three equal sections. Place one of the pieces on a plate or platter and, with a palette knife, slather on one of the spreads (see below). Top with the second layer and slather on more of the filling. Top with the third layer and glaze or ice (see below). Refrigerate until needed. You could also layer the cake with sliced fruit, such as strawberries or peaches (see the photograph opposite page 210).

FILLINGS AND TOPPINGS

Fillings for Swiss Rolls and Layer Cakes

Chocolate Icing (opposite)
Orange Ricotta Cream (page 218)
Lemon Cream (page 219)
Apricot Spread (page 73)
Honey or Maple Vanilla Cream, when made
    with ricotta (page 228)
Mango Cream (page 228)

Toppings for Swiss Rolls and Layer Cakes

Chocolate Icing (opposite)
Old Fashioned Dark Chocolate Icing (page
    218)
Make a glaze by melting marmalade or jam
    (with a tablespoon of liqueur, if desired)
    and spread it on the cake.

CHOCOLATE ICING (MICROWAVE)

MAKES 2 PINTS (1.1 LITRES)
V ⊙

This icing is more like a thick, fudgy chocolate pudding, but is useful for filling and icing cakes, or as the creamy chocolate layer in a trifle. And it is also useful (useful! It's pure heaven), eaten with a spoon, to soothe those chocolate longings. Use the best cocoa powder and chocolate you can find (see page 242).

9 tablespoons unsweetened cocoa powder
3 tablespoons cornflour
5 tablespoons skimmed milk powder
8 tablespoons sugar

½ oz (15 g) high-cocoa-solids dark chocolate, grated
½ teaspoon vanilla extract
about 18 fl oz (500 ml) skimmed milk

1 Sift the cocoa, cornflour, milk powder and sugar into a 3½ pint (2 litre, 7 inch (18 cm) top diameter, opaque white plastic or 3½ pint (2 litre), 7½ inch (19 cm) diameter Pyrex clear glass measuring jug. Sprinkle in the grated chocolate.

2 Using a wire whisk, whisk the vanilla and milk into the dry ingredients. Whisk well to avoid lumps (and vigorous whisking helps alleviate the chance of volcanic eruptions). Cover the jug tightly with cling film.

3 Microwave on high (full power) for 3 minutes, then carefully pierce the cling film (avert your face, be careful – the steam is hot) to release the steam. Uncover (begin with the side *away* from you), and whisk thoroughly. Re-cover tightly, with a fresh piece of cling film, and microwave for another 2 minutes. Carefully pierce the film, uncover, whisk, re-cover tightly and microwave for a final 1½–2 minutes or until boiled, thickened and smooth.

4 Whisk again and leave to stand for 5 minutes, whisking occasionally. Store in the refrigerator with a sheet of microwave cling film directly over the surface of the pudding.

OLD-FASHIONED DARK CHOCOLATE ICING

MAKES 1 ¾ PINTS (1 LITRE)

V ☺

If you don't have a microwave, this is your filling or icing. Use it also as a pudding to satisfy your chocolate-loving soul.

8 tablespoons unsweetened cocoa powder
½ oz (15 g) high-cocoa-solids dark chocolate, grated
8 tablespoons caster sugar

4 tablespoons cornflour
tiny pinch of salt
1½ pints (900 ml) skimmed milk

1 Whisk together all the ingredients, then put in a blender, in batches, and blend until *very* smooth.

2 Rinse a heavy-bottomed, non-stick saucepan with cold water. Pour out the water, but do not dry the saucepan (this helps reduce scorching). Pour the chocolate mixture into the pan, and heat on medium heat, stirring, until it begins to bubble strenuously. As you stir, do not scrape the bottom: if any scorching does occur on the bottom of the saucepan, you do not want to stir the scorched bits into the pudding. Continue stirring and cooking for 1 minute or until thickened, then remove from the heat.

3 Immediately pour into a bowl. Cover with cling film and refrigerate until needed.

ORANGE RICOTTA CREAM

MAKES ½ PINT (300 ML)

V ☺

This fluffy cream makes a lovely filling for Swiss rolls and layer cakes. It can also be used as a topping for desserts.

two 9 oz (250g) cartons ricotta cheese (or half quark, half ricotta)
1–2 heaped tablespoons orange marmalade

1 teaspoon vanilla extract
1 tablespoon orange liqueur (Grand Marnier or Cointreau)

Combine all the ingredients in a food processor. Process until well mixed and fluffy. Taste and add a little more marmalade or a touch of icing sugar, if you think it's needed.

LEMON CAKE

SERVES 8
V

This is a layer cake filled with lemon cream and glazed with lemon glaze. Yes, it's low-fat, but who's going to believe you?

2 oz (50 g) self-raising flour
3½ oz (100 g) caster sugar
5 egg whites (at room temperature)
pinch of cream of tartar
½ teaspoon lemon extract (page 242)
½ teaspoon lemon juice

LEMON 'CREAM'
1 lb (450 g) ricotta
about 2 tablespoons lemon marmalade
½ teaspoon lemon extract
GLAZE
1½ tablespoons lemon marmalade

I Preheat the oven to 180°C, 350°F, Gas Mark 4.

2 Sift the flour and 1½ oz (40 g) sugar together into a bowl, and set aside.

3 Beat the egg whites until foamy. Add the cream of tartar and beat until they hold soft peaks. Continue beating, adding the remaining sugar, 2 tablespoons at a time, until the sugar is dissolved and the whites are stiff and glossy. Fold in the lemon extract and the lemon juice.

4 A little at a time, sprinkle the flour mixture over the whites and fold in gently but thoroughly.

5 Spread the mixture in a Swiss roll tin lined with non-stick (silicone) baking paper.

6 Bake in the oven for 15–18 minutes or until the surface feels firm but springy.

7 Place the tin on a wire rack and leave to cool. When cooled, spread a tea-towel on the work surface, turn the cake out on to it, and gently peel off the silicone paper.

8 For the lemon 'cream', combine the ingredients in a food processor. Process until well mixed and fluffy. Taste and add a little more marmalade if needed. Chill until serving time.

9 For the glaze, melt the marmalade in a bowl over boiling water.

10 Cut the cake crossways into three equal sections. Place one section on a plate and spread with a generous amount of lemon cream. Cover with the second piece and slather on more filling. Top with the last third and brush the top with the glaze. If not serving within 1 hour, store in the fridge, then allow to come to room temperature before serving in slices.

FRUIT LOAVES

The following three 'tea' loaves are based on a no-fat flour, sugar and egg white mixture with added fruit. They all keep well, and make great snacks or packed-lunch additions.

BANANA CAKE

MAKES ABOUT 16 SLICES

V

It is important that you use very ripe bananas for this deliciously moist cake. When cool, wrap in foil and keep for one day before eating (if you can bear to wait!). The flavour develops beautifully and seems to improve with age.

2 very *ripe bananas*
8 *fl oz (225 ml) orange juice*
5 *oz (150 g) soft brown sugar*
10 *oz (275 g) self-raising flour*
pinch of salt

½ *teaspoon ground cinnamon*
1 *teaspoon ground mixed spice*
2 *egg whites, lightly beaten*
oil spray (page ix)

1 Preheat the oven to 170°C, 325°F, Gas Mark 3.

2 Peel the bananas and mash with the orange juice.

3 Sift the sugar, flour, salt and spices together into a bowl, and add the banana and juice mixture and the egg whites. Mix together and combine well.

4 Line an 8 inch (20 cm) non-stick cake tin with greaseproof paper. Spray with oil spray. Scrape the mixture into the tin, smooth the top and bake in the oven for about 1 hour.

5 When the cake is risen and golden brown, check that it is done by inserting a fine metal skewer or cake tester into the centre. When it comes out clean, the cake is done.

6 Cool in the tin on a wire rack for a few minutes. With a palette knife, loosen the cake carefully all around the sides, and turn out. Peel off the greaseproof paper. Cool thoroughly. To store, wrap in foil.

APPLE LOAF

MAKES ABOUT 16 SLICES

V

With this Apple Loaf, as with all the fruit loaves, measure and mix each batch separately if you plan to make several at once, or you will end up with a gluey mess!

10 oz (275 g) Granny Smith apples (about 2), or other tart eating apples, cored and diced
6 fl oz (175 ml) orange juice
10 oz (275 g) self-raising flour

5 ½ oz (160 g) soft brown sugar
2 egg whites, lightly beaten
oil spray (page ix)

1 Soak the apple cubes in the orange juice for 1 hour or so, or overnight.

2 Preheat the oven to 170°C, 325°F, Gas Mark 3. Drain the apples, reserving the juice.

3 Sift the flour and sugar together into a bowl. Add the drained apple pieces with 3 fl oz (75 ml) of the reserved orange juice and the egg whites. Mix together and incorporate well.

4 Line a 2 lb (900 g) non-stick loaf tin with greaseproof paper. Spray with oil spray. Scrape the mixture into the tin, smooth the top and bake in the oven for about 2 hours. During the last 30 minutes or so, cover loosely with foil to prevent overbrowning.

5 When the loaf is risen and golden brown, check that it is done by inserting a fine metal skewer or cake tester into the centre. When it comes out clean, the loaf is done.

6 Cool in the tin on a rack for a few minutes, then loosen the loaf carefully all around the sides with a palette knife, and turn out. Peel off the paper. Cool thoroughly. To store, wrap in foil.

SPICY VARIATION Add 1 teaspoon ground cinnamon, ⅛ teaspoon ground cloves and ½ teaspoon ground allspice when sifting the flour.

FRUIT CARROT LOAF

MAKES ABOUT 16 SLICES
V

An old-fashioned carrot cake (very rich) is usually iced with a sweet cream cheese frosting (even richer). Instead, serve one of the ricotta or quark creams (pages 218 and 228) for spreading on each slice of this beautiful, low-fat carrot loaf.

8 oz (225 g) sultanas or raisins, soaked
  overnight in 8 fl oz (225 ml) orange juice
5 oz (150 g) Granny Smith apples (about 2),
  peeled, cored and diced
6 oz (175 g) carrots, (about 5 peeled carrots),
  peeled and finely grated
5½ oz (160 g) soft brown sugar

10 oz (275 g) self-raising flour
pinch of salt
1 teaspoon ground cinnamon
3 teaspoons ground mixed spice
2 egg whites, lightly beaten
oil spray (page ix)

1 Preheat the oven to 170°C, 325°F, Gas Mark 3.

2 Stir the apples and carrots into the sultanas and their juice. Sift the sugar, flour, salt and spices together into a bowl. Add the soaked sultanas, apples, carrots and their juices, then add the egg whites. Mix together and incorporate well.

3 Line a 2 lb (900 g) non-stick loaf tin with greaseproof paper and spray with oil spray. Scrape the mixture into the tin, smooth the top and bake in the oven for about 2 hours. During the last 30 minutes or so, cover loosely with foil so that the loaf does not overbrown.

4 When the loaf is risen and golden brown, check that it is done by inserting a fine metal skewer or cake tester into the centre. When it comes out clean, the loaf is done.

5 Cool in the tin on a wire rack for a few minutes, then with a palette knife, loosen carefully all around the sides. Turn out and peel off the greaseproof paper. Cool thoroughly. To store, wrap in foil.

TIRAMISU

Tiramisu (it means 'pick-me-up') has become something of a cliché, turning up on the dessert displays of most of the Italian restaurants and wine bars in the known world. (At least, that's how it seems!) There is a reason for this phenomenon – tiramisu is an impossibly seductive and delicious pudding. It's soggy/boozy (liqueur-drenched sponge fingers), and sweet and creamy (sweetened whipped cream and mascarpone cheese). These elements meld into each other so the whole forms a tipsy, soggy, creamy mass – part cheesecake, part trifle – that has to be tasted to be believed.

The problem with tiramisu (you don't need to be told – I'm sure you know already) is that it contains enough fat to choke a brontosaurus. I don't usually go into graphic detail about fat and calorie comparisons, but this is just too over-the-top to resist. Marscarpone cheese is more than 80 per cent fat – actually higher in fat than double cream. A traditional tiramisu contains 602 Calories (no, it is not a misprint) and almost 40 grams of fat *per serving*. I'll give you a moment for those frightening numbers to sink in. Yes, the damned thing is delicious, but really! You might as well plaster it all over your hips and thighs and have done with it – you might as well just go ahead and butter your arteries!

Does this mean a tiramisu-deprived lifestyle? Or does it mean an occasional indulgence, followed by guilt and uncontrolled longing for just one more piece, and another, and another . . . of course not, on both counts. A streamlined, lean tiramisu is not only possible, it is delicious. I'll repeat that: It . . . is . . . delicious. I'm shouting, because no one believes me until they try it for themselves. The secret is to get rid of the mascarpone and the cream. Replace it with ricotta cheese (15 per cent fat) or a combination of ricotta and quark (0 per cent fat). Beaten with icing sugar or a tablespoon or two of marmalade, these cheeses taste as rich and creamy as you could possibly wish for. Sponge fingers form the base of a tiramisu – they contain whole eggs but no other added fat. The following tiramisu recipes use sponge fingers, but if you must (or you cook for someone who must) avoid fat and cholesterol altogether, use one of the following bases:

Bread Base Instead of sponge fingers, use 3 or 4 slices of non-fat or low-fat bakery white bread, ¾ inch (1.5 cm) thick, trimmed of crusts and cut into fingers 1 inch (2.5 cm) wide. Decrease the amount of coffee (when applicable) to 1–2 tablespoons. Any of the fillings can be used with this base.

Angel Sheet Cake Base Use the chocolate or plain Angel Sheet Cake (pages 215, 216 and 219). Cut the cake into 1 inch (2.5 cm) fingers. Decrease the amount of coffee (when applicable) to 3 tablespoons.

TIRAMISU

SERVES 6–8

V ○

This tiramisu retains the tipsy, creamy seductive qualities of the original but the calorie count of a single portion is 154 (compared to 602). And the fat grams measure 4 (compared to 40). So enjoy yourself. In this recipe and the following one, water-processed decaffeinated filter coffee can be substituted for the strong coffee with absolutely no loss of quality. If you are planning to serve tiramisu to children, substitute fruit juice for the liqueurs and coffee.

15–16 sponge fingers
¼ pint (150 ml) strong black coffee
1½ teaspoons vanilla extract
1 tablespoon Amaretto di Saronne or dark rum
1 tablespoon brandy

three 9 oz (250 g) cartons ricotta cheese, or use
half ricotta, half quark
3½–4½ tablespoons icing sugar
1 heaped tablespoon unsweetened cocoa
powder

1 Line the bottom of a shallow rectangular (12 × 7 inches/30 × 18 cm) or oval baking dish with one layer of sponge fingers (you may have to break a few in half). Stir together the coffee, ½ teaspoon vanilla extract, Amaretto di Saronne or rum, and brandy. A tablespoon at a time, sprinkle this mixture over the sponge fingers.

2 Combine the ricotta cheese, 3–4 tablespoons icing sugar and 1 teaspoon vanilla in a food processor, and process until smooth and fluffy. Spread this mixture over the sponge fingers.

3 Combine the cocoa and remaining icing sugar. Sift it evenly over the surface of the pudding, cover the dish and chill.

CHOCOLATE TIRAMISU

SERVES 6–8

V ○

Cocoa powder is an extremely low-fat form of chocolate (to produce cocoa powder, much of the cocoa butter is separated from the chocolate solids). Cocoa powder turns tiramisu into a chocolate delight. Pure heaven!

15–16 *sponge fingers*
¼ *pint (150 ml) strong black coffee*
1½ *teaspoons vanilla extract*
1 *tablespoon Amaretto di Saronne*
1 *tablespoon dark rum*

12 oz (350 g) *each of ricotta cheese and quark*
6½ *tablespoons icing sugar*
3 *tablespoons unsweetened cocoa powder*
½ oz (15 g) *high-cocoa-solid dark chocolate,*
  melted and cooled slightly

1 Line the bottom of a shallow rectangular (12 × 7 inches/30 × 18 cm) or oval baking dish with one layer of sponge fingers (you may have to break a few in half.) Stir together the coffee, ½ teaspoon vanilla extract, the Amaretto di Saronne and rum. Sprinkle over the fingers.

2 Combine the ricotta and quark, 6 tablespoons icing sugar, 2 tablespoons cocoa, the melted chocolate and 1 teaspoon vanilla in a food processor, and process until smooth and fluffy. Spread over the fingers.

3 Sift together the remaining cocoa and icing sugar, and sprinkle over the top. Cover and chill.

CHERRY RICOTTA TIRAMISU

SERVES 6–8
V

The cherry conserve tints the top creamy layer a blushing pink. This is a beautiful tiramisu for a summer party.

2 lb (900 g) *cherries, stoned and halved*
1 lb (450 g) *raspberries*
juice of 2 large oranges
4 *tablespoons each of Cointreau and Amaretto*
  di Saronne
1 *tablespoon each of Kirsch and vanilla extract*

about 16 sponge fingers
three 9 oz (250 g) cartons ricotta cheese
7 oz (200 g) *carton quark*
4–6 *tablespoons cherry conserve*
2 *pairs amaretti biscuits, crushed*

1 Gently toss together the fruit, juice, liqueurs and vanilla. Leave to macerate for 30 minutes.

2 Line the bottom of a clear glass baking dish (12 × 7 inch/30 × 18 cm) with a layer of sponge fingers (breaking some in half if necessary). Spread the fruit mixture evenly over the fingers, making sure that all the juices go in as well.

3 Scrape the ricotta and quark into the processor. Process with the cherry conserve until fluffy and beautifully pink. Taste, and add more conserve or a pinch or two of icing sugar if needed.

4 Evenly spread the ricotta mixture over the fruit. Sprinkle with the amaretti crumbs. Cover and refrigerate overnight. To serve, cut into squares.

CHEESECAKES

Thanks to ricotta and quark, low-fat cheesecakes that are actually good to eat are not just a fond dream. In the following recipe, the cheesecake filling is swirled into a crumb crust made from Grape Nuts cereal and crushed amaretti biscuits. Any of the tiramisu toppings (pages 223–225) can be swirled into such a crust to create other low-fat cheesecakes.

CHOCOLATE CHEESECAKE

SERVES 8

Yes! It *is* possible to have a luxurious, sinful-tasting chocolate cheesecake that is low in fat. You have to taste it to believe it.

CHOCOLATE SAUCE
1½ oz (40 g) cocoa powder
3½ oz (85 g) caster sugar

8 tablespoons skimmed milk powder
4 fl oz (110 ml) cold water
1 teaspoon vanilla extract

1 Sift together the cocoa, sugar and milk powder, and put in a blender with the water and vanilla. Blend, stopping to scrape the sides, until very well combined and perfectly smooth. Strain into a 3½ pint (2 litre) glass bowl or measuring jug. Cover tightly with cling film.

2 Microwave on high (full power) for 1 minute. *Carefully* uncover, (begin with the side away from you, and avert your face) and whisk well. Re-cover and microwave for 30 seconds, then whisk again. Re-cover and microwave for another 30 seconds. Uncover and whisk well. Cool with cling film on the surface of the sauce, and refrigerate overnight. (It may go solid when chilled – don't worry, it's not a problem.)

CHOCOLATE FILLING
two 9 oz (250 g) cartons ricotta cheese
7 oz (200 g) carton quark

½ oz (15 g) high-cocoa-solids dark chocolate,
melted and cooled slightly
1 quantity Chocolate Sauce (see above)
Crumb Crust (opposite)

1 Put the ricotta, quark, melted chocolate and Chocolate Sauce in a food processor, and process until very smooth and fluffy.

2 Spread and swirl the mixture in the crumb crust. Chill for several hours or overnight.

CRUMB CRUST

MAKES ONE 10 INCH (25.5 CM) CRUST

V ⊙

2½ oz (60 g) amaretti biscuits
2½ oz (60 g) Grape Nuts cereal

2 egg whites
oil spray (page ix)

I Preheat the oven to 180°C, 350°F, Gas Mark 4.

2 Put the dry ingredients into a blender or food processor, and process to coarse crumbs.

3 Lightly beat the egg whites, and mix with the crumb mixture until thoroughly combined.

4 Lightly spray a 10 inch (25.5 cm) round non-stick flan tin with oil spray. Scrape the crumb mixture into the pan. With the back of a serving spoon, spread it evenly over the bottom and up the sides.

5 Bake in the oven for 7–10 minutes, then cool in the tin on a wire rack. When cool, loosen all around and down the sides with a palette knife, to facilitate later serving. Set aside until needed.

CREAMY TOPPINGS

Whipped cream, crème fraîche and soured cream are not options for those who must control their dietary fat, but there are plenty of other possibilities. Quark, ricotta or fromage frais can be whipped with a sweetener (icing sugar, honey, marmalade, jam or preserves, or maple syrup) and used very successfully to top fruit salads or puddings. Whip fromage frais with a wire whisk and ricotta or quark in the processor or with an electric mixer. Several examples follow, but you will come up with many more of your own. Another appears on page 218.

HONEY OR MAPLE VANILLA CREAM

MAKES 18 FL OZ (500 ML)

V ⊙

1 vanilla pod
1 lb 2 oz (500 g) very low-fat fromage frais or
  ricotta cheese

2 tablespoons runny honey or pure maple syrup

1 With a small, sharp knife, split the vanilla pod lengthways. With the tip of the knife, scrape the soft pulp from each half into the fromage frais or ricotta. (Save the scraped pod to store in a canister of caster sugar, or to simmer in dried fruit compote.)

2 Whisk the honey into the fromage frais. Or if you are using ricotta, swirl it in a food processor with the honey. Stir so that the black vanilla bean specks are evenly distributed through the fromage frais. Store in the refrigerator.

MANGO CREAM

MAKES ABOUT ½ PINT (300 ML)

V ⊙

If you whip a dead-ripe mango into ricotta you will produce a spectacular cream topping. I especially like this spooned on top of warm fruit.

1 very ripe mango, peeled and cubed (page 69)
9 oz (250 g) carton ricotta cheese

½–1 tablespoon icing sugar

In the processor, combine the cubed mango and ricotta, and process until puréed. Taste and process in a little icing sugar if needed.

FRUIT-BASED DESSERTS

FRESH FRUIT SALAD

V ⊘

A simple fruit salad is one of the most luscious things to serve for summer dessert. When berries are at their best, peaches are fragrant and silky, and plums are bursting with juicy pulp, this can hardly be bettered.

Put as many kinds of berries as you can find into a big bowl. Hull and halve or quarter any strawberries. Stone and cube peaches and plums over a bowl to catch their juices. Add cubes of ripe melon, mango – whatever you like and looks good. Add 1 teaspoon vanilla extract, a few tablespoons orange juice, and a few tablespoons Crème de Pêche (peach liqueur) and Cointreau. Mix gently together, and leave to stand for 15–30 minutes. Serve with Raspberry Coulis (page 232) and Honey Vanilla Cream (opposite).

In winter, use apples, pears and peeled diced oranges. Add drained canned lychees in natural juice, and a bit of slivered (use scissors) crystallized ginger. Dress with orange juice, Cointreau, Crème de Pêche and vanilla extract, as described above.

PEACHES AND CREAM

SERVES 4
V ⊘

A one-fruit salad can end a meal elegantly, when the fruit in question is absolutely perfect. Instead of Honeyed Vanilla Cream, you might want to top the peaches with a scoop of Peach Ice Cream or Peach Sorbet (pages 210–211).

6 large, ripe peaches
2–3 tablespoons Crème de Pêche or orange
  liqueur (Cointreau or Grand Marnier)

1 teaspoon vanilla extract
Honey Vanilla Cream (opposite)
brown sugar, to serve

1 Halve and stone the peaches. Cut into ¾–1 inch (1.5–2.5 cm) cubes. Work over a large bowl, to catch the juices. Combine the peach cubes in the bowl with the liqueur and vanilla extract.

2 To serve, heap the peaches and their juices in clear glass goblets and top each with a *very* generous dollop of Honey Vanilla Cream. Sprinkle with a pinch of brown sugar.

STUFFED PEACHES

MAKES 12 HALVES

As long as we're talking about perfect peaches, they are delicious lightly baked as well, stuffed with peach pulp and crumbled amaretti biscuits. They look beautiful on their pool of scented juices.

7 ripe, firm peaches
3 pairs amaretti biscuits
½ teaspoon vanilla extract
3 fl oz (75 ml) orange liqueur (Cointreau or
*   Grand Marnier)*

6 fl oz (175 ml) medium sweet red vermouth or
*   sherry*
Orange Ricotta Cream (page 218), optional

1 Preheat the oven to 190°C, 375°F, Gas Mark 5.

2 Carefully halve the peaches and remove the stones. (Work over a bowl to catch any juices.) Trim any bits of peach flesh off the stones and add them to the juices. Chop two of the peach halves and put them in the bowl with the juices. Use a teaspoon to hollow out the depressions in the remaining peach halves, so that they will hold the filling. Add the scooped-out peach pulp to the bowl. Place the peaches, skin-side down, in a baking dish that holds them snugly in one layer.

3 Crumble the amaretti biscuits and stir them into the peach juices and chopped peach pieces. Stir in the vanilla and ½ teaspoon orange liqueur. Combine the remaining orange liqueur with the vermouth or sherry.

4 Fill each peach half with an equal amount of the amaretti mixture. Pour 4–6 fl oz (110–175 ml) of the orange liqueur and vermouth mixture around the peaches. Sprinkle them with another 2–3 tablespoons of the mixture.

5 Bake, uncovered, in the oven for 10–12 minutes. Sprinkle them evenly with another 3–4 tablespoons of the vermouth mixture, and bake for 8–10 minutes more. The peaches should not lose their shape.

6 With a slotted spoon, remove the peaches to a pretty serving dish. Simmer the pan juices briefly to reduce slightly. Serve the peaches warm or at room temperature, on a pool of the cooking juices. If you wish, spoon a dollop of Orange Ricotta Cream on to the centre of each peach half.

BAKED PEARS

MAKES 8 HALVES

v

Even under-ripe pears taste good when they've been baked. The halved pears are served in a puddle of their pan juices, with a scoop of Pear Ice Cream (or Orange Ricotta Cream) nestled in their hollows.

4 fl oz (110 ml) medium sweet sherry
juice and slivered zest of 1 large orange
juice and slivered zest of ½ lemon

4 ripe but firm pears
Pear Ice Cream (pages 210–211) or Orange
  Ricotta Cream (page 218)

1 Preheat the oven to 190°C, 375°F, Gas Mark 5.

2 Pour the liquids into a shallow, non-reactive baking dish and add the citrus zests.

3 Peel the pears and cut off the stems. Dip in the sherry mixture to prevent the pears darkening. Halve each pear and dip again. With a teaspoon, scoop out the cores. Rub the cavities with the sherry mixture. Place the pears, cored sides up, in the dish.

4 Bake, uncovered, in the oven for 20–30 minutes or until just tender. With a slotted spoon, transfer the pears to a plate. Drain all the juices into a small saucepan and boil until thickened and syrupy. Pour the juices over and around the pears (reserve a bit of the juices). Serve warm or at room temperature. Fill each pear half with either Pear Ice Cream, or Orange Ricotta Cream. Drizzle some of the reserved syrupy juices over the filling in each pear.

COEURS À LA CRÈME WITH RASPBERRY COULIS

SERVES 8

V

ACoeur à la Crème mould is a pierced white porcelain, heart-shaped mould used to produce a romantic, creamy pudding – just the thing for Valentine's day. Many houseware shops and departments sell them, but you could also prepare this in an ordinary colander. The resulting pudding will be domed rather than heart-shaped, but still delicious, and still very attractive.

*three 9 oz (250 g) cartons ricotta cheese (or a
    mixture of quark and ricotta)*
2 heaped tablespoons orange marmalade
icing sugar, to taste
2 teaspoons vanilla extract

*2 tablespoons orange liqueur (Grand Marnier
    or Cointreau)*
Raspberry Coulis (below)
*fresh raspberries or thawed frozen raspberries,
    to decorate*

1 Combine all the ingredients, except the coulis and raspberries, in a food processor. Process until well mixed and fluffy. Taste and add a little more marmalade and/or a touch of sugar if you think it's needed.

2 Place the mixture in a muslin- or jelly-bag-lined, heart-shaped, pierced *coeur à la crème* mould, set over a bowl, to drain for about 2 hours, or overnight. If you do not have a coeur à la crème mould, use a colander.

3 Unmould on to a plate, surround with Raspberry Coulis (below), and decorate with raspberries.

RASPBERRY COULIS

This suave, scarlet sauce – pure raspberries with a bit of sweetener – decorates the coeurs à la crème dramatically, but it is delicious ladled over the food processor ice creams and sorbets (pages 210–211) as well. And it is an elegant and beautiful addition to fruit salad. When strawberries are big, juicy and flavourful, serve them whole with this sauce for dipping.

*two 12 oz (350 g) boxes frozen raspberries,
    thawed*

icing sugar, to taste
a few drops of lemon juice, to taste

Drain the berries and purée the fruit in a food processor or blender. Sieve the purée to eliminate the pips. Sweeten to taste, and add a few drops of lemon juice, if necessary, to sharpen the taste. Refrigerate until needed.

CARAMELIZED BANANAS AND PEARS WITH MANGO CREAM

SERVES 1–2
V ☉

The combination of thick, mango-drenched, cold cream on the hot, syrupy, tender fruit, will send you into a frenzy. Well, maybe not quite – not everyone reacts quite so intensely to food pleasure. But it *will* send the odd frisson up and down your spine.

1 ripe, firm banana, peeled and sliced
1 ripe, firm pear, peeled, cored and cubed
8 fl oz (225 ml) orange juice
½ tablespoon lemon juice

3 tablespoons orange liqueur
1 teaspoon vanilla extract
1–2 teaspoons soft brown sugar
Mango Cream (page 228)

1 In a heavy-bottomed frying pan, combine everything except the Mango Cream. Simmer briskly for 5–7 minutes or until the juices are thickened and reduced, but the fruit is still firm. Stir constantly. With a slotted spoon, scoop out the fruit and divide the fruit between two glass goblets.

2 Boil the juices down to a syrup, then scrape and pour them over the fruit. Top the fruit and syrup with cold Mango Cream. Serve at once.

SUMMER PUDDING PARFAIT

SERVES 4
V

This is an easy-to-make summer pudding served in a glass. It looks enchanting served in clear glass goblets, garnished with extra fruit and sprigs of mint.

1 punnet strawberries, quartered
2 punnets raspberries
1 punnet blueberries
6 fl oz (175 ml) orange juice

2 fl oz (50 ml) Cointreau
1 teaspoon vanilla extract
1–2 tablespoons maple syrup
12 slices firm white bread

1 Combine the berries, juice, Cointreau, vanilla and maple syrup, and leave to stand for 1 hour.

2 With a glass, cut out a circle from each slice of bread. Layer the bread, fruit and their juices in four wine glasses in this order: a slice of bread, fruit and juice, bread, fruit and juice, bread, juice. Cover each glass with cling film, and place the glasses in a shallow baking dish (to catch the drips). Weight each glass with jarred foods (one jar each glass) and refrigerate for several hours.

COLD ORANGES WITH HOT SULTANAS

V ⊙

Afrozen orange tastes like orange sorbet. Keep juicy, seedless oranges in the freezer. When you want to make this recipe, remove the oranges from the freezer while the sultanas simmer. Then, when it is time to slice them, they will have thawed just enough to be sliceable with a good sharp, serrated knife. (Be careful! Grip the orange with an oven glove.) The shock of hot/cold makes this a dramatic dessert.

orange juice
grated orange zest
grated zest and juice of ½ lime

Cointreau or Grand Marnier
several handfuls of sultanas
partially frozen large juicy seedless oranges

1 Combine all the ingredients, except the oranges, in a frying pan, and simmer until the sultanas are plump and coated in a thick syrup.

2 Carefully slice the oranges. Quickly trim the peel and pith from each slice. Arrange overlapping slices on individual serving plates. Pour and scatter some sultanas with their syrup over the slices. Serve at once.

APPLE CRUMBLE

SERVES 4–6
V

Lower-fat crumbles can be made with a ricotta–flour–maple syrup (or honey) topping as here, or with an amaretti, Grape Nuts and egg topping (page 237). For the apple crumble, I prefer the apples to keep their shape, but if you like a fluffy apple purée for your crumble, use Bramleys, and add a touch more maple syrup (or honey).

1½ lb (700 g) tart apples, peeled, cored and
  diced
3 oz (75 g) dried apricots, chopped (use scissors)
3 oz (75 g) sultanas
juice of ½ lemon
juice of ½ orange
3 tablespoons maple syrup

2 teaspoons vanilla extract
¼ teaspoon ground mixed spice
3 oz (75 g) ricotta
3 oz (75 g) plain flour
1 oz (25 g) whole oats with their bran
1 tablespoon orange marmalade
1 tablespoon brown sugar

1 Preheat the oven to 190°C, 375°F, Gas Mark 5.

2 Combine the apples, dried fruit, citrus juices, maple syrup, half the vanilla and the spices in a baking dish. Bake, uncovered, in the oven for 30 minutes.

3 Process the remaining ingredients, including the remaining vanilla, in a food processor until the mixture forms damp, pebbly clumps.

4 Sprinkle the clumps evenly over the apples and bake for a further 20–30 minutes or until the crumble is browned.

PEAR COMPOTE

MAKES 1¼ PINTS (750 ML)
V

Use this compote to make a pear crumble (see the Apple Crumble recipe opposite for topping and method, or use the amaretti topping on page 237). Or use the compote to make delightful little pear tarts (see below).

2½ lb (1.1 kg) pears
juice of 1 orange
juice of ½ lemon
1 tablespoon orange marmalade
2 tablespoons maple syrup
1 tablespoon Cointreau

1 tablespoon dark rum
1 teaspoon vanilla extract
½ teaspoon each of ground ginger and
  cinnamon
3 tablespoons dried sour cherries

1 Preheat the oven to 190°C, 375°F, Gas Mark 5.

2 Peel and core the pears, and cut them into chunks. Toss the pears with the remaining ingredients and spread out in a baking dish. Bake in the oven for 30–45 minutes or until tender.

FRUIT TARTS

Either the apple compote from the Apple Crumble (steps 1 and 2, pages 234–5) or the Pear Compote (above) can be served in goblets with a cloud of Honey or Maple Vanilla Cream or Orange Ricotta Cream (pages 218 and 228). Or make a simple apple or pear tart: Cut a circle from a slice of excellent quality white bread. Repeat with additional slices of bread to make as many as you need. Each circle will form the base of a single tart.

Dry the bread on a baking sheet in the oven at 150°C, 300°F, Gas Mark 2, for about 15 minutes, turning occasionally. When the bread is dried through (but not browned) it will keep for days in an airtight tin.

Put one circle on a plate. Warm the compote. Spoon some of the compote on the circle, covering it completely. Drizzle on some of the juices. Serve with a knife and fork. Marvellous!

BLUEBERRY CRUMBLE

SERVES 4–6

V

Either the amaretti topping (below) or the ricotta-flour topping (page 234) can be used with the blueberries. Frozen blueberries are available in many supermarkets. When fresh berries are out of season, the frozen work just fine.

18 oz (500 g) blueberries
3–4 tablespoons caster sugar
1 tablespoon cornflour
½ teaspoon vanilla extract
½ tablespoon lemon juice
juice of ½ orange

pinch each of ground cinnamon and freshly
  grated nutmeg
6 pairs amaretti biscuits
3 oz (75 g) Grape Nuts cereal
1 whole egg
2 egg whites

1 Preheat the oven to 190°C, 375°F, Gas Mark 5.

2 Mix together the blueberries, sugar, cornflour, vanilla, lemon and orange juices, cinnamon and nutmeg. Put the mixture into a glass or ceramic baking dish and bake, uncovered, in the oven for 15 minutes or until thick, bubbly and juicy.

3 Put the amaretti and cereal into a food processor, and process to coarse crumbs. Add the whole egg to the crumbs and process until well mixed. Pour and scrape the mixture over the blueberries and spread with the back of a large spoon to cover the surface of the blueberries, leaving a ½ inch (1 cm) border all around. Raise the oven temperature to 200°C, 400°F, Gas Mark 6, and bake for an additional 7–10 minutes or until the topping is set and the juices are bubbling. Serve warm or cold.

NEW WAVE BANOFFEE

SERVES 8

V ⊙

Banoffee Pie is a concoction of buttered crumb crust, banana-toffee filling and whipped cream topping. The toffee is made by boiling down condensed milk, and the whipped cream topping is usually several inches thick. Not, as you can imagine, a suitable recipe for a low-fat lifestyle. Recently, I was asked to come up with a slim-line version, so I have spent quite a bit of time and effort over the past few months trying to tame the Banoffee. I found that a syrup of orange juice, orange liqueur and brown sugar makes a perfectly gorgeous substitute for the toffee; and ricotta or ricotta/quark stands in splendidly for the whipped cream, in fact it has quite a bit more character than the whipped cream. The intense banana activity in my kitchen resulted in the Caramelized Bananas and Pears with Mango Cream (page 233), in addition to this New Wave Banoffee. I *do* love my work!

½ pint (300 ml) orange juice
juice of ½ lemon
1½ tablespoons orange liqueur (Cointreau or
*   Grand Marnier)*
2 tablespoons dark brown muscovado sugar
5 ripe, firm bananas, peeled and sliced

two 7 oz (200 g) cartons quark
9 oz (250 g) carton ricotta cheese
2 tablespoons orange marmalade
2 tablespoons Grape Nuts cereal
2 amaretti biscuits

1 Combine the juices, orange liqueur and 1 tablespoon sugar in a heavy-bottomed saucepan. Bring to the boil, and boil, stirring, until syrupy and reduced to a little less than half. Add the sliced bananas to the mixture, and stir to coat thoroughly. Leave to cool slightly.

2 Combine the quark, ricotta, marmalade and remaining sugar in a food processor, and process until thoroughly combined.

3 Spoon the banana and orange mixture into a pretty glass bowl, or into individual glass goblets. Top with the creamy mixture.

4 Put the Grape Nuts and amaretti into a plastic bag. Pound with a kitchen mallet or the bottom of a bottle to reduce to crumbs. Sprinkle evenly over the cream topping. Refrigerate for several hours.

INDEX

ADDRESSES

The following will all supply their goods by mail order.
Contact them by phone or fax for details.

Low fat cocoa
Good quality high cocoa
solids whole chocolate
Terence Fisher
Chocolate Wholesaler
The Chestnuts
Earl Soham
Woodbridge
Suffolk
IP13 7RN

Tel: 01728 685529
Fax: 01728 685843

Cookware
Divertimenti
45–47 Wigmore Street
London
W1H 9LE

Tel: 0171 935 0689
Fax: 0171 224 0058

Cookware
Natural vanilla extract
Lemon and almond
extracts
Lakeland Plastics
Alexandra Buildings
Windermere
Cumbria
LA23 1BQ

Te: 015394 88100
Fax: 015394 88300

Oil sprays
Pure natural vanilla
extract
Made in America
Hathaway Retail Park
Chippenham
SN15 1JG

Tel: 01249 447558
Fax: 01249 446142